# Grow Your Own
# FRUIT
— *Ken Muir* —

**Ken Muir Ltd, Honeypot Farm, Rectory Road, Weeley Heath,**
**Clacton-on-Sea, Essex CO16 9BJ**
**Telephone: 01255 830181   Fax: 01255 831534**
**Email: info@kenmuir.co.uk   Web: www.kenmuir.co.uk**

Grow Your Own Fruit

First edition 1994
Second edition 1999
Third edition 2003
Fourth edition 2007

Published in the United Kingdom by Ken Muir Ltd
Honeypot Farm, Rectory Road, Weeley Heath, Clacton-on-Sea, Essex CO16 9BJ

British Library Cataloguing in Publication Data. A catalogue record for this book is available from the British Library.

ISBN 0-9555101-0-6

# GROW YOUR OWN FRUIT

## PREFACE

Ever since I began to supply strawberry plants and other fruit stocks to the amateur gardener forty years ago, I recognised the importance of providing up-to-date information on cultural practices, in a clear and concise manner that could be understood by even the less experienced person who had never grown fruit before. I also appreciated the necessity of keeping the gardener advised of the latest selection of improved varieties of fruit as they became available from breeders.

I have been informed on numerous occasions by gardeners how difficult it is for them to obtain practical advice on fruit from garden centres and what advice was forthcoming, more often than not proved to be insufficient, inconclusive and inaccurate. This still applies equally to some organisations who supply fruit stocks by mail order and where the cultural instructions provided are perhaps no more than reference to digging a hole to plant the tree or bush, the planting distance and the more obvious advice to water the plant during dry weather but omitting to say with how much and how frequently.

Proper advice given at the time of purchasing fruit stocks is just as important as buying healthy, well grown plants. Good quality plants are not cheap to buy and it must therefore be worthwhile for the amateur fruit grower to read this book, to help ensure he, or she, gets the best results. This is what the book sets out to do. After all, nobody would buy a new lawnmower without ensuring that a manual on its maintenance came with it!

This fourth edition has been completely revised and contains an additional 19 pages of information.

KEN MUIR
January 2007

# GROW YOUR OWN FRUIT

## FORWARD

The admirable booklets, originally compiled by Ken Muir and given freely to help gardeners in the planting and care of fruit plants purchased from him, have now been revised, updated, enlarged and brought together in this one publication by Ken Muir and Jim Arbury.

Ken Muir and Jim Arbury are professional growers of high repute and long experience, both dedicated to serving the amateur fruit grower. Jim Arbury, employed by the Royal Horticultural Society at Wisley, is responsible for the Model Fruit Gardens and for the care and well being of the large range of temperate fruits in the Fruit Field. The Model Fruit Gardens demonstrate the many ways of growing hardy fruits in a British garden and are an inspiration to fruit growers world wide.

Ken Muir is a nurseryman, propagator and commercial fruit grower. He has, over the years, introduced many kinds of varieties of fruit from British Research Stations and the Continent, varieties of superior flavour, heavier cropping and more resistance to pests and diseases. He has, nevertheless, remained loyal to good old varieties worthy of a place in a British garden. His speciality is the strawberry and his introductions have greatly enhanced the strawberry industry.

This book details the care of tree and soft fruits in many forms and explains in simple terms the craft of fruit growing from planting to fruition and continuing success thereafter.

There can be few nurserymen, if any, who give so much good advice in printed form or such impartial information about their varieties than Ken Muir.

HARRY BAKER
Fruit Officer (1969-1991)
The Royal Horticultural Society's Garden
Wisley, Surrey.

# CONTENTS

# CONTENTS

7

## SITE

Fruit can be successfully grown out in the open in most parts of the United Kingdom. The site should be sunny, sheltered and ideally, though not essentially, in full sun. Some fruits will tolerate partial shade and this is mentioned in the text. On exposed sites, however, and at high altitudes, cropping will be poorer unless some kind of protection is provided. With increasing altitudes, above 600ft, winds become stronger and the growing season is shorter; nonetheless with proper shelter, soft fruits as well as dwarf trees of the early maturing tree fruits can be planted because they are quicker to mature and being smaller are more easily protected. Culinary varieties of tree fruits can also can be grown in such situations.

## SOIL

Fruit plants will tolerate a wide range of soils providing they are well drained and preferably at least 45cm (18in) deep for tree, bush and cane fruits and not less than 30cm (12in) deep for strawberries. A deep, well drained, medium loam of about pH 6.7 (slightly acid) is best for most fruits. Blueberries and related plants however, require very acid conditions. Sandy, gravelly and shallow soils over chalk, all of which tend to dry out quickly, are unsatisfactory but they can be improved by various means such as increasing the depth of shallow soil, the incorporation of bulky organics to increase moisture retention, or regular mulching and irrigation when necessary. Water-logged land must be drained before planting (see page 14).

## SHELTER

The provision of shelter will improve yields by approximately 15% in gardens slightly exposed to wind and by as much as 50% in very exposed gardens. Shelter can take the form of living barriers e.g. trees and hedges or non-living e.g. walls or fences. Generally a semi-permeable windbreak is best, e.g. a hedge, windbreak of trees or slatted fence, all of which reduce the wind speed. Solid barriers e.g. walls, fences or dense hedges can create turbulence and trap cold air to form a frost pocket. Living windbreaks do compete with the other plants so in a small garden walls or fences are probably best; they can also be used for growing trained fruit up against them. Ideally, shelter should be provided before the fruit is planted.

## ROTATION

Ideally when fruit stocks have to be replaced, for various reasons it is better to replant on a fresh site. If this is not possible then soil from the planting row or hole should be exchanged with fresh soil from another part of the garden or a mixture of soil with compost or peat brought in from outside. This is particularly important in the case of strawberries, which should not be grown on land that has previously grown potatoes. There is no disinfectant or fumigant on the market for gardeners to purchase legally which will give effective sterilization of the soil.

## POLLINATION

Most tree fruits are not self-fertile and, therefore, consideration must be given to the question as to whether it will be necessary to have one or more other varieties of the same fruit growing close at hand in order to achieve adequate pollination of the flower parts, without which there can be little or no fruit set. Bees as well as other insects and the wind itself, play an important part in transferring pollen from one flower to another (see pages 17-18).

## THE PURCHASE OF HEALTHY PLANTING STOCK

The only way of ensuring that healthy blackcurrants, raspberries and strawberries are planted and are of the variety being offered for sale is to obtain those certified by the Department for Environment, Food and Rural Affairs (DEFRA) as being true to type and healthy. All certified stocks have a certification number and if the nurseryman cannot quote the number for the plants being ordered, it would be safer to buy from a nurseryman who can.

A few varieties of hybrid berries, blackberries, redcurrants and gooseberries are also available within the certification scheme. With the last two fruits virus infection is rarely a problem and it will be quite acceptable to obtain uncertified plants as long as they come from a reputable source.

Some varieties of tree fruits can be obtained as certified plants but many of the old varieties cannot. As in the case of gooseberries and red currants, there is no need for concern as long as the trees are bought from a reliable source.

## TIME OF PLANTING

Planting of cane, bush and tree fruits (not strawberries) other than those growing in pots, which can be planted at any time, should only be undertaken during the period when they are dormant. Usually this would be between November and early April provided the soil is in a suitable condition. When plants have started into spring growth before planting, they do not grow as well during their first growing season as they would have done had they been planted earlier.

## WEED CONTROL BEFORE PLANTING

Sometimes fruit trees and bushes have to be planted in either a new garden or a neglected one. Both of these are likely to be seriously infested with weeds, particularly perennial ones which must be got rid of before planting. If the infestation is not too bad it is possible to pick out every root whilst digging. Alternatively the plot can be fallowed for one year, removing weeds as they appear throughout the summer or it can be treated with a suitable herbicide in accordance with the manufacturer's recommendations.

# GENERAL CONSIDERATIONS

## MULCHING

The application of bulky organic surface mulches such as farmyard manure, peat, straw, coconut fibre, coco shells, compost — or alternatively black polythene — besides suppressing weeds, will greatly assist in the retention of soil moisture to the benefit of the crop. With the exception of black polythene these materials will also help in maintaining the soil structure and fertility.

Mulches up to 10cm (4in) thick are best applied during the winter months and should cover at least 1m (1yd) around individual plants or 45cm (18in) both sides of a row of plants. Mulching should continue for the first three to four years on good soils and every year on poor, sandy soils and for wall-trained trees which otherwise tend to dry out more quickly.

## FERTILIZERS

As a general rule it would be more convenient to apply one of the all purpose proprietary compound fertilizers such as Ken Muir Fruit Tree Feed, Growmore, Phostrogen or Miracle Gro', all of which contain fixed amounts of nitrogen, phosphoric acid and potash, according to the brand. A cheaper alternative would be to use straight fertilizers such as sulphate of ammonia, superphosphate and sulphate of potash, where the ratios between the plant foods can be varied to best suit the requirements of the crop and soil conditions. The important point to remember is only to apply the fertilizer at the rate advised by the manufacturer. This means accurately weighing out the fertilizer and measuring the area of land over which it is to be applied beforehand.

On newly planted bushes and trees, fertilizers should be applied in mid-March as the buds begin to burst, or if planted later than this, immediately after planting. The fertilizer should be applied in a circle 45cm (18in) diameter around each bush or tree. Bushes planted over one year ago should receive applications of fertilizer each year in February or early March and broadcast 90cm (36in) both sides of the rows of bushes or in a circle 90cm (36in) diameter around individual bushes.

## FROST PROTECTION

It is important to protect early flowering fruits against spring frosts if a worthwhile crop is to be obtained.

The yield of strawberries can be seriously reduced by spring radiation frosts that can occur during the month of May when strawberries are in flower. Frost damage can be prevented by covering the plants with fleece, straw, sheets of polythene or hessian on frosty nights. The television meteorologists forecast very accurately when damaging frosts are likely to occur and therefore when these precautions should be taken. Some frost protection during the flowering period can be provided by putting a top net over a fruit cage.

Wall fruit can be protected by rolling down a cover of fleece, hessian or thick netting at night when frost is likely and rolling it up during the day. This should be supported away from the plants by bamboo canes (see fig. 1). Alternatively a clear polythene cover as recommended for peaches and nectarines to control peach leaf curl (see page 67) can be used and left on during the day but this restricts access for pollinating insects, so hand pollination may be necessary. This cover should be open at the ends and have a gap of 30cm (1ft) at the bottom to provide ventilation.

Bush fruits and small free-standing trees can be protected against frost by making a temporary framework of bamboo canes and draping this with a cover of fleece, hessian or thick netting.

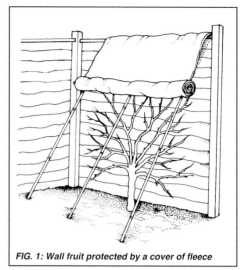

**FIG. 1: Wall fruit protected by a cover of fleece**

## BIRD PROTECTION

To achieve maximum yields, ripening fruit should be protected against birds. This is particularly important for soft fruit and vines. A 'walk-in' fruit cage is the best solution as this can also prevent finches from pecking out the fruit buds in winter. Fruit grown against walls or fences can easily be protected by hanging a net down in front of the plants, secured to the top of the fence with staples and pegged to the ground, held away from the plants by long canes.

## YIELDS

Subject to variety and climatic conditions, with proper management and given reasonably fertile soil, the average amount of fruit that it should be possible to pick annually from well-grown bushes and trees outdoors is as follows:

| | | |
|---|---|---|
| **Blackberry** | 9.0kg (20lb) per bush | early July/Oct |
| **Blackberry (var. Fantasia)** | 36.0kg (80lb) per bush | mid-Aug/early Nov |
| **Blackberry/raspberry hybrids** | 5.4-6.8kg (12-15lb) per bush | July/Sept |
| **Blackcurrant** | 4.5kg (10lb) per bush | late July/Aug |
| **Blueberry** | 2.7kg (6lb) per bush | July/Sept |
| **Gooseberry** | 4.5kg (10lb) per bush | late May/Aug |
| **Grape (outdoor)** | 3.6kg (8lb) per vine | late Aug/Nov |

| | | |
|---|---|---|
| **Jostaberry** | 3.6-4.5kg (8-10lb) per bush | July/late Aug |
| **Kiwi fruit** | 11.3-13.6kg (25-30lb) per vine | Oct/Nov |
| **Raspberry (summer)** | 2.7kg per m (6lb per yd) of row | July/early Aug |
| **Raspberry (autumn)** | 0.7-1.8kg per m (1½-4lb per yd) of row | Aug/late Nov |
| **Red & White Currants** | 4.5kg (10lb) per bush | July/Aug |
| **Strawberry (summer)** | 225-450g (½-1lb) per plant | early June/late July |
| **Strawberry (autumn)** | 225-450g (½-1lb) per plant spread over two cropping periods | early June/mid-Oct |

In the case of tree fruits the rootstock onto which the tree is budded or grafted and the way the tree is trained will have an important influence on yield.

| | Bush | Espalier/Fan | Minarette/Cordon |
|---|---|---|---|
| **Apple** | 15-25kg (33-55lb) | 10-12kg (22-26lb) | 2.5-5kg (6-11lb) |
| **Pear** | 10-20kg (22-44lb) | 8-10kg (18-22lb) | 2-4kg (5-9lb) |
| **Plum** | 15-30kg (33-66lb) | 7-13.5kg (15-30lb) | 3.5-7kg (7-15lb) |
| **Cherry (Sweet)** | 13.5-45.5kg (30-100lb) | 5-15kg (11-33lb) | 2.5-7kg (6-15lb) |
| **Cherry (Acid)** | 13.5-18kg (30-40lb) | 5-15kg(11-33lb) | 2.5-7kg (6-15lb) |
| **Apricot** | 13.5-45.5kg (30-100lb) | 5-15kg (11-33lb) | |
| **Fig** | 5-22.5kg (11-50lb) | 2-10kg (4-22lb) | |
| **Peach/Nectarine** | 13.5-27kg (30-60lb) | 5-10kg (11-22lb) | |
| **Quince** | 15-30kg (33-66lb) | | |

# SOIL PREPARATION

**C**lean, well cultivated land in a good state of fertility will not need much initial preparation apart from the forking in of a slow release fertilizer such as Vitax Q4 or Osmocote at the rate of 105g/m² (3oz/yd²) over the whole plot for soft fruits and closely planted fruit trees. Widely spaced trees should have each planting site prepared (see page 26).

Virgin land, compacted soils and those low in fertility and organic status should be double dug to ensure good drainage and to enable bulky organics such as farmyard manure or turves, in the case of grassland, to be incorporated.

Compaction is a problem that should always be addressed as it leads to the death of plants. Compacted soil will prevent surplus water from draining away in periods of heavy rain and will prevent plant roots from penetrating it in their search for water during dry spells.

## DOUBLE DIGGING

Double digging is best done several weeks before planting, in the autumn or winter when the ground is moist but not waterlogged or frozen. The ground then has time to settle and on heavy soils the frost will break down the clods before planting.

Double digging may sound like a complicated process, but it is in fact very straightforward. Basically you need to work on two layers of soil, hence the name 'double digging.' The top layer is dug with a spade and the soil is set to one side so the layer underneath is exposed. This can then be forked over whilst incorporating some bulky organic matter.

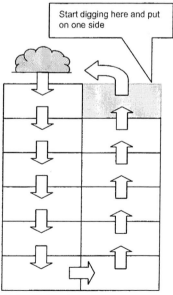

Start digging here and put on one side

Use a line to mark out the area you intend to dig. Once you have marked out the width, dig a trench 25-30cm (10-12in) deep and 60cm (2ft) back from the line, half way across the width of the bed. (See fig 2). Set the soil temporarily to one side as this will be used to fill the top layer of the final trench. Lightly fork into the subsoil a 5-7.5cm (2-3in) layer of rotted manure or compost.

Using a cane to mark where to dig to, dig a second trench next to the first trench 25-30cm (10-12in) deep and 2ft wide. This time, move the soil into the space created when the first trench was dug. Once again fork into the subsoil a 5-7.5cm (2-3in) layer of rotted manure or compost.

This process should be repeated until the whole planting area has been dug. In the final trench, replace the top layer with the topsoil that was removed from the first trench.

*FIG. 2: Double Digging*

13

After digging, a 5-7.5cm (2-3in) layer of rotted manure or compost should be spread on top and forked or rotovated in.

## DOUBLE DIGGING GRASSLAND

The procedure for double digging grassland is exactly the same as for double digging, with the exception that the turf is incorporated into the bottom layer. The turf should be considered the 'cream off the top of the milk' as when it breaks down it will feed the soil. It should therefore never be removed from the planting site.

After the plot has been marked out, the turf should be sprayed with a suitable herbicide to kill the grass and skimmed off the first trench to a depth of 5cm (2in). The skimmed off turf should be set to one side (just outside the area that is going to be dug). When the second trench is dug the turf should be skimmed off and placed grass downwards on the loosened subsoil in the first trench. It should be chopped up before the top soil from the second trench is placed on top. When the final trench is dug, incorporate into the bottom layer the turf that was removed from the first trench.

## CONSTRUCTING A DRAIN

Badly-drained land which cannot be improved by double digging should be drained by placing a 10cm (4in) tile or plastic drain in the centre of the plot at a depth of 60cm (24in) and covered with 10cm (4in) of coarse gravel and emptying into a ditch or soakaway (see fig. 3). Such a drain would take surplus water away from a plot 5m (16ft) on both sides of it.

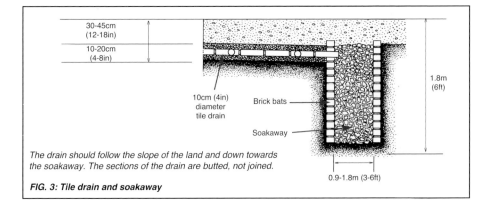

30-45cm (12-18in)

10-20cm (4-8in)

10cm (4in) diameter tile drain

Brick bats

Soakaway

1.8m (6ft)

0.9-1.8m (3-6ft)

The drain should follow the slope of the land and down towards the soakaway. The sections of the drain are butted, not joined.

**FIG. 3: Tile drain and soakaway**

# SOIL PREPARATION

## CONSTRUCTING A RAISED BED

If the soil is inclined to be heavy or shallow a raised bed should be constructed.

The height of the raised bed will depend on the type of crop to be grown and how poor the soil is. The soil needs to be 45cm (18in) deep for tree, bush and cane fruits or 30cm (12in) deep for strawberries. If the soil is fairly workable, the bed will need raising just a few inches. However, if the soil is is impenetrable below a few inches, the bed will require raising considerably more, in which case a box will need to be constructed to enclose the bed.

If the bed is to be raised by just a few inches, the existing topsoil should be loosened and improved by incorporating some bulky organic matter such as compost or well-rotted manure and some additional topsoil. Using a sturdy garden rake, drag the soil mix up to form a bed to the required depth for the crop that is to be grown.

If the bed is to be raised by more than a few inches then you will need to construct a box out of almost any solid material, such as brick, pressure treated timber or plastic. It is important that the material used is not toxic to the soil, especially when an edible crop is being grown (railway sleepers that have been treated with creosote, for example, are not suitable). If the bed is longer than 3m (10ft), crossbraces should be used to prevent the bed from wobbling. The box should be positioned on the level and slightly below the surface of the soil to improve stability. Once in place, it should be filled with topsoil mixed with some bulky organic matter such as compost or well-rotted manure.

## LIMING & ACIDIFYING

With the exception of blueberries and cranberries, all bush, cane and top fruits grow better when the soil pH is between 6.5 and 6.7 (slightly acid). Before (and preferably a year before) planting, the soil should be tested with a meter or chemical testing kit. If the pH is lower than 6.5, ground chalk or carboniferous limestone should be applied at the rates indicated in the following table.

| pH before liming | $kg/m^2$ | $oz/yd^2$ |
|---|---|---|
| 6.5 | nil | nil |
| 6.0 | 0.25 | 7 |
| 5.5 | 0.50 | 14 |
| 5.0 | 0.90 | 26 |
| 4.5 | 1.25 | 37 |

A pH of 5.5 may not appear to be very serious but it is ten times more acid than one of 6.5. The lime should be broadcast over the soil after it has been dug and then forked or rotovated into the ground as deeply as possible. Lime should not be applied at the same time as fertilizers as it can adversely react with some of them. It is best applied earlier in the winter or autumn and preferably a year in advance.

Fruit stocks growing on alkaline soils, especially shallow soils with a pH of 7.0 or above, may suffer from lime-induced chlorosis caused by deficiencies of iron or manganese or both. Alkaline soils can be acidified by the application of Flowers of Sulphur. For details on reducing the pH, please refer to the section on 'Lime Induced Chlorosis' (pages 164-165).

# HANDLING PLANTS AFTER PURCHASE

**P**lanting should be undertaken as soon as possible after delivery of the plants but only provided the ground has been properly prepared beforehand and is not too wet or frozen for planting. If the soil sticks to your boots, then it is too wet. No attempt should be made to plant under such adverse conditions; it is imperative to delay the operation until the ground is somewhat drier, even if this means waiting several weeks or even months! There is no reason why planting should not be undertaken when there is light frost on the soil surface when about to dig the planting hole.

## PLANTING IN WET OR FROZEN CONDITIONS

Should the fruit trees or bushes arrive from the nursery and the planting conditions are not favourable, the best plan would be to follow one of the following options.

**Option 1** — Store the plants under cover in an unheated garage or garden shed but before doing so, inspect the roots to ascertain that they have not dried out in transit. If necessary the roots may be stood in water for 30 minutes (and no longer) before being repacked in their polythene sleeve. They may need to be protected from frost, in spite of being under cover. This is best done by covering the roots with several layers of sacking or fleece. The plants can be stored like this for up to 2 weeks and inspected every few days to make sure the roots have not dried out. If you think planting will be delayed for more than 2 weeks then you should pot the plants up or heel them in (see options 2 & 3).

**Option 2** — Dig a shallow trench and lay the plants in the trench at an angle of 45 degrees or less to the horizontal. The plants can be spaced apart as little as a few inches in this temporary accommodation (depending on the type of fruit). Moist friable soil or compost should be placed over the roots afterwards and with the hands gently pressed against the roots but not firmed against them with the feet, as this could effectively prevent oxygen from reaching the roots. This is especially important with raspberries which need to be heeled in as shallowly as possible. The purpose of tilting the plants in the trench at an angle of 45 degrees when 'healing in' is to bring the roots closer to the surface where they are less likely to get waterlogged or deprived of oxygen. Care must be taken not to expose any of the roots above the surface of the soil, otherwise they will dry out. The plants can be left in the trench whilst they remain dormant after which they should either be planted in their permanent positions or if the ground is still not ready, potted up into containers (see option 3).

**Option 3** — Pot the plants up into containers using a free-draining compost. If this is only likely to be a very temporary measure, then the container only needs to be big enough to accommodate the roots of the plant. If it is likely to be a more permanent measure, further consideration should be given to the size of pot and choice of compost. As a very temporary measure, raspberry canes can be potted up in bundles. Otherwise they should be potted up individually. The compost should be kept just damp (but not saturated) at all times. The containers are best kept in a sheltered position or cold greenhouse to protect the roots from severe freezing conditions. Of all the options listed above, potting into containers can be the most permanent solution. If the ground is still not ready by the end of March, the plants should remain in the containers until they again become dormant the following autumn, or until they have rooted sufficiently so as not to disturb the rootball too much when they are eventually transferred from the container into the ground.

# POLLINATION

**P**ollination is achieved by the transfer of pollen from the male part of the flower (anthers) to the female part of the flower (stigmas). The end result is fertilization followed by fruit set. The majority of flowers on plants grown for their fruits have both anthers and stigmas, whilst a few (e.g. cobnuts) bear separate male and female flowers on the same plant and those of kiwi fruits do so on different plants.

Some fruits (and these include apricots, peaches and nectarines as well as certain varieties of plums, gages, damsons and cherries) can be fertilized by their own pollen; these are described as being self-fertile, self-compatible or self-pollinating. Most varieties of soft fruit also fall into this category. Those fruits which require another variety of the same fruit flowering at the same time to achieve fertilization are said to be self-incompatible and include most varieties of apples and pears.

## APPLES, PEARS & PLUMS

The various varieties of apples, pears, plums, gages and damsons are separated into pollination groups according to when they flower, starting with the earliest flowering varieties as group A, group B a little later and so on.

Varieties within the same pollination group will usually cross pollinate one another because they flower at the same time. For example, the apple variety 'Discovery' (group B) will pollinate the apple variety 'Fiesta' (group B) and vice versa.

Varieties in adjacent groups will also serve as pollinators for one another because in most seasons there is sufficient overlap of pollen resulting from an overlap in the flowering period. For example the apple variety, 'Egremont Russet' (group A) will pollinate the apple variety 'Bountiful' (group B) and vice versa.

Different types of fruit however will not pollinate one another. For example apples will not pollinate pears and vice versa.

Self-fertile varieties and partially self-fertile varieties will set fruit without a pollinator but the fruit set will always be improved when a pollinator is present. They will also act as pollinators for self-incompatible varieties.

The majority of apple and pear varieties are what are known as diploids. That is to say they contain two sets of chromosomes. There are several varieties of pear which even though they are diploids and in the same or overlapping pollination groups, are unable to pollinate each other. For example 'Onward' will not cross pollinate with 'Doyenne du Comice'.

There are a few triploid varieties such as the apples 'Bramley's Seedling' and 'Crowngold' which have three sets of chromosomes. These make poor pollinators and should be grown with two diploid varieties that will not only pollinate each other but also the triploid variety. Alternatively, they can be grown with a self-fertile variety.

# POLLINATION

## CHERRIES

Some acid cherries are self-fertile and all would appear to be capable of pollinating one another. Sweet cherries do not make satisfactory pollinators for acid or Duke cherries but acid cherries will pollinate sweet cherries on the rare occasions when their flowering periods overlap.

With a few notable exceptions, namely the varieties 'Celeste', 'Cherokee', 'Stella', 'Summer Sun', 'Sweetheart' and 'Sunburst', all sweet cherries are self-incompatible and require specially defined pollinators.

## OTHER FRUITS

The majority of these are self-fertile and this includes most varieties of soft fruits. Most varieties of blueberries are partially self-incompatible and therefore should be grown alongside a second variety. As a general rule apricots, peaches and nectarines need to be hand pollinated. The pollination of cobnuts and filberts can be helped by pruning them whilst they are in flower. The pollination of grapes can be improved by tapping the rods during flowering.

## HAND POLLINATION

There are occasions when some fruits should be pollinated by hand. This is necessary when there are likely to be few insects about, or when for example the fruit is being grown under glass and the pollinating insects are prevented from reaching the flowers.

Hand pollination should be undertaken daily, when the weather is warm and dry and the flowers are fully open. The pollen is best transferred from the anther to the stigmas with the aid of a soft camel hair brush or rabbit's tail.

## POLLINATION PETS

Besides the honeybee, Britain has more than 250 species of native bee, many of which help your garden by pollinating flowers, but with fewer wild flowers and suitable nest sites, about 25% of our native bees are now endangered species. Finding nest sites has become crucially important for our bee population and bee nest kits are now available to gardeners. By attracting bees to your garden not only will you notice improved fruit crops but the bees will also visit a wide range of garden flowers.

The Red Mason Bee is a docile, friendly, solitary bee, safe around children and pets. It is also a more efficient pollinator of fruit crops than the honeybee. Nest boxes designed specifically for the Red Mason Bee are available. All you need to do is place the nest boxes in a sunny, sheltered, south facing position in the garden and you will attract Red Mason Bees in early spring.

# FRUIT TREE FORMS

Fruit trees can be trained into almost any shape but several recognised forms have been developed. Some forms are free growing, and will require little pruning, where others will need pruning to maintain shape. Some forms are completely free standing, where others will require permanent staking or support against a fence or wall. The choice of tree form is as important as the choice of rootstock. This will depend on several factors including the availability of space, the intended planting site, and the degree of maintenance required.

## BUSH, HALF-STANDARD & STANDARD

Bush trees are traditional open-centred goblet-shaped trees with a clear stem of 60cm (24in) for a dwarf bush and 75cm (30in) for a bush. Bush apple trees on M26 and bush pears on Quince 'C' grow to 2.4-3.5m (8-12ft) in height and spread and should be spaced 3-4.5m (10-15ft) apart. They should be staked for the first four to five years. Plums grown on St. Julien 'A' rootstock will make a bush 3.5-4.5m (12-15ft) in height and spread and need to be spaced 3.5-4.5m (12-15ft) apart and if grown on Pixy rootstock, will make a bush 2.4-3m (8-10ft) in height and should be spaced 2.4-3m (8-10ft) apart. They should be staked for the first four to five years for St Julien 'A' and permanently for Pixy.

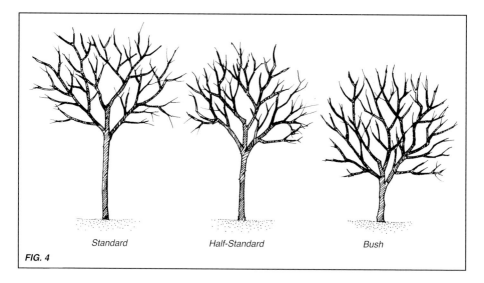

*Standard*　　*Half-Standard*　　*Bush*

**FIG. 4**

The half-standard is similar to the bush tree, but on a taller clear trunk of approximately 1.4m (4ft 6in). A vigorous rootstock is necessary for this tree type. It is not recommended for most gardens since the extra height makes maintenance and harvesting more difficult.

The standard has an even taller clear trunk of 1.8m (6ft), and can only be grown on the most vigorous rootstocks. This form is not recommended for most gardens since it is too big to be practicable.

*Minarette*

*Pyramid*

## PYRAMID

A pyramid is similar to a bush but the main stem leader is maintained to give an overall conical shape. The tree tapers to allow the lower branches to receive plenty of sun.

## MINARETTE

Minarettes are vertical, columnar-trained trees that bear fruit on short spurs up and down the length of a single upright stem, rather than on long spreading branches. They are particularly suitable for today's smaller garden where space is limited and for growing in tubs and for these reasons have become immensely popular. A wide range of well known, proven varieties are now available. Minarette apples and pears should be maintained at 1.8-2.4m (6-8ft) in height and can be spaced as close as 60cm (2ft) apart. Minarette plums, gages and damsons and cherries should be spaced 90cm (3ft) apart. Their ultimate height should be restricted to 1.8-2.4m (6-8ft).

## CORDON

Cordons are single-stemmed trees which are usually grown as oblique cordons at an angle of about 45°. The cordon is intended for growing against a low fence. If planted closely, many varieties can be grown in a relatively small space. They should be grown to a height of 1.8m (6ft) which gives a stem length of about 2.4m (8ft) and should be spaced 75cm (2ft 6in) apart.

## DOUBLE & MULTIPLE CORDONS

The Double ('U') cordon is a variation on the single cordon but is more usually grown upright. It is more easily situated against a narrow area of wall or fence than two single oblique cordons. Multiple cordons with three, four or even more vertical arms are suitable for certain varieties of apples and pears but require intricate training and maintenance.

*Double 'u' cordon*

*A row of cordons*

# FRUIT TREE FORMS

*Espalier*

## ESPALIER

Espalier trees consist of a vertical stem with one or more tiers of horizontal branches at intervals of 38-45cm (15-18in). The tree is trained in one plane and can be used to cover walls or fences. This form is ideal for apples and pears, but does not really suit stone fruits. Espalier apples on M26 rootstock and pears on Quince 'C' rootstock should be spaced at 3.6-4.5m (12-15ft) apart and should have two or three tiers of branches.

## FAN

The fan is widely used for plums, gages, damsons, cherries, peaches, nectarines and apricots where space is limited, especially in colder districts. The main stem is short, and the ribs of the fan emanate from two low angled arms. A fan-trained tree on St. Julien 'A' needs a space of at least 4.5m (15ft) wide and 2.1-2.4m (7-8ft) high, and on Pixy 3.6m (12ft) wide and 1.8m (6ft) high (the size of two standard fence panels). Trees should be planted 15-23cm (6-9in) away from the wall or fence and the stem inclined slightly towards it. The wall should be fitted with horizontal wires 15cm (6in) apart.

*Fan*

# FRUIT TREE FORMS

## STEPOVER

Stepovers are cordons bent at right angles and then trained horizontally in one direction. Alternatively they can be trained as a one-tier espalier to produce two arms. They are usually supported by wires. Stepovers are often planted at the front of a border to form an attractive low edging.

*Stepover*

## FAMILY TREES & DUO-MINARETTES

The need for a pollination partner can create difficulties in a small garden where there is room for only one tree. Growing a family tree or Duo-Minarette can be the solution. Family trees are single trees composed of more than one variety growing on the same single root system — three varieties is usual for a bush tree. Duo-Minarettes consist of two varieties on a single vertical stem, one above the other.

A significant advantage to family trees and Duo-Minarettes is the ease with which bees will pollinate the whole tree and hence all varieties get a good fruit set. The rootstock must be chosen very carefully and the varieties should be of similar vigour so that the tree is well balanced and one variety does not outgrow the others.

Most tree fruits with the exception of figs, mulberries and cobnuts are budded or grafted onto rootstocks. Rootstocks are chosen for their dwarfing effect, their fruitfulness (this affects the cropping of the variety grafted onto them), for resistance to pests and diseases and for a good root system. Trees grown on their own roots (cuttings), and seedling trees are variable in size and vigour and slow to come into bearing. The correct rootstock should be chosen to provide the size of tree required and for the tree form required. The following are some of the best and more commonly available rootstocks.

## APPLES

There is a wide selection of rootstocks available. They are listed in order of ascending vigour.

**M27: Extremely dwarfing** — Trees grown on this rootstock require very careful cultivation. It is only suitable for trees grown on fertile soils and should be kept free from weeds and competitive plants. The trees should be staked throughout their lives. It is particularly suitable for vigorous triploid varieties such as 'Bramley's Seedling' and 'Blenheim Orange'. It can be used for stepovers, dwarf bush and pyramid trees and as oblique cordons for triploid varieties. Maximum height and spread 1.8m (6ft).

**M9: Dwarfing** — Requires good soil conditions and will require careful cultivation. Trees must be kept free from weeds and competitive plants. The root system is brittle and the tree will require permanent staking. Suitable for cordons, dwarf bush trees and pyramids. Maximum height and spread 1.8-3m (6-10ft).

**M26: Dwarfing** — One of the most useful rootstocks, suitable for small gardens. It will require staking for the first four or five years. It is probably the best rootstock for Minarettes, cordons and is also suitable for bush trees and for two and three-tier espaliers. Maximum height and spread 2.5-3.6m (8-12ft).

**MM106: Semi-dwarfing** — This is generally too vigorous for trees in a small garden but is useful for cordons on poor soils and for espaliers and bush trees. It is a good rootstock where there is more space available, or conditions are less favourable. It will require staking for the first four or five years. Maximum height and spread 3.6-5.6m (12-18ft).

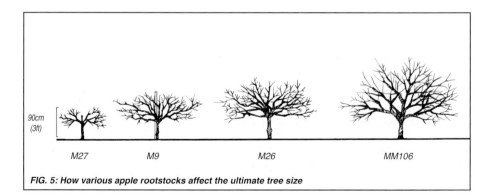

90cm
(3ft)

M27      M9      M26      MM106

*FIG. 5: How various apple rootstocks affect the ultimate tree size*

# ROOTSTOCKS FOR TOP FRUIT

## PEARS

Pears are usually grafted onto quince rootstocks to produce small trees which are earlier into cropping than those grown on pear stocks.

**QUINCE 'C': Semi-dwarfing** — This is early into cropping, and suitable for Minarettes, cordons, bush trees and two or three tier espaliers. Unsuitable when soil conditions are poor. Maximum height and spread 2.5-5.5m (8-18ft).

**QUINCE 'A': Semi-dwarfing** — This is only slightly more vigorous than Quince 'C' and suitable for cordons on poorer soils; also for bush trees and larger espaliers. Maximum height and spread 3-6m (10-20ft).

## PLUMS, GAGES & DAMSONS

There are two rootstocks suitable for growing plums in the garden (other available rootstocks are too vigorous).

**PIXY: Dwarfing** — The only dwarfing plum rootstock, this is suitable for bush, pyramid, fan-trained trees and cordons. Trees grown on Pixy require permanent staking and require very fertile soil. The fruit tends to be smaller than that grown on St Julien 'A'. Maximum height and spread 1.8-3m (6-10ft).

**ST JULIEN 'A': Semi-dwarfing** — The most useful rootstock for garden planting and the only one to choose if conditions are less than ideal. More vigorous than Pixy, this is suitable for larger pyramid, bush and fan-trained trees and Minarettes. Maximum height and spread 3-6m (10-20ft).

## PEACHES, NECTARINES & APRICOTS

**ST JULIEN 'A': Semi-dwarfing** — This is the only rootstock dwarf enough for most gardens and is suitable for pyramid, bush and fan-trained trees.

## CHERRIES

The main problem with growing cherries in the past has been that only vigorous rootstocks have been available. With some modern rootstocks small trees suitable for the garden can be produced.

**GISELA 5 & TABEL: Dwarfing** — These rootstocks make a very small tree suitable for cordons, pyramids, fan-trained trees and Minarettes. Maximum height and spread 1.8-3m (6-10ft).

**COLT: Semi-dwarfing** — This produces too large a bush tree for small gardens but is a reliable rootstock and useful for larger fan-trained trees. Maximum height and spread 4.5-6m (15-20ft).

# PLANTING & STAKING TOP FRUIT

**C**orrect planting and staking is important. Planting can be carried out between November and early April for bare-rooted trees provided the ground is not waterlogged or frozen. Container-grown trees can also be planted in the summer months but care should be taken that they are well watered. The ground should be well prepared beforehand for planting (see pages 13-15).

## MINARETTES, BUSH & PYRAMID TREES

A stake should be driven or planted 45cm (18in) into the ground. For Minarettes and pyramids the stake should be 1.5-1.8m (5-6ft) out of the ground and for bush trees 60-90cm (2-3ft). Use a telescopic tree stake made of 100% anti-corrosive materials (available from Ken Muir) or a pressure treated stake of minimum length 2 metres (6ft 6in) and 5cm (2in) in diameter (or flat side of square). The tree should be planted on the side of the stake away from the prevailing wind.

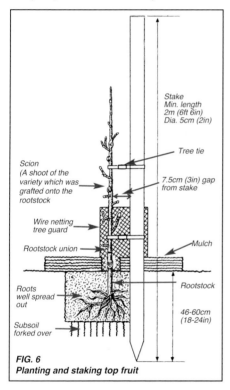

Stake
Min. length
2m (6ft 6in)
Dia. 5cm (2in)

Tree tie

Scion
(A shoot of the
variety which was
grafted onto the
rootstock

7.5cm (3in) gap
from stake

Wire netting
tree guard

Rootstock union

Mulch

Roots
well spread
out

Rootstock

Subsoil
forked over

46-60cm
(18-24in)

**FIG. 6**
**Planting and staking top fruit**

A hole should be taken out wide and deep enough for the roots to be spread out evenly. Plenty of well-rotted manure, compost or peat should be forked into the bottom of the hole (particularly if on heavy or dry soils) and in addition a slow-release fertilizer, such as Vitax Q4 or Osmocote, should be mixed into the soil removed from the hole, at the recommended rate — usually about 105g/m² (3oz/yd²), before the soil is replaced.

The tree should be positioned in the hole 7.5cm (3in) away from the stake and the roots spread out carefully. The tree should be planted at the depth it was in the nursery making sure that the rootstock union is above soil level — usually between 15-30cm (6-12in). The soil should then be firmed thoroughly around the roots.

The tree should be secured to the stake using two ties for Minarettes and pyramids, one near the top of the tree and one about halfway down. For bush trees a tie positioned below the top four or five buds or just below the crotch of an older tree. It is best to use a cushion tree tie, which will form a figure of eight around the tree and the stake. If a simple tie is used, then a cushion should be placed between the tree and the stake. The tie should not be over-tightened and some excess should be left for adjustment. Ties should be checked each spring and adjusted or replaced as necessary.

A mulch of manure, compost or straw should be applied around the tree 7.5cm (3in) deep in a 45cm (18in) radius but not touching the stem.

## TREES GROWN AGAINST WALLS OR FENCES

When planting trees against walls or fences, a semi-circular hole should be dug and the roots spread out away from the wall. Fan, espalier and cordon trained fruit trees should always be secured to a supporting framework of horizontal wires. These are either fixed to the wall or fence against which the trees are trained or to a series of posts if they are grown in the open away from a wall. Galvanized wire is best. For trees trained against a wall or fence horizontal wires should be fixed 5-10cm (2-4in) away from the wall to allow for air circulation. This can be achieved by securing them to wooden battens fixed at 1.5-1.8m (5-6ft) intervals, or lead vine eyes can be used at 1.5-1.8m (5-6ft) intervals, or galvanized screw vine eyes can be used at 1.5-1.8m (5-6ft) intervals — these are particularly suitable for wooden fences. The spacing and gauge of the wires depends on the training system being used.

### *FANS*

Fan-trained trees grown against a wall or fence should be planted about 15cm (6in) away from the wall and slightly inclined towards it. Fan-trained trees require closely spaced wires 15cm (6in) apart with the first wire at 38cm (15in) from the ground. Light straining wire (1.2mm [14 gauge]) is sufficient and straining bolts are not needed.

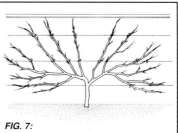

**FIG. 7:**
**A fan growing on wire supports**

### *CORDONS, ESPALIERS & STEPOVERS*

Espalier trees grown against a wall or fence should be planted about 15cm (6in) away from the wall and the arms should be secured to horizontal wires using soft string or chainlock ties. Espaliers require heavier wire than fans — 2.5mm (12 gauge) — and should be spaced further apart. Wires for supporting espaliers should be spaced to coincide with the arms, usually at about 38-45cm (15-18in) apart. Three wires are required for supporting cordons and should be spaced at about 60cm (2ft) apart with the first wire 60cm (2ft) from the ground. Stepovers only require one wire 30-60cm (1-2ft) off the ground

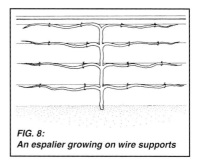

**FIG. 8:**
**An espalier growing on wire supports**

For cordons, stepovers and espaliers, straining bolts should be used so that tension can be maintained over the years. 15cm (6in) straining bolts are suitable and can be fed through holes drilled in battens or posts, or can be slotted through screw vine eyes.

Oblique cordons should be planted out at an angle of about 45°. Care should be taken that the graft union is above soil level and that the scion is uppermost. The trees should be tied using soft string to canes fixed to horizontal wires.

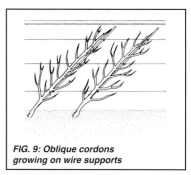

**FIG. 9: Oblique cordons growing on wire supports**

# GROWING FRUIT IN CONTAINERS

**C**ontainerised fruit trees are decorative as well as fruitful. They make an attractive feature for a patio so fruit growing is possible even without a garden. Almost all fruit trees and bushes can be grown in containers and there are valid reasons for growing them in containers whatever size your garden.

*Minarettes in containers*

Container growing is particularly useful for less hardy subjects such as peaches, nectarines, apricots and figs, which may need some protection at flowering time or in the winter. Even citrus and olives can be grown provided they can be given protection over winter in a glasshouse or conservatory. The pots should be positioned to make the best use of the microclimate such as in sunny sheltered corners; but remember these areas can also be subject to eddying and turbulence.

Growing fruit in containers enables fruit with special soil requirements to be grown, for example blueberries, which prefer an acid soil. It is also an ideal way to restrict the growth of more vigorous fruits such as figs.

Most tree forms can be used for pot grown trees; Minarettes, pyramids and dwarf bush trees being particularly suitable. The container limits the size of the tree and so most rootstocks are suitable but the more dwarfing rootstocks are generally best. A maiden or two year old tree should be used  and the pot size increased as the tree develops.

## SIZES & TYPES OF CONTAINER

Plants should be potted into containers slightly larger in diameter than their root area - up to 7.5cm (3in) larger, and repotted in to a larger container each year until the final desired size has been reached. It may be tempting to put a small plant into a large container straight away but this is not advisable as the volume of compost in relation to the roots is too great to create water movement and air circulation through the soil, which will result in stagnant compost and may in turn cause root death. A wide range of containers are available and most are suitable provided they have adequate drainage holes.

## TYPES OF COMPOST

For most fruit trees and bushes a proprietary loam-based compost such as John Innes No. 3 is best. Never use garden soil as it is not sufficiently well drained for pot culture. Plants requiring acid conditions (e.g. blueberries) must be grown in either a proprietary ericaceous compost or a mixture of peat and sand.

## POTTING

Bare rooted or container grown plants can be used. Any thick, thong-like roots should be cut back and at the same time any broken roots trimmed off, so that the root ball fits the pot. If the roots are a little too large for the pot, they may be trimmed back so that they sit freely in the pot without curling up. The roots on the outside of the rootball of container grown plants should be teased away to prevent a pot-bound effect.

Clay pots should be crocked to provide good drainage, using broken pot fragments. Plastic pots usually have adequate drainage but should be crocked if necessary. The stem of the plant should be positioned in the centre of the pot at the same depth as it was previously, at about 2.5-5cm (1-2in) below the rim to allow for watering. The pot should be filled carefully, firming as it is filled. Once potting is complete, the pot should be stood on two bricks to ensure good drainage.

## STAKING

Container grown fruit trees should be staked to keep the tree straight. This is best achieved by plunging a telescopic tree stake or stout bamboo cane 2.5cm (1in) in diameter and of suitable length into the container to its fullest extent and tying the tree to it loosely to allow for expansion of the trunk. Tree ties should be inspected once a year to make sure they have not become too tight and if necessary they should be slackened. In an exposed site, the top of each cane should be secured to a horizontal wire, held in place by two supporting posts.

## REPOTTING

The tree or bush should be repotted each year to a larger pot until it has reached the final desired size. Thereafter, it should be kept in the same container but the compost changed each autumn. If a slow-release fertilizer is used (for example Osmocote or Vitax Q4), it should be mixed with the compost when repotting is carried out.

Repotting should be carried out in late autumn by turning the pot upside down and by tapping the rim, gently knocking the plant out of the pot. The thicker, thong-like roots should be trimmed by about one tenth and if it is becoming pot bound, by teasing out and trimming off up to 10% of the secondary roots. Any loose soil should be removed from the rootball.

## FEEDING & WATERING

The watering requirement of potted plants varies according to the size of the plant, time of year and the weather. During the winter months, little or no watering is required although the compost must not be allowed to dry out completely. During the spring, the need for water increases and at the height of the summer, pots may need watering once or twice every day. They should be watered when the surface of the compost starts to dry out. Over-watering should be avoided, especially with small plants that do not have the capacity to get rid of excessive amounts of water around the roots through transpiration through the leaves. Contraction of the compost away from the side of the pot is a sign that it has become extremely dry.

Liquid feeding should be carried out every seven to ten days during the spring and summer, using a high potash feed such as Ken Muir Fruit Tree Feed or Tomato fertilizer. However, if an 'Osmocote' slow-release fertilizer is used according to manufacturer's recommendation then this will not be necessary for a period of time.

Watering can be time consuming but it is possible to install an automatic system which, although not perfect, will enable the task to be carried out without an operator.

## FROST PROTECTION

During periods of severe frosts which can occur during the winter, containerised fruits can be killed by freezing winds which penetrate the wall of the container and kill the roots. The tree or bush should therefore be moved to the side of the house, away from the prevailing wind. For extra root protection the container should be lagged with sacking or other suitable insulation.

# APPLES & PEARS

**A**pples are the most reliable and popular of the tree fruits with varieties suitable for almost all parts of Britain. The wide range of varieties means good quality and fine flavoured fruit can be provided over a long season.

Pears are juicy and delicious but more temperamental than apples. They flower early and so are liable to damage by spring frosts and cold winds. In more favoured areas of the country they can be grown as bush trees in the open but elsewhere it is better to grow them in restricted forms such as Minarettes, cordons and espaliers on warm south, south-west, south-east or west facing walls or fences. They have the reputation of being slow to come into bearing but come into bearing much quicker when grown on the less vigorous rootstocks such as Quince 'A' and Quince 'C'.

## APPLE VARIETIES

*A.G.M. signifies the Award of Garden Merit, the Royal Horticultural Society's most prestigious award.*

### *DESSERT*

*Ashmead's Kernel*

**ADAM'S PEARMAIN** — Picking time: Early to mid-October. Season: November to March. Mr Robert Adams first brought this dessert apple to notice in 1826 under the name of Norfolk Pippin. It produces heavy crops of high quality apples which have a rich, aromatic nutty flavour. The tree has good scab resistance, making a good choice for wet areas. Partial tip-bearer. Pollination group A.

**ASHMEAD'S KERNEL** — Picking time: Mid-October. Season: December to February. Almost 300 years old but still one of the best late dessert apples. Medium-sized, crisp flesh, superb aromatic flavour, good resistance to scab but not for exposed northern gardens. Cropping is erratic. Spur-bearer. Pollination group C. *A.G.M.*

*Braeburn*

**BRAEBURN** — Picking time: Late-October. Season: January to March. This variety from New Zealand is becoming increasingly popular in the U.K. The fruit is refreshing, crisp and juicy. Heavy cropping. Requires a sheltered sunny spot. Unsuitable for the north. Spur-bearer. Pollination group C.

**CHIVERS DELIGHT** — Picking time: Mid-October. Season: November to January. An attractive late dessert apple raised in England about 1920. Fairly hardy and suitable for growing in the north. Produces good crops of sweet, juicy fruit often with a honey-like flavour. Prone to canker. Spur-bearer. Pollination group C.

*Chivers Delight*

*Cox*

*Crowngold*

*Discovery*

*Egremont Russet*

**CORNISH GILLIFLOWER** — Picking time: Mid October. Season: November to March. Discovered about 1800 growing in a garden in Cornwall. Considered a high quality dessert apple, possessing an intensely sweet, rich, aromatic flavour. Tip-bearer. Pollination group C.

**COX (SELF-FERTILE CLONE)** — Picking time: Early to mid-October. Season: Late October to January. Usually considered the finest flavoured English apple. The medium-sized fruit is crisp and juicy. Crops can be inconsistent and yields low. Susceptible to mildew, scab and canker in cold, wet, areas. Unsuitable for the north and wet areas. Requires good soil conditions. Spur-bearer. Self-fertile. Pollination group B.

**CROWNGOLD** — Picking time: Mid-October. Season: November to March. An improved clone of Jonagold. A very large, late apple with light yellow-green skin flushed, mottled and striped with red. Crisp, juicy and full of flavour. Precocious and high yielding. Triploid (will not act as a pollinator). Spur-bearer. Pollination group C. *A.G.M.*

**D'ARCY SPICE** — Picking time: Late October to early November. Season: December to April. This apple was discovered in Colchester, Essex, around 1785. It requires a hot dry summer to gain the spicy, almost nutmeg like flavour for which it is named. The fruit is richly aromatic, with a nice balance of sweetness and acidity. Partial tip-bearer. Pollination group C.

**DISCOVERY** — Picking time: Mid-August. Season: Mid-August to mid-September. A well flavoured, crisp dessert apple with a surprisingly long shelf life for such an early variety. The tree will bear heavy, regular crops of medium-small apples. The skin is yellow, almost entirely covered with bright crimson. The blossom shows good tolerance to frost. Suitable for growing nationwide. Partial tip-bearer. Pollination group B. *A.G.M.*

**EGREMONT RUSSET** — Picking time: Late September. Season: October to December. The classic russet apple with a rich sweet nutty flavour. Young trees bear good, regular crops of medium-sized apples. Mature trees can show a tendency towards biennial cropping under some circumstances. Suitable for growing in the north and west but susceptible to frost damage when in flower. Fruit resistant to scab but prone to bitter pit. Needs minimum of spraying for disease control and little pruning. Spur-bearer. Pollination group A. *A.G.M.*

**ELLISON'S ORANGE** — Picking time: Mid-October. Season: September to October. This variety produces heavy crops of red flushed apples which are crisp yet have a soft, juicy, melting flesh. It has a glorious, rich aromatic flavour and a taste of aniseed which develops after picking. The blossom is particularly attractive. The tree is hardy but dislikes wet areas. Spur-bearer. Pollination group C. *A.G.M.*

**ELSTAR** — Picking time: October. Season: Mid-October to January. Becoming a popular variety since it crops heavily, stores until January and combines an outstanding juiciness and flavour. The medium sized fruit is greenish-yellow flushed with bright red. Spur-bearer. Pollination group B. *A.G.M.*

*Elstar*

**FALSTAFF** — Picking time: Early October. Season: October to December. This new dessert apple was bred at the Institute of Horticulture, East Malling. As a bush it forms a medium sized open tree of medium vigour and drooping habit. The fruit is fairly large, yellow with orange-red stripes. The flesh is crisp and juicy and has a very good flavour. Very heavy cropping. Good scab and mildew resistance. Spur-bearer. Self-fertile. Pollination group B. *A.G.M.*

*Falstaff*

**FIESTA (RED PIPPIN)** — Picking time: Mid-September. Season: Late October to January. An excellent new dessert apple with a rich and refreshing Cox-like flavour and crisper texture. It is a reliable cropper and excellent keeper. Easier to grow successfully than Cox. A first rate choice for the garden. The flowers are resistant to frost damage, making the tree suitable for northern districts. Bears heavy crops of medium-large apples. The fruit is yellow, flushed and striped with bright red. Spur-bearer. Partially self-fertile. Pollination group B. *A.G.M.*

**GALA** — Picking time: Early October. Season: October to early January. A highly coloured dessert apple, with a sweet and interesting flavour often reminiscent of pear drops. The skin is yellow, heavily flushed with red. The crisp and juicy fruits are excellent when picked straight from the tree but the flavour may fade with keeping. Fairly heavy crops of medium-sized fruits. Suitable for growing in the north. Prone to canker and scab. Spur-bearer. Pollination group C. *A.G.M.*

*Fiesta*

*Gala*

*Greensleeves*

*Herefordshire Russet*

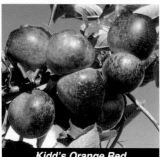

*Katy*

*Kidd's Orange Red*

**GOLDEN DELICIOUS** — Picking time: Late October. Season: November to February. Originating in America in 1890, this variety is now the most widely planted in the world. Heavy and regular cropping. The medium sized yellow fruits have a sweet, refreshing flavour. Requires a sunny position. The blossom is fairly frost resistant. Fruits from an early age. Spur-bearer. Pollination group C. *A.G.M.*

**GREENSLEEVES** — Picking time: Mid to late September. Season: Late September to mid-November. A new, medium sized, crisp, green apple. The quality is excellent and it has a pleasant flavour. The tree is hardy, reliable and easy to manage. It will crop heavily from the first or second year in the garden. The blossom is fairly frost tolerant and the tree is therefore suitable for growing countrywide. Partial tip-bearer. Self-fertile. Pollination group B. *A.G.M.*

**HEREFORDSHIRE RUSSET** — Picking time: Early October. Season: October to late December. A new russet variety with good disease resistance. The medium-sized fruit is crisp and juicy with a good, sweet aromatic flavour. Heavy cropping. Spur-bearer. Self-fertile. Pollination group B.

**JAMES GRIEVE** — Picking time: Early September. Season: September and October. A heavy and regular cropping variety. The medium-sized fruit is yellow, speckled with orange. Can be used as a cooking apple in July. Excellent flavour. Prefers the north, disliking the humid west where it is prone to canker and scab. The flowers are resistant to frost damage. Spur-bearer. Partially self-fertile. Pollination group B. *A.G.M.*

**KATY** — Picking time: Early September. Season: September to early October. Gives high yields of very attractive apples. The medium sized fruit is greenish-yellow, heavily flushed with bright red. The flesh is white and crisp but the flavour is only fair. A wise choice for northern gardens. Spur-bearer. Pollination group B.

**KIDD'S ORANGE RED** — Picking time: Mid-October. Season: November to January. One of the finest flavoured dessert apples, sweet and aromatic. Produces good crops of medium sized fruits but can be small unless thinned. Prone to canker and excessive russeting. Spur-bearer. Pollination group B. *A.G.M.*

**LAXTON'S SUPERB** — Picking time: Early October. Season: November to January. Raised in 1871, this variety is highly valued for its sweet flavour. Greenish-yellow apples almost completely covered with purplish-red. Heavy cropping but can be biennial. Prone to scab. Suitable for the north. Spur-bearer. Pollination group C.

**LORD LAMBOURNE** — Picking time: Late September. Season: Late September to mid-November. This variety crops heavily and regularly almost anywhere. Medium sized, sweet, juicy and aromatic fruit, greenish-yellow, flushed and striped with red. Spur-bearer. Pollination group A. *A.G.M.*

*Malling Kent*

**MALLING KENT** — Picking time: Late October. Season: November to February. The skin is pale green flushed with orange-red. A good alternative to Cox as it is easier to grow and is much heavier cropping. The flavour is rich and slightly aromatic with lots of juice and acidity. Stores very well. Prone to excessive russeting. Spur-bearer. Pollination group C.

**MERIDIAN** — Picking time: September. Season: September to March. A new trouble-free Cox-like variety. The fruits are striped orange-red and are crisp and juicy with an aromatic flavour. Stores very well. Spur-bearer. Pollination group B.

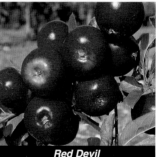

*Meridian*

**PIXIE** — Picking time: mid-October. Season: December to March. Raised in the U.K, this apple is a popular garden variety. The fruits are yellow with red stripes and an orange/red flush. Finely flavoured, intensely rich and aromatic with a good balance of sugar and acidity. Stores very well. Spur-bearer. Pollination group C. *A.G.M.*

**RED DEVIL** — Picking time: Late September. Season: October to December. This relatively new variety is easy to manage and is resistant to scab and mildew. The highly decorative medium-sized bright red fruits can partially tinge the flesh pink. The apple is crisp and juicy and its excellent flavour is reminiscent of strawberries. Suitable for small gardens. Spur-bearer. Self-fertile. Pollination group B.

*Red Devil*

**RED WINDSOR (SWEET LILLIBET)** — Picking time: September. Season: September to October. This new variety has been described as 'the early Cox'. It has a superb Cox-like flavour but does not suffer from any of the problems associated with Cox. Frost hardy and very heavy cropping. Spur-bearer. Self-fertile. Pollination group A.

*Red Windsor*

# APPLES & PEARS

*Scrumptious*

*Sunset*

*Sweet Society*

*Tydeman's Late Orange*

**RIBSTON PIPPIN** — Picking time: Late September. Season: October to January. This late variety is thought to have been raised from a pip c1707 and was highly prized in Victorian times. The fruits are sweet and juicy with an aromatic flavour, slightly reminiscent of pear drops. Self-fertile. Spur-bearer. Pollination group A. Triploid (will not act as a pollinator). *A.G.M.*

**SATURN** — Picking time: September. Season: September to February. This new variety produces heavy crops of large, red-flushed fruits. Crisp and very juicy with a good sweet flavour. Resistant to scab and mildew. Suitable for growing countrywide. Spur-bearer. Self-fertile. Pollination group B.

**SCRUMPTIOUS** — Picking time: September. Season: September to October. This new variety, bred in the U.K., was named 'Scrumptious' for its wonderful complexity of flavours. The fruits are thin skinned, crisp, sweet and aromatic. Frost hardy and suitable for planting in all areas of the U.K. It will produce heavy crops even as a young tree. Spur-bearer. Self-fertile. Pollination group B.

**SUNSET** — Picking time: Late September. Season: October to December. The usual choice where a Cox-like apple is required. The tree is easy to grow and a reliable cropper. Will perform well in areas unsuited to the culture of Cox and is tolerant to a moist climate. Prone to canker. Medium-sized fruit. Spur-bearer. Pollination group B. *A.G.M.*

**SWEET SOCIETY** — Picking time: Late September. Season: Early October to late December. An attractive classic Cox type apple with a superb, aromatic, rich sweet flavour. The appearance is similar to a good coloured Cox with attractive russet streaks and a red flush on a yellow-green background. Tip-bearer. Pollination group C.

**TYDEMAN'S LATE ORANGE** — Picking time: Mid-October. Season: December to April. This Cox cross is intensely rich and aromatic, with a perfect balance of sugar and acidity. The flavour is stronger than Cox. Heavy cropping. Spur-bearer. Pollination group C.

**WINTER GEM** — Picking time: Mid-October. Season: November to March. A new late dessert apple producing very heavy crops of large, pink flushed fruits. Excellent flavour, rich and aromatic. Partial tip bearer. Pollination group B.

## DESSERT/CULINARY

**BARDSEY** — Picking time: Early October. Season: Mid-October to late November. Recently discovered growing on the Welsh island of Bardsey and thought to be the only survivor from an orchard tended by monks up to 1000 years ago. The fruits are striped pink and have a distinct scent of lemon. It cooks to a delicate light golden fluff and requires no added sugar. Spur-bearer. Pollination group B.

*Bountiful*

**BLENHEIM ORANGE** — Picking time: Early October. Season: November to January. One of the best of all dual-purpose apples. Skin is pale yellowish-green. The creamy flesh is crisp and dry with an excellent nutty, distinctive flavour. Mildew resistance is good. The trees bear shyly when young but improve with age. Prone to biennial cropping. Partial tip-bearer. Triploid (will not act as a pollinator). Pollination group B. *A.G.M.*

**BOUNTIFUL** — Picking time: Late September. Season: September to January. A new large cooker producing heavy crops of sweet, good-flavoured apples which will keep until January. The fruit is pale-green, striped with orange-red. Cooks to a yellow fluff. In late winter it can be eaten as a dessert apple. Good mildew resistance. Very suitable for small gardens. Spur-bearer. Pollination group B.

*Broadholme Beauty*

**BROADHOLME BEAUTY** — Picking time: Late September. Season: Late September to early March. This new variety was raised from a James Grieve pip. The fruits have an extraordinarily thin skin and are naturally sweet and therefore do not require added sugar when cooked. It can be grown nationwide and has good disease resistance. Spur-bearer. Pollination group B.

**CHARLES ROSS** — Picking time: Mid-September. Season: Late September to December. The fruits are crisp, juicy, sweet and flavoursome but become flavourless by late October. When cooked, the flesh stays fairly intact. Fairly resistant to scab. Suitable for growing nationwide. Spur-bearer. Pollination group B. *A.G.M.*

*Charles Ross*

**JUMBO** — Picking time: Mid-September. Season: Mid-September to late February. This new variety produces exceptionally large fruits that are particularly good for baking. For eating fresh it has a good aromatic flavour. The green fruits are flushed and striped red. It appears to have good disease resistance. Triploid (will not act as a pollinator). Spur-bearer. Pollination group B.

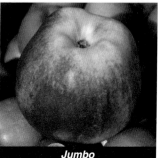
*Jumbo*

## CULINARY

**Arthur Turner**

**ARTHUR TURNER** — Picking time: Late September to early October. Season: September to November. A large cooker with especially beautiful blossom. Hardy and therefore suitable for the north. A heavy, regular cropper. Fairly resistant to scab but prone to mildew. An excellent baker. When cooked the fruit breaks up completely but not to a fluff. Pleasant, though not strong, acidic flavour. Spur-bearer. Partially self-fertile. Pollination group B. *A.G.M.*

**Bramley's Seedling**

**BRAMLEY'S SEEDLING** — Picking time: Mid-October. Season: November to March. The premier variety for cooking. Fruit is large, flat and round in shape but may be irregular. Skin is a pale yellowish-green flushed and striped with brownish red. Flesh is of coarse texture, juicy and has an acid flavour. Cooks to a pale, cream fluff. Fruit is prone to bitter pit. Tolerant to wet conditions — can be grown nationwide. Heavy cropping but sometimes biennial. Partial tip-bearer. Triploid (will not act as a pollinator). Pollination group B. *A.G.M.*

**Howgate Wonder**

**HOWGATE WONDER** — Picking time: Early October. Season: October to March. A very large fruited variety that is useful for exhibition and garden purposes. The fruits are pale green, becoming yellow, partly flushed and striped with brownish-red. Flesh is creamy white, fine and juicy and breaks up almost completely when cooked. Flavour is less intense than Bramley but the fruit stores well. Resistant to mildew. Suitable for the north. Spur-bearer. Pollination group C.

**LORD DERBY** — Picking time: Late September. Season: October to December. A cooker that will keep until December and does well on cold wet soils in the north and at the same time is resistant to scab. The green fruit has a good flavour and stays intact when cooked. A prolific and regular cropper. Spur-bearer. Partially self-fertile. Pollination group C.

**Lord Derby**

**NEWTON WONDER** — Picking time: Mid October. Season: November to March. Discovered growing in Norfolk in the 18th century, this is one of the best cookers with an extremely good fruity flavour. The fruits are very large. When baked it has a creamy texture and requires very little sugar. Spur-bearer. Pollination group C. *A.G.M.*

## CRAB APPLES (MALUS)

Crab apples (Malus) are probably the most popular flowering trees, brightening up our gardens in the spring with a mass of lovely pink and white blossom followed by large clusters of colourful fruits suitable for making crab apple jelly. They are also very useful universal pollinators for other varieties of apple.

**BUTTERBALL** — A stunning tree with large single white flowers and arching branches due to the heavy crops of large glowing butter coloured fruits. Spur-bearer. Self-fertile.

*Golden Hornet*

**EVERESTE** — Large soft to white flowers in the spring followed by small red and yellow fruits, holding well into winter. Spur-bearer. Self-fertile. *A.G.M.*

**GOLDEN HORNET** — White flowers, mid-season, followed by bright yellow almost conical fruits persisting until December. Spur-bearer. Self-fertile. *A.G.M.*

**HARRY BAKER** — This variety has exceptionally large dark pink flowers combined with large ruby red fruit with deep pink flesh lasting into mid-October. Makes a superb jelly. Spur-bearer. Self-fertile.

*Harry Baker*

**JOHN DOWNIE** — Snowed under in early spring with a mass of lovely pink-budded white flowers, followed by beautiful clusters of conical bright orange-scarlet fruit of refreshing flavour. Spur-bearer. Self-fertile. *A.G.M.*

**LAURA** — The flower is a unique bi-colour of pink and white and the persistent maroon to bright red fruits make a superb crab apple jelly. The tree is very compact reaching a maximum height of 2m (6ft) in ten years. Ideal for the patio. Spur-bearer. Self-fertile.

*John Downie*

**PINK GLOW** — The single white flowers are followed by bright pink fruits that look like large plums and make a superb jelly. A more disease resistant alternative to John Downie. Spur-bearer. Self-fertile.

**RED SENTINEL** — An excellent fruiting tree with white flowers and large clusters of bright red fruits that remain on the branches throughout the winter. Spur-bearer. Self-fertile. *A.G.M.*

*Laura*

# APPLES & PEARS

*Beth*

*Concorde*

*Conference*

*Doyenné du Comice*

## PEAR VARIETIES

*A.G.M. signifies the Award of Garden Merit, the Royal Horticultural Society's most prestigious award.*

**BETH** — Picking time: Early September. Season: Mid to late September. A small-medium sized pear with a rich sweet flavour. The flesh is melting, fine and creamy. Pale yellow with spots of russet. It crops very freely and early, often after two years. Spur-bearer. Pollination group D. *A.G.M.*

**BEURRÉ HARDY** — Picking time: Mid-September. Season: Mid to late October. Raised about 1820, this is one of the best garden varieties. Produces large handsome russet pears. The flesh is white, very smooth, juicy, sweet and aromatic. Will produce heavy crops given a good, sheltered position. Spur-bearer. Pollination group C. *A.G.M.*

**CONCORDE** — Picking time: Early October. Season: Late September to January. This new variety produces pale green, medium to large sized pears with excellent flavour and firm flesh. It is a heavy cropper, even on young trees. Spur-bearer. Self-fertile. Pollination group C. *A.G.M.*

**CONFERENCE** — Picking time: Late September. Season: Mid-October to late November. Raised in 1894, this remains the most widely grown pear. Produces long and narrow, olive green fruits with large patches of russet. The flesh is firm and of pleasant flavour. Stores well. Suitable for northern districts. It is by far the most reliable variety for garden planting. Spur-bearer. Partially self-fertile. Pollination group C. *A.G.M.*

**DOYENNÉ DU COMICE** — Picking time: Mid-October. Season: Late October to December. Raised in 1849, this late pear has an excellent rich, sweet and aromatic flavour. It has creamy white, melting, very juicy flesh. The skin is golden-yellow flushed with brownish-red. The fruits are large but cropping can be irregular. The tree needs a warm and sheltered site for successful fruit production and is therefore unsuitable for northern districts. Spur-bearer. Pollination group D. *A.G.M.*

**GLOU MORCEAU** — Picking time: Mid-November. Season: December to January. Raised in the eighteenth century, this is considered to be one of the best dessert pears, particularly when in season at Christmas. Produces good crops of medium to large fruits with white flesh, very smooth texture and a sweet, excellent flavour. The tree requires a sheltered position. Spur-bearer. Pollination group D.

**INVINCIBLE\*** — Picking time: September. Season: Mid-September to early December. This new heavy cropping variety is very hardy and reliable, setting crops each year. It will often produce a second flowering if the first flowers are destroyed after a heavy frost. The fruits are very large and can be used for dessert and culinary purposes. Self-fertile. Pollination group C.

**ONWARD** — Picking time: Mid-September. Season: Late September to early October. Often described as 'the early Comice.' This variety has a good, sweet flavour and creamy white, fine, melting, juicy flesh. The medium-large sized fruit is yellowish-green flushed with red and patches of russet. It is a good, reliable cropper, but has a short season and does not store well. Spur-bearer. Pollination group D. Will not pollinate Comice or vice versa. *A.G.M.*

*Red Williams'*

**RED WILLIAMS'** — Picking time: Early September. Season: September. A sport of Williams' with red skinned fruit. Creamy white, fine texture, melting and juicy. Crops early. Spur-bearer. Pollination group C. Will not pollinate Williams' or vice versa.

**WILLIAMS' BON CHRETIEN** — Picking time: Early September. Season: September. Raised about 1770, this is an early pear of excellent, sweet flavour. The flesh is white, soft and very juicy. The skin is pale yellow, faintly striped with red. Crops of medium-large sized fruits are regular, but not particularly heavy. The season is short and the fruit does not store well. Susceptible to scab. Spur-bearer. Pollination group C. *A.G.M.*

*Williams' Bon Chrétien*

## TREE FORMS

Bush trees and Minarettes can be grown in the open. Oblique cordons and espaliers should be grown against walls or fences or trained to freestanding posts and wires. Where space is limited, Minarettes, cordons and espaliers are the best choice.

## BUSH TREES

Bush apple trees on M26 and bush pears on Quince 'C' grow to 2.5-3.5m (8-12ft) in height and spread and should be spaced 3-4.5m (10-15ft) apart. They should be staked for the first four to five years.

## FORMATIVE PRUNING OF BUSH TREES

Formative pruning is essential and should be carried out in the dormant season, November-March. Its purpose is to produce a well-balanced tree with a strong branch framework capable of carrying heavy crops of fruit. Hard pruning is therefore carried out in the early years to produce strong growth *instead* of fruit. If formative pruning is not carried out the tree will tend to be weak, of poor shape with drooping branches and bare wood. Pruning in later years should be lighter to encourage fruiting.

**THE MAIDEN TREE** — If it is a maiden whip (a one year old tree with no side shoots) the tree should be pruned to a bud with at least two good buds just below it at about 75cm (30in) from ground level following planting. These buds should produce the primary branches during the tree's first growing season. If it is a feathered maiden with several well-balanced side shoots, the main stem should be pruned back to leave three or four good shoots at about 75cm (30in) from the ground. Shorten these side shoots by two thirds of their length to an outward facing bud and remove completely any shoots lower down on the main stem (see fig. 10). In the second year prune it as if it were a three year old tree.

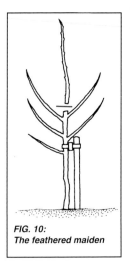

**FIG. 10:**
**The feathered maiden**

**THE TWO YEAR OLD TREE** — Prune three to five of the best placed shoots by half to an outward facing bud, to form the primary branches (see fig. 11). Remove any shoots lower down on the main stem and any inward growing shoots. The topmost shoot is often too upright to keep as a primary branch and should be removed. If left in it would tend to become dominant and crowd the centre of the tree.

**THE THREE YEAR OLD TREE** — Prune the leading shoots (leaders) of branches selected to extend the framework by half to a bud facing in the desired direction (see fig. 12). Select up to four good laterals to fill any gaps in the framework and shorten these by half to form secondary branches. Prune any remaining laterals to four buds to form fruiting spurs.

**THE FOUR YEAR OLD TREE** — Only limited formative pruning will be necessary. The tree should now be fruiting. Shorten leaders by one third and prune laterals (side shoots arising from a branch or leader) not required to extend the framework, to four buds (see fig. 13). From the fifth year onwards, the tree may be regarded as being established and should be pruned annually as described below.

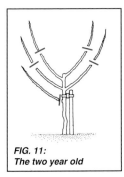

**FIG. 11:**
**The two year old**

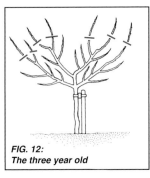

**FIG. 12:**
**The three year old**

**FIG. 13:**
**The four year old**

## WINTER PRUNING OF ESTABLISHED BUSH TREES

*AIMS*

(1)  To improve air circulation and light penetration in order to ripen wood and encourage fruit bud production and at the same time reduce the incidence of pests and diseases.
(2)  To control the size and shape of the tree for ease of picking, spraying, pruning etc.
(3)  To produce regular crops of fruit of a good size.

Unpruned trees tend to produce large crops of small, worthless fruit often damaged by pests and diseases. The main part of the crop is often out of reach at the top of the tree. Branches are often broken by the weight of the crop and cropping may become biennial. Overpruned trees tend to produce light crops of large, flavourless fruits which do not store well, and too much vegetative growth. Pruning is therefore done to achieve a good balance between shoot growth and fruit production.

*SPUR BEARERS & TIP BEARERS*

Apples and pears fall into two groups according to their fruiting habit — spur bearers and tip bearers. Spur bearers produce most of their fruit on short spurs on the older wood, for example the apple variety 'James Grieve' and the pear variety 'Conference'. Tip bearers produce most of their fruit on the tips of the previous season's growth (although they produce some spurs). Some apple varieties, like 'Bramley's Seedling' and 'Discovery', are partial tip bearers, producing some spurs and some fruit on the tips. Spur bearers and tip bearers should be pruned differently.

*PRUNING OF SPUR BEARERS*

Spur bearers are pruned by a combination of regulative pruning and spur pruning. The tree is composed of a main framework of branches with secondary branches about 38-45cm (15-18in) apart with spur systems about 23cm (9in) apart.

**REGULATIVE PRUNING**

Regulative pruning involves shortening or removing dead, diseased, broken, crowded and crossing branches, keeping the centre clear and controlling the height and spread of the tree. Branch leaders are normally tipped. If the tree becomes too large it may be necessary to remove an entire branch. If this is the

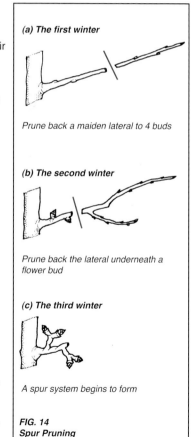

**(a) The first winter**

*Prune back a maiden lateral to 4 buds*

**(b) The second winter**

*Prune back the lateral underneath a flower bud*

**(c) The third winter**

*A spur system begins to form*

**FIG. 14**
**Spur Pruning**

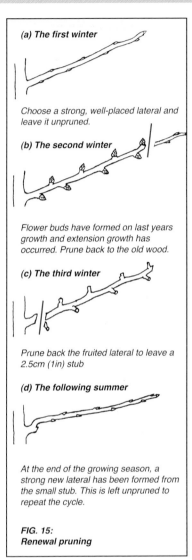

**(a) The first winter**

*Choose a strong, well-placed lateral and leave it unpruned.*

**(b) The second winter**

*Flower buds have formed on last years growth and extension growth has occurred. Prune back to the old wood.*

**(c) The third winter**

*Prune back the fruited lateral to leave a 2.5cm (1in) stub*

**(d) The following summer**

*At the end of the growing season, a strong new lateral has been formed from the small stub. This is left unpruned to repeat the cycle.*

**FIG. 15:**
**Renewal pruning**

case the branch should be cut out either at its point of origin or to a suitably placed secondary branch which is at least one third of the diameter of the branch being removed.

## SPUR PRUNING

Spur pruning involves shortening lateral shoots produced in the previous summer to four to six buds to encourage fruit bud formation close to the framework branches. As the tree gets older it may be necessary to thin out the number of fruiting spurs, or small fruit will result. This is done by pruning back to a fruit bud on two year old wood or removing portions of the spurs (see fig. 14).

## *PRUNING OF TIP BEARERS*

### REGULATIVE & SPUR PRUNING

Tip bearers are also pruned on the regulative system, but only limited spur pruning is required. The previous year's shoots of 23cm (9in) or less (roughly secateurs length) should be left unpruned. Longer shoots are spur pruned to prevent crowding and to stimulate the production of more short tip-bearing shoots in the following years. The branch leaders are 'tipped', removing the top three to four buds, pruning to a bud facing in the desired direction to make them branch out and so produce more tip-bearing shoots. Partial tip bearers require some light spur pruning.

### RENEWAL PRUNING

Renewal pruning involves cutting back a proportion of old branches that have produced fruit to a young strong shoot or a basal bud to promote fresh growth. This ensures that plenty of new growth is produced the following season (see fig. 15).

## PRUNING & TRAINING OF MINARETTES

Minarettes are supplied already pruned; further pruning will not be required before midsummer. With proper management a Minarette will continue to grow as a single column to about 1.8-2.5m (6-8ft) high with short fruit bearing spurs up and down its length. A small amount of trimming of the shoots to make sure it keeps to the desired size and shape will be necessary during the summer, as well as a minimum amount of pruning in the winter or early spring. This will help to ensure that the tree bears well-coloured, good sized, ripe fruit every year. With Minarettes practically all the pruning is carried out in the summer with the purpose of retarding their growth and encouraging the formation of fruit buds.

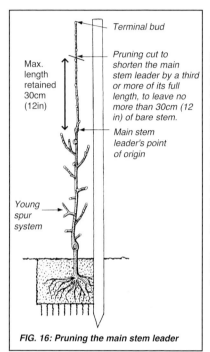

Terminal bud

Pruning cut to shorten the main stem leader by a third or more of its full length, to leave no more than 30cm (12 in) of bare stem.

Max. length retained 30cm (12in)

Main stem leader's point of origin

Young spur system

**FIG. 16: Pruning the main stem leader**

## PRUNING THE MAIN STEM LEADER

The term 'main stem leader' refers to the new growth which leads a Minarette upwards at the top of the tree (see fig. 16). The leader of a Minarette should be tied to a stake or cane at intervals throughout the summer months whilst it is soft and pliable and still growing, to keep it upright and from growing out at an angle to the main stem. This leader is only pruned in the winter or early spring and involves the removal of one third or more of the growth it made during the previous summer. It should be cut to a bud on the opposite side to the stake. The length of bare stem left after pruning should be no more than 30cm (12in). Once the tree has reached the required height, the leader should be shortened during winter or early spring to about 1cm (½in) from the point of origin. The leader is not pruned during the summer months. Pruning of the leader encourages the furnishment of side shoots along its length from which fruiting spurs are made.

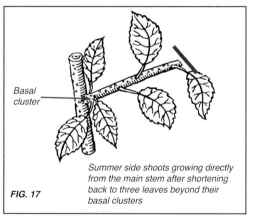

Basal cluster

*Summer side shoots growing directly from the main stem after shortening back to three leaves beyond their basal clusters*

**FIG. 17**

## PRUNING THE SIDE SHOOTS

This task is carried out in the summer. A Minarette will start to produce these side shoots from May onwards. The side shoot from a Minarette apple tree will have matured by early to mid-August in the south of England and approximately ten days later in the north. With pears, the shoots will have matured a week or so earlier. When this stage has been reached, summer pruning should commence. The shoots will have woody bases with a basal cluster of leaves and then light green leaves from the young shoots. Any shoots which are less than 20cm (8in) in length should not be pruned. New shoots growing **directly from the main stem** which are more than 20cm (8in) in length should be cut back to about three leaves above the basal cluster (see fig. 17). Any shoots growing **from existing side shoots or spurs** which are similarly in excess of 20cm (8in) in length should be cut back to **one leaf**, about

2.5cm (1in) or more beyond their basal cluster (see fig. 18). The basal cluster is easy to recognise — it is a small cluster of two to four closely spaced leaves at the base of a shoot.

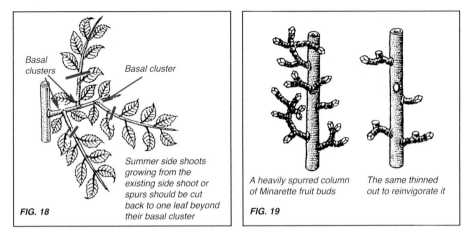

Basal clusters

Basal cluster

Summer side shoots growing from the existing side shoot or spurs should be cut back to one leaf beyond their basal cluster

FIG. 18

A heavily spurred column of Minarette fruit buds

The same thinned out to reinvigorate it

FIG. 19

*THINNING THE FRUIT SPURS*

As the tree gets older it may be necessary to thin out the number of fruiting spurs, if there are too many (see fig. 19). They should be thinned out during winter months. Reducing the number of fruit buds increases the size of fruit but it must not be overdone.

## PRUNING & TRAINING OF CORDONS

Cordons are usually grown as oblique cordons at an angle of about 45° (see fig. 9). They are trained to canes fixed to horizontal wires 60cm (2ft) apart (three wires for a 1.8m [6ft] fence). Cordons can be trained against fences, walls or on freestanding posts and wires in which case ideally they should be orientated north-south. The tree should be planted with the top of the cordon towards the north so the sun reaches all along its length. If an east-west orientation is unavoidable, the cordon should be inclined towards the east. The tree should be planted at an angle with its scion uppermost; the leader should be pruned by one third to a suitable bud and any side shoots greater than 15cm (6in) in length should be pruned to three or four buds beyond their basal cluster. Formative pruning is largely the same as for Minarettes.

## PRUNING & TRAINING OF ESPALIERS

Espaliers can be trained against fences or walls or on freestanding posts and wires. They consist of a central stem with a series of horizontal tiers of branches at intervals of 38-45cm (15-18in). They should have a space of 3.5 to 4.5m (12-15ft) wide (see page 27).

## FIRST YEAR

It is best to start off with a maiden whip (a one year old tree without side shoots). In April following planting cut back the central stem to a bud at about 37cm (15in) from the ground, ensuring there are two more good buds below on either side facing parallel with the wall. These will form the first two ribs (see fig. 20). In the summer, three shoots should be produced. The topmost should be trained vertically to a cane and the other two to canes at 45°. Any other shoots should be summer pruned to three leaves from the basal cluster of leaves, in early to mid-August (see fig. 21).

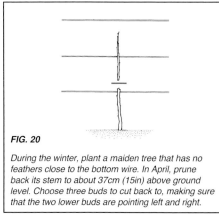

**FIG. 20**

*During the winter, plant a maiden tree that has no feathers close to the bottom wire. In April, prune back its stem to about 37cm (15in) above ground level. Choose three buds to cut back to, making sure that the two lower buds are pointing left and right.*

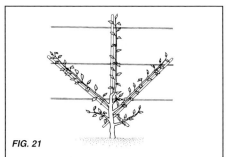

**FIG. 21**

*From June to September, train the shoot from the top bud vertically up a bamboo cane. The two lower buds should have their shoots trained at an angle of 45° to the main stem. They should be tied to canes fixed to the wire support.*

Where a feathered maiden is used, if there are two suitably placed side shoots one on each side at around 37-45cm (15-18in) from the ground, these can be used to form the first tier and tied horizontally. The leader should be pruned to three good buds at 37-45cm (15-18in) above this tier. All other side shoots should be shortened to about three buds. Using a feathered maiden effectively saves one year of training but the results might not be so good.

## SECOND YEAR

In the second winter the leader should be pruned back to the second wire to three good buds (normally 37-45cm [15-18in] above the

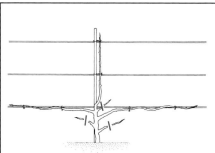

**FIG. 22**

*In November attach the two side branches to the bottom wire and tie them to the wire with soft string. Any surplus of laterals on the main stem should be shortened to three buds.*

first tier). The side branches should be lowered to the horizontal (see figs. 22 & 23). In the summer the second horizontal tier should be trained in the same way and the extension shoots at the ends of the first tier should be trained at 45°. Any other laterals should be summer pruned to three leaves from the basal cluster of leaves if they arise from the main stem and one leaf from the basal cluster if they arise from an existing spur. This process is repeated until the required number of tiers has been produced (see figs. 24-26).

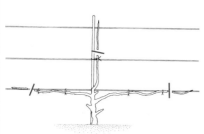

**FIG. 23**

At the same time, prune back the main stem leader to within 45cm (18in) at the middle wire, ensuring that three good buds are left to form the main leader and two new horizontal branches. If the side branches have not grown well, they should be cut back to one third to downward pointing buds.

**FIG. 24**

From July to September, the second tier of branches are trained in the same way as in the previous year. Any growths arising from the main side branches should be pruned back to three or four leaves above the basal cluster. Growths arising from the main stem should be shortened back to three leaves.

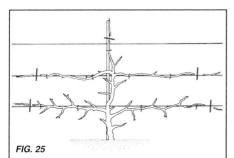

**FIG. 25**

In the autumn cut back the main stem leader to within 45cm (18in) of the uppermost side branch, ensuring that three good buds are left to form both a new leader and two horizontal branches. Continue as before.

**FIG. 26**

In late spring, when the last of the tiers have been formed and the tree has covered the space allotted to it, the new terminal growths of the vertical and horizontal branches should be cut back to their origins. Thereafter the side branches should be pruned as if they were cordons.

## FRUIT THINNING

**IN THE FIRST SUMMER** — After planting, fruitlets should be removed at an early stage.

**IN SUBSEQUENT YEARS** — If there is a good fruit set, thinning should be carried out after the natural thinning of fruits (the June drop) at the end of June to the beginning of July. Failure to thin can result in small, poor quality fruit and a tendency for the tree to crop biennially. The small, diseased and misshapen fruit should be removed, leaving the large, well-shaped ones. Thin to one or two fruits per cluster 10-15cm (4-6in) apart for dessert apples and pears, and 15-23cm (6-9in) apart for culinary apples.

# APPLES & PEARS

## MANURING

In early February each year broadcast over the rooting area:

$25g/m^2$ *(1oz/yd²) of sulphate of potash.*

and in late February for dessert apples:

$35g/m^2$ *(1¼oz/yd²) of Nitro-Chalk (calcium ammonium nitrate)*
*or sulphate of ammonia;*

and for trees grown in grass, pears and culinary apples:

$70g/m^2$ *(2½oz/yd²) of Nitro-Chalk (calcium ammonium nitrate)*
*or sulphate of ammonia;*

and every third year:

$70g/m^2$ *(2½oz/yd²) of superphosphate.*

Alternatively a compound fertilizer may be used annually following the manufacturer's recommendations.

If magnesium deficiency is a persistent problem, in early April each year apply:

$50g/m^2$ *(1¾oz/yd²) of magnesium sulphate (Epsom salts).*

## HARVESTING & STORAGE

*APPLES*

To assess when to pick, watch for the first true windfalls (not premature drop due to codling moth). Lift the fruit in the palm of the hand and if it leaves the spur easily with its stalk intact, it is ready for picking. Early apples should be picked before they are fully ripe, and before they become soft and mealy (the pips are often not fully brown when picked). Pick the ripest, best coloured fruits first, usually those near the top of the tree on the south (sunny side). Late varieties should be allowed to hang on the tree as long as possible and their pips should be fully brown when picked but most should be harvested by the end of October except the very late varieties. Fruit should be stored in a cool, dark but frost-free place such as a garage or shed. Apples are best laid on trays and inspected regularly for rot. They will keep longer if wrapped in tissue paper. Apples can also be stored in polythene bags which reduces shrivelling and keeps the fruit clean. Thin polythene bags which hold about 2.5kg (5½lb) of fruit should be used. After filling the bag, the mouth of the bag should be folded over, but not sealed. One 5mm (¼in) diameter hole should be made for every 1kg (2¼lb) of fruit. The holes should be made in different parts of the bag. If the variety 'Bramley's Seedling' is stored in this way twice as many holes should be made, as the fruit can be spoiled by an excessive build up of carbon dioxide. As with other methods of storage, it should be kept in a cool, dark, frost-free place and inspected regularly for rot.

## PEARS

It is difficult to judge when to pick pears. Early and mid-season varieties should be picked when they are almost ready but still hard. If they are left on the tree too long they become soft and mealy in the centre. There is a very slight colour change from green to pale green with many varieties when they are ready for harvesting. Lift the pear in the palm of the hand and give it a slight twist and a tug. If it is ready it should leave the spur with the stalk intact. The fruit should be stored in a cool, dark place and inspected regularly for rot; early pears ripen a week or so after picking; late pears are picked when they leave the spurs easily and windfalls are a good indication that they are ready. They should be stored in a cool, dark, frost-free place until ripe. Ripening can be hastened, if desired, by subjecting them to normal living room temperatures.

## PESTS, DISEASES & DISORDERS

Some of the most troublesome pests, diseases and disorders are listed in the following table. See chapters on 'Common Fruiting Problems' and 'Pests & Diseases' for details.

| Symptoms | Possible problem | Symptoms | Possible problem |
|---|---|---|---|
| Leaf distortion/ marking on leaves | Aphids<br>Apple mildew<br>Pear leaf blister mite<br>Pear leaf midge<br>Spider mite | Maggots in fruit | Apple sawfly<br>Codling moth<br>Pear midge |
| Leaves/shoots dying off | Apple/pear canker<br>Apple mildew<br>Fireblight<br>Frost damage | Marked/ distorted fruit | Aphids<br>Apple sawfly<br>Apple/pear scab<br>Bitter pit<br>Brown rot<br>Green capsid bug<br>Winter moth |
| Holes in leaves | Green capsid bug<br>Winter moth | Fruit drop | Apple sawfly<br>Codling moth<br>Frost damage<br>Incomplete pollination<br>Pear midge<br>Winter moth |
| Disfigured/ cracking bark | Apple/pear canker<br>Fireblight<br>Woolly aphid | | |
| Blossom damage | Apple blossom weevil<br>Apple mildew | | |

# PLUMS, GAGES, DAMSONS
# CHERRY PLUMS & BULLACE

**P**lums, gages and damsons (referred to as plums from now on) are excellent as fresh fruit and for cooking and preserving. Plums are a valuable fruit not always easy to obtain from the shops. They flower early and so need shelter from cold winds. Because of this, in years with severe spring frosts the crop can be much reduced or non-existent unless some form of protection is given.

## VARIETIES

*A.G.M. signifies the Award of Garden Merit, the Royal Horticultural Society's most prestigious award.*

*PLUMS*

**BLUE TIT** — Raised in the U.K. and introduced in 1938, this dual-purpose plum is one of the best garden varieties, cropping heavily and reliably, even when there are spring frosts. The medium-sized blue plums have a dense blue bloom and are juicy and well flavoured. Ripens early to mid-August. Self-fertile. Pollination group C. *A.G.M.*

Blue Tit

**COE'S GOLDEN DROP** — Raised in Suffolk in 1800, this is an excellent large yellow dessert plum. The fruits are very juicy and very sweet, having an apricot-like flavour. Cropping is erratic, sometimes heavy but usually light. It will benefit from being grown as a fan against a warm, south facing wall. Ripens mid to late September. Requires a pollinator. Pollination group B.

Czar

**CZAR** — This heavy cropping culinary variety was raised in c1870 and was at one time grown extensively commercially in the U.K. It produces medium-sized dark purple plums. The fruits are very juicy and have a good acid flavour. It crops heavily and reliably even in years when there are spring frosts. Ripens early August. Self-fertile. Pollination group B. *A.G.M.*

**JUBILEE** — This new variety, raised in Sweden is similar to Victoria in flavour and appearance but with much larger fruits, often twice the size of Victoria. It ripens one week earlier than Victoria but flowers at the same time. Self-fertile. Pollination group B.

Jubilee

# PLUMS, GAGES, DAMSONS CHERRY PLUMS & BULLACE

**Marjorie's Seedling**

**MARJORIES SEEDLING** — Introduced in 1928, this is the main late dessert/culinary plum variety grown commercially in the U.K. It produces heavy crops of large, purplish fruits with blue bloom. The yellow flesh is soft and juicy with good flavour. The tree is very resistant to disease and is suitable for colder districts. Ripens late September. The fruits will hang on the tree until the end of October. Self-fertile. Pollination group C. *A.G.M.*

**OPAL** — Raised in Sweden in 1925, this early dessert plum is heavy cropping and reliable. The medium-sized red fruits have a distinct 'gage like' texture and excellent taste. Ripens late July to early August. Self-fertile. Pollination group B. *A.G.M.*

**VICTORIA** — Introduced about 1840, this dessert/culinary plum is the most widely grown commercial variety in the U.K. It is one of the best varieties for cooking and when fully ripe it is of good flavour for dessert. The large fruits are pale-red and juicy. One of the most heavy cropping plums. Frost resistant. Ripens late August to early September. Self-fertile. Pollination group B. *A.G.M.*

**Victoria**

## GAGES

**CAMBRIDGE GAGE** — An excellent flavoured, dessert/culinary gage, very similar to the old fashioned Green Gage. It crops more reliably than the old Green Gage. The small fruits are yellow-green and very juicy, Ripens mid to late August. Partially self-fertile. Pollination group C. *A.G.M.*

**DENNISTON'S SUPERB (IMPERIAL GAGE)** — Raised around 1790, this variety is one of the most reliable gages. It produces heavy crops of sweet gages with transparent flesh. Suitable for midland and northern regions. Ripens late August. Self-fertile. Pollination group B. *A.G.M.*

**Cambridge Gage**

**EARLY TRANSPARENT GAGE** — Introduced in 1873, this gage is of the highest quality. Suitable for all purposes. Produces small golden juicy fruits. Excellent rich flavour. Prone to splitting. Heavy cropping and reliable. Self-fertile. Pollination group B.

**Early Transparent Gage**

# PLUMS, GAGES, DAMSONS
# CHERRY PLUMS & BULLACE

**GREEN GAGE** — Introduced to France in the reign of Francis I (1494-1547) this is usually considered the finest flavoured plum. It produces small yellowish-green fruits that are very juicy, rich and aromatic and ideal for all purposes. It is prone to splitting and attacks by birds and wasps. Requires a pollinator. Pollination group C.

**OULLIN'S GOLDEN GAGE** — Introduced to the U.K. before 1856, this variety is reliable and heavy cropping, but slow to start bearing. The fruits are large, round and yellow. The flesh is pale yellow and transparent. Sweet flavour. Slow to bear. Vigorous growth. Ripens mid-August. Self-fertile. Pollination group C. *A.G.M.*

*Merryweather Damson*

## DAMSONS

**MERRYWEATHER DAMSON** — Introduced in 1907, this variety is an excellent all round performer producing large, juicy, acidic fruits for dessert and culinary use in September. Self-fertile. Pollination group B.

**PRUNE DAMSON (SHROPSHIRE DAMSON)** — First recorded in 1676, this variety produces heavy crops of small, oval, blue-black fruits with green-yellow flesh. Ripens September to October.  Dwarfish growth. Excellent flavour. Self-fertile. Pollination group C. *A.G.M.*

*Prune Damson*

## CHERRY PLUMS (MIRABELLES)

**GYPSY** — This new variety was bred in the Ukraine and produces very large, dark carmine fruits with an orangey flesh. Firm and juicy with a sugary, rich flavour. Requires a pollinator. Pollination group A.

**GOLDEN SPHERE** — Bred in the Ukraine, this variety produces large yellow, almost translucent fruit. Firm and juicy with a good fresh 'plum' flavour. Requires a pollinator. Pollination group A.

*Gypsy*

## BULLACE

**LANGLEY BULLACE** — Raised in 1920, this old variety is generally considered the best bullace producing small blue-black fruits which should be cooked and make excellent jam. Crops heavily and reliably.  Ripens late September. Self-fertile. Pollination group B.

*Golden Sphere*

53

# PLUMS, GAGES, DAMSONS
# CHERRY PLUMS & BULLACE

## TREE FORMS

In the more favourable areas of the British Isles plums can be grown as bush, Minarette or pyramid trees but in the colder regions they are best grown as oblique cordons or as a fan on a warm south, south-west or south-east facing wall or fence. The best flavoured and late season plums and gages such as 'Coe's Golden Drop' and 'Cambridge Gage' are best grown as a fan on a warm wall or fence, even in the warmer regions. Minarettes and pyramids are a better form for the garden than bushes since their low angled branches are less liable to break and they are easier to pick, prune, spray and net. They also occupy less space than a bush tree. Damsons make particularly good pyramids.

## THE TIME FOR PRUNING

Stone fruits (plums, gages, damsons, cherries, peaches, nectarines, apricots and sweet almonds) should not be pruned during the dormant season because of the risk of silver leaf and bacterial canker infection. For this reason pruning after planting is delayed until April to June. All pruning cuts in the initial training should be protected with a wound paint.

## PRUNING & TRAINING OF BUSHES

Plums grown on St. Julien 'A' rootstock will make a bush 3.6-4.5m (12-15ft) in height and spread and need to be spaced 3.6-4.5m (12-15ft) apart and if grown on Pixy rootstock, will make a bush 2.4-3m (8-10ft) in height and should be spaced 2.4-3m (8-10ft) apart. They should be staked for the first four to five years for St Julien 'A' and permanently for Pixy.

### INITIAL TRAINING

The formative pruning is much the same as for the apple for the first two to three years but should be carried out in April (see page 42). They are normally grown on a slightly longer leg than apples; in the first year the main stem should be pruned to a bud or well-placed lateral at about 90cm (3ft) from ground level.

If it is a feathered maiden, the main stem should be pruned back to leave three or four good side shoots at about 90cm (3ft) from the ground. Shorten these side shoots by two thirds of their length to an outward-facing bud and remove any shoots lower down on the main stem.

### PRUNING OF THE CROPPING TREE

Pruning of the cropping tree is lighter than for apples and pears. In April, crossing, crowding, dead, diseased and broken branches are removed as necessary. A plum can tolerate a more crowded head than apples and pears.

# PLUMS, GAGES, DAMSONS
# CHERRY PLUMS & BULLACE

## PRUNING & TRAINING OF PYRAMIDS

A pyramid plum on St. Julien 'A' rootstock will grow to 2.4-2.7m (8-9ft) and should be spaced 3-3.6m (10-12ft) apart. A pyramid on Pixy rootstock will grow to 1.8-2.1m (6-7ft) and should be spaced 2.4-3m (8-10ft) apart. Trees should be staked for the first five years using a 2.4m (8ft) stake driven 60cm (2ft) into the ground.

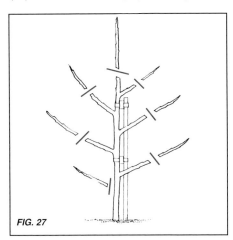

FIG. 27

### INITIAL TRAINING

Prune the main stem to a good bud at about 1.2m (4ft) from ground level for St Julien 'A' and 1m (3ft 3in) for Pixy. Remove any feathers (side shoots) within 45cm (18in) of the ground and shorten the rest to half their length to a downward facing bud. In the summer the central leader should be tied to the stake but not pruned (see fig. 27).

In late July the young current season's shoots should be pruned by shortening the branch leaders to 20cm (8in) to a downward facing bud (see fig. 28) and branch laterals to 15cm (6in).

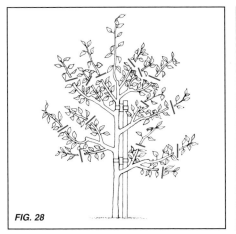

FIG. 28

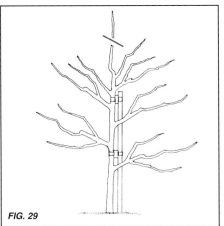

FIG. 29

Each April the central leader's previous summer's growth should be cut back by two thirds until it has reached the desired height (see fig. 29).

If the side branches are not growing at a very low angle they should be tied down to 30° above the horizontal in late July. They can be tied to pegs in the ground, or to the stake, or even weighted bags can be used. This is particularly suitable for the side branches of

**FIG. 30**

vigorous varieties such as 'Marjorie's Seedling' as well as for upright side-branch growth at the top of the tree but not the central leader. The strings can be removed once the branches have set in position in late autumn. The aim should be to achieve a weeping habit to the tree as far as possible.

## PRUNING IN SUBSEQUENT YEARS

Once the desired height has been reached, the central leader should be pruned to 2.5cm (1in) in May. In late June, any vertical shoots competing with the central leader are removed. In late July the current season's growth should be pruned by shortening the branch leaders to 20cm (8in) to a downward facing bud (see fig. 30) and laterals to 15cm (6in).

## PRUNING & TRAINING OF MINARETTES

Minarettes are supplied already pruned; further pruning in the case of Minarette stone fruits will not be required before the late spring. With proper management a Minarette will continue to grow as a single column to about 1.8-2.4m (6-8ft) high with short fruit bearing spurs up and down its length. A certain amount of trimming and pruning to make sure it keeps to the desired size and shape will be necessary during the summer as well as a minimum amount of pruning in late spring. This will help to ensure that the tree bears well-coloured, good sized, ripe fruit every year. With Minarettes practically all the pruning is carried out in the summer with the purpose of retarding their growth and encouraging the formation of fruit buds.

### PRUNING THE MAIN STEM LEADER

The term 'main stem leader' refers to the new growth which leads a Minarette upwards at the top of the tree (see fig. 16). The main stem leaders of stone fruits grow very rapidly and must therefore have their respective growing points pinched out **when they have reached a length of 30cm (12in)**. A new leader will grow from the point where the initial leader was pinched out and this in turn should have its growing point similarly pinched out **as soon as it also has attained a length of 30cm (12in).** This pinching out of the leader is repeated until the late summer but is not pruned back to 30cm (12in) **until May of the following year.**

The reason for the delay in pruning the final leader is to help avoid the risk of silver leaf or bacterial canker gaining entry to the tree through a pruning cut made in the autumn or winter. The risk is minimal when pruning of stone fruits is delayed until the late spring or summer. Once a Minarette has reached its desired height the leader should be pruned in the same way as if it were a side shoot.

# PLUMS, GAGES, DAMSONS
# CHERRY PLUMS & BULLACE

## PRUNING THE SIDE SHOOTS

In the case of stone fruits, all current season's shoots emanating directly from the main stem should have their growing points pinched out once they have made six leaves beyond their basal clusters; this is likely to be some time during May (see fig. 31). Secondary growth will appear and as soon as they have made six leaves they too should be pinched or cut back but this time to one leaf from their respective points of origin (see fig. 32). Any further secondary growth should be dealt with similarly. Any secondary growth occurring in the late summer should be shortened to one leaf the following spring, otherwise spring pruning (March-April) should only ever be carried out to stone fruits if a tree is making too much secondary growth or to renovate a neglected tree.

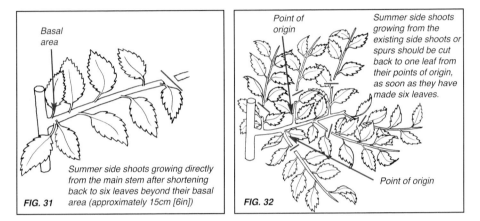

Basal area

Summer side shoots growing directly from the main stem after shortening back to six leaves beyond their basal area (approximately 15cm [6in])

**FIG. 31**

Point of origin

Summer side shoots growing from the existing side shoots or spurs should be cut back to one leaf from their points of origin, as soon as they have made six leaves.

Point of origin

**FIG. 32**

## THINNING THE FRUIT SPURS

As the tree gets older it may be necessary to thin out the number of fruiting spurs if there are too many (see page 46). Unlike apples, they should be thinned out during the late spring. Reducing the number of fruit buds increases the size of fruit but it must not be overdone.

# PRUNING & TRAINING OF CORDONS

Unlike Minarettes, cordons may need some initial pruning and training. Cordons should be planted at an angle of around 45° with the scion uppermost and should be spaced 75cm-90cm (2½-3ft) apart (see page 27). They are trained to canes fixed to horizontal wires 60cm (2ft) apart (three wires for a 1.8m [6ft] fence). They should ideally be orientated north-south. The trees should be planted with the top of each cordon inclined towards the north so the sun reaches all along their length. If an east-west orientation is unavoidable the cordons should be inclined towards the east.

Pruning should be delayed until March or April when the leading shoot should be pruned by one third to a suitable bud and any side shoots greater than 15cm (6in) in length should be pruned to three or four buds. Formative pruning is largely the same as for Minarettes.

# PLUMS, GAGES, DAMSONS CHERRY PLUMS & BULLACE

## PRUNING & TRAINING OF FANS

This is the best form to train stone fruits where space is limited, especially in colder districts. A fan-trained tree on St. Julien 'A' needs a space of at least 4.5m (15ft) wide and 2.1-2.4m (7-8ft) high and on Pixy 3.6m (12ft) wide and 1.8m (6ft) high (the size of two standard fence panels). Trees should be planted 15-23cm (6-9in) away from the wall or fence and the stem inclined slightly towards it. The wall should be fitted with horizontal wires 15cm (6in) apart.

During the first three years the pruning of a plum fan is the same as for a peach fan and should only be undertaken in the spring and summer. This procedure also applies to cherries.

### *THE FIRST YEAR*

Where a maiden whip is used (a tree without side shoots), cut back the central stem in April, following planting, to a bud at about 60cm (2ft) from the ground ensuring that there are two more good buds below on either side, facing parallel with the wall. These will form the first two ribs (see page 47, fig. 20). In early to midsummer, once the two laterals have formed, cut back the central stem to the uppermost lateral. Train the two shoots along canes fixed to the wires at 45°. Pinch back any other shoot on the main stem to one or two leaves (see page 47, fig. 21).

Where a feathered maiden is used (a tree with side shoots), cut back the central stem in April following planting, to the uppermost of five strong laterals growing parallel with the fence on alternate sides of the main stem. The topmost should be about 60cm (2ft) above the ground. Prune the bottom four selected shoots back to the first upward facing bud, leaving the topmost lateral unpruned (see fig. 33). in the early summer, choose three strong shoots. Train the top one vertically, one to the left and one to the right. Cut back all other buds and shoots (see fig. 34). In June, tie the lengthening side shoots to canes set at an angle of 45° to the horizontal. In the late summer remove the central shoot and paint the cut with a wound paint to avoid infection (see fig. 35). This method usually produces the best result.

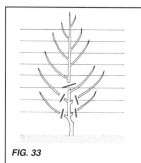

**FIG. 33**

*During April a feathered maiden should be cut back to a lateral about 60cm (2ft) from the ground, leaving two good laterals on each side. These four laterals should be cut back to one bud.*

**FIG. 34**

*During the early part of the summer, three shoots should be selected. The uppermost one should be trained vertically and the other two, trained left and right. All other buds or shoots should be removed.*

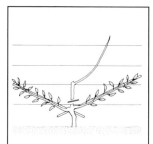

**FIG. 35**

*In June the lengthening side shoots should be tied to canes fixed at an angle of 45° to the horizontal. In September the central shoot should be removed, painting the cut with a wound paint.*

# PLUMS, GAGES, DAMSONS
# CHERRY PLUMS & BULLACE

Alternatively, for a quicker result, the main stem of a feathered maiden can be cut back to two strong laterals (one on either side). The two selected laterals should be shortened to 30-45cm (12-18in) from the main stem. These will form the first two ribs, and effectively saves one year (see fig. 36). The tree can now be treated as a two year old.

## THE SECOND YEAR

The following April the ribs should be cut back by about half, each to an upward facing bud (see fig. 36). During the summer the leaders are tied to the canes. Two more shoots spaced 10-15cm (4-6in) apart on the upper side of each rib and one below should be selected and tied in as they grow. Any shoots growing inwards towards the wall should be rubbed out. Any other shoots should be pinched back to one to two leaves (see fig. 37).

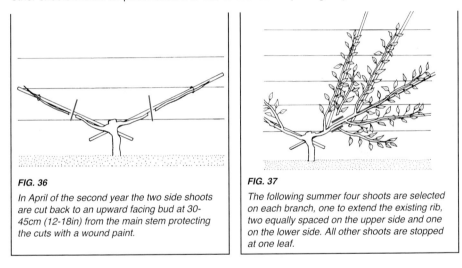

**FIG. 36**

*In April of the second year the two side shoots are cut back to an upward facing bud at 30-45cm (12-18in) from the main stem protecting the cuts with a wound paint.*

**FIG. 37**

*The following summer four shoots are selected on each branch, one to extend the existing rib, two equally spaced on the upper side and one on the lower side. All other shoots are stopped at one leaf.*

## THE THIRD YEAR ONWARDS

In April of the third year, the ribs should be cut back by one third to a half of the previous summer's growth (see fig. 38). This process is repeated until the required area against the wall is filled.

In the summer, the leading shoots on each rib are allowed to extend (see fig. 39). Train three shoots on each branch to extend the framework and tie to bamboo canes every 10cm (4in). Any shoots growing inwards towards the wall should be rubbed out. Any other shoots not required for the framework should have their growing points pinched once they have made six leaves. Any sub laterals should be stopped at one leaf. Later in the summer, the pinched out shoots should be pruned back to three leaves to help develop fruit buds to form.

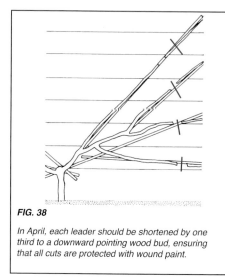

**FIG. 38**

*In April, each leader should be shortened by one third to a downward pointing wood bud, ensuring that all cuts are protected with wound paint.*

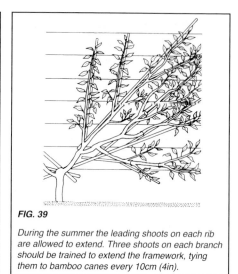

**FIG. 39**

*During the summer the leading shoots on each rib are allowed to extend. Three shoots on each branch should be trained to extend the framework, tying them to bamboo canes every 10cm (4in).*

## PRUNING THE ESTABLISHED FAN

During the summer any shoots growing inwards towards the wall should be rubbed out as they appear. Any required to extend the fan are tied in. The remaining laterals need to be kept pinched back to six leaves (see fig. 40). After picking they should be shortened back to three leaves (see fig. 41). Any very vigorous vertical shoots must be removed entirely or bent over to fill a gap and any that are dead, diseased or making poor growth should be removed. As growth begins in the spring, any shoots growing directly towards or away from the fence should be rubbed out (see fig. 42).

**FIG. 40**

*From late June to late July, new shoots should have their growing points pinched out when they have made six or seven leaves and are not wanted for the framework. This will result in the formation of a fruit-bearing spur system.*

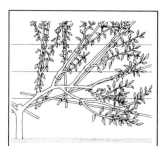

**FIG. 41**

*After harvest, between mid-August and mid-September, the pinched-out shoots should be pruned back to three leaves to help develop fruit buds to form at their bases the following year.*

**FIG. 42**

*From the fourth year onwards, as growth begins in the spring, side shoots growing directly towards the fence or outwards in the opposite direction should be rubbed out.*

# PLUMS, GAGES, DAMSONS
# CHERRY PLUMS & BULLACE

## FRUIT THINNING

If there is a heavy crop, the fruits should be thinned when they are about hazelnut size and again when they are twice that size. Small, misshapen and diseased fruits should be removed to leave the rest 5-7.5cm (2-3in) apart or 10cm (4in) apart for large fruited varieties.

## MANURING

In early February each year, broadcast over the rooting area:

*15g/m² (½oz/yd²) of sulphate of potash,*
*and 50g/m² (1¾oz/yd²) of sulphate of ammonia or Nitro-Chalk*
*(calcium ammonium nitrate);*

and every third year:

*70g/m² (2½oz/yd²) of superphosphate.*

Alternatively, a compound fertilizer may be used annually following the manufacturer's recommendations.

## HARVESTING & STORAGE

Plums should be picked when fully coloured and ripe, at which stage they part easily from the spur. It will be necessary to pick over the tree several times, as not all the fruit ripens at once. Fruit for bottling, jam or cooking should be picked when slightly underripe but dessert fruit should be fully ripe. Most plums will not keep long and are best used straightaway. But some late plums can be stored; the variety 'Coe's Golden Drop' will keep up to a month if stored in a cool, dark place.

## PESTS, DISEASES & DISORDERS

Some of the most troublesome pests, diseases and disorders are listed in the following table. See chapters on 'Common Fruiting Problems' and 'Pests & Diseases' for details.

| Symptoms | Possible problem | Symptoms | Possible problem |
|----------|------------------|----------|------------------|
| Leaf distortion/ marking on leaves | Aphids<br>Apple leaf miner<br>Rust<br>Silver leaf<br>Spider mite | Maggots in fruit | Codling moth<br>Plum fruit moth<br>Plum sawfly<br>(see apple sawfly) |
| Leaves/shoots/ branches dying off | Bacterial canker<br>Frost damage<br>Silver leaf | Marked/ distorted fruit | Aphids<br>Brown rot<br>Green capsid bug<br>Winter moth |
| Holes in leaves | Bacterial canker<br>Green capsid bug<br>Winter moth | Fruit drop | Codling moth<br>Frost damage<br>Incomplete pollination<br>Plum fruit moth<br>Winter moth |
| Discoloured/ cracking bark | Bacterial canker | | |

# APRICOTS

Richly flavoured and delicious, apricots need a warm sheltered situation to succeed. In colder regions of the U.K. they should only be grown under glass. They flower very early, so frost protection may be necessary. They are self-fertile, so only one tree needs to be grown but hand pollination using a soft brush or rabbit's tail may be necessary as there may be few pollinating insects around at flowering time.

*Alfred*

*Tomcot*

## VARIETIES

There are several varieties from which to choose and some of the best are:

**ALFRED** — This is an orange coloured apricot of good flavour and moderately juicy, ripening in July/August. Its great value is that it is less prone to dieback than other varieties.

**GOLDEN GLOW** – This new variety found on the side of the Malvern Hills in Worcestershire is very hardy, cropping well as a free standing tree in U.K. conditions. Large fruits. Very good flavour.

**MOORPARK** — Moorpark is an orange apricot with firm, juicy, orange flesh of good flavour, ripening in August. It is reliable and the most commonly grown apricot in England. It was raised in 1760. *R.H.S. Award of Garden Merit.*

**TOMCOT** — This new variety is far more reliable than other apricots producing masses of flower and very large fruits with a strong red blush on an orange background. The fruits have a sweet, aromatic flavour. A wise choice for northern gardens.

## TREE FORMS

Although often associated with peaches, apricots in fact have a similar growth habit to plums and so can be pruned and trained in the same way (see pages 54-60). In most areas they will only crop well if grown as a fan on a warm south, south-west or west facing wall or fence but in warmer parts of the country they can be grown as bushes or pyramids. Apricots are grown on St. Julien 'A' rootstock. As a fan, a space of about 4.5m (15ft) wide by 2.1-2.4m (7-8ft) high is required. Pyramids should be spaced 3.0-3.6m (10-12ft) apart and bushes 3.6-4.5m (12-15ft) apart.

# APRICOTS

## FRUIT THINNING

Thinning should be carried out gradually, starting when the fruits are the size of hazelnuts. Remove small, misshapen and awkwardly placed fruit to leave fruits 7.5-10cm (3-4in) apart.

## MANURING

In early February each year, broadcast over the rooting area:

$35g/m^2$ *(1¼oz/yd²) of sulphate of potash,*
*and $25g/m^2$ (1oz/yd²) of Nitro-Chalk (calcium ammonium nitrate)*
*or sulphate of ammonia;*

and every third year:

$70g/m^2$ *(2½oz/yd²) of superphosphate.*

Alternatively, a compound fertilizer may be used following the manufacturer's recommendations.

## HARVESTING & STORAGE

Apricots should be picked for dessert when fully coloured and ripe, when they part easily from the spur. They will require picking over several times. Apricots can be picked slightly under-ripe for jam, cooking or bottling. They will not keep for any length of time.

## PESTS, DISEASES & DISORDERS

Some of the most troublesome pests, diseases and disorders are listed in the following table. See chapters on 'Common Fruiting Problems' and 'Pests & Diseases' for details.

| Symptoms | Possible problem | Symptoms | Possible problem |
|---|---|---|---|
| Leaf distortion/ marking on leaves | Aphids Silver leaf Spider mite | Holes in leaves | Bacterial canker |
| | | Discoloured/ cracking bark | Bacterial canker |
| Leaves/shoots/ branches dying off | Apricot dieback Bacterial canker Frost damage Silver leaf | Marked/ distorted fruit | Aphids Brown rot |
| | | Fruit drop | Frost damage Incomplete pollination |

# PEACHES, NECTARINES & ALMONDS

**P**eaches and nectarines can be grown successfully outdoors provided they are situated in a warm, sunny and sheltered position. Nectarines are smooth skinned forms of the peach and are grown in exactly the same way but are slightly less hardy. They are best grown as a fan against a south, south-west or west facing wall or fence where they can be easily protected against spring frosts and peach leaf curl. In sheltered positions in the south they can also be grown as a bush tree, which is much less labour intensive than a fan.

The almond tree is not dissimilar to the peach in its size, habit of growth, leaf form and flower. Because it comes into flower even earlier than the peach, the risk of blossom being damaged by frost is much greater. When it can be grown without the flowers being damaged by frost, satisfactory yields can be obtained. It is grafted onto St. Julien 'A' rootstock and trained either as a bush, half-standard or standard.

*Peregrine*

*Rochester*

## VARIETIES

Only varieties of peach and nectarine which will ripen early, during July or August, are suitable for growing outdoors. Later varieties will not ripen successfully unless grown under glass. ***A.G.M. signifies the Award of Garden Merit, the Royal Horticultural Society's most prestigious award.***

### PEACHES

**PEREGRINE** — This is one of the best flavoured peaches with juicy, white flesh ripening in mid to late August. It crops well and reliably. Self-fertile. *A.G.M.*

**ROCHESTER** — Rochester is a large yellow-fleshed peach of good flavour ripening early to mid-August. It crops heavily and is probably the most reliable peach for growing outdoors in this country. Self-fertile. *A.G.M.*

**SATURNE** — A peento (flat shaped) peach from China with very good honey taste and white flesh. Extremely sweet and juicy. Self-fertile.

### NECTARINES

**EARLY RIVERS** — One of the earliest nectarines ripening in mid-July. Pale yellow flesh. Good flavour. Self-fertile. *A.G.M.*

**LORD NAPIER** — Richly flavoured with pale green flesh, ripening in early August. One of the best nectarines, ripening early enough to be grown outdoors. Self-fertile. *A.G.M.*

*Saturne*

# PEACHES, NECTARINES & ALMONDS

## PRUNING & TRAINING OF BUSHES

### INITIAL TRAINING

A bush tree on St. Julien 'A' will grow to 3.5-4.5m (12-15ft) in height and spread and should be spaced 4.5-5.5m (15-18ft) apart. Formative pruning is much the same as for the apple during the first two to three years and should be carried out in April (see page 42). They are normally grown on a slightly longer leg than apples. The main stem should be pruned to a bud or well-placed lateral at about 90cm (3ft) above ground level in April following planting.

### PRUNING OF THE CROPPING TREE

Pruning of the cropping tree differs from other fruits as peaches produce most of their fruit on wood produced the previous year. In April each year cut out some two and three year old wood back to young replacement shoots and remove any dead, diseased, crossing, crowded or broken branches. Pruning cuts must be protected with a wound paint.

## PRUNING & TRAINING OF FANS

### INITIAL TRAINING

A fan-trained tree on St. Julien 'A' needs a space of at least 3.5m (12ft) wide by 1.8m (6ft) high. The formative pruning of peaches and nectarines during the first two years is the same as for a fan-trained plum (see pages 58-59). The pruning and training from the third year onwards is different because the peach fruits on wood made the previous year and so replacement pruning is necessary.

### THIRD SUMMER

Any buds growing directly towards the wall should be rubbed out. Allow the leading shoots on each rib to extend — these will add to the framework. Shoots should also be allowed to grow out from the ribs every 10-15cm (4-6in) on the upper and lower sides. These selected shoots should be stopped at 45cm (18in) and tied in. The remainder should be pinched back to one or two leaves (see page 66, fig. 43).

### TRAINING THE ESTABLISHED CROPPING TREE

This is a labour intensive task as there is regular disbudding, pinching back and tying in to be done during the summer. Any shoots growing directly towards the wall as growth commences should be rubbed out. Any shoots growing directly away from the wall should be stopped at two leaves. This is the same technique as for plums (see page 60, fig. 42).

The young flowering laterals should be dealt with next. At the base of these will be one or more shoots. One of these should be allowed to develop as the replacement shoot and one in the middle kept as a reserve. The fruiting lateral should also be allowed to extend. The basal and reserve laterals should be allowed to grow out until they are 45cm (18in) long, and

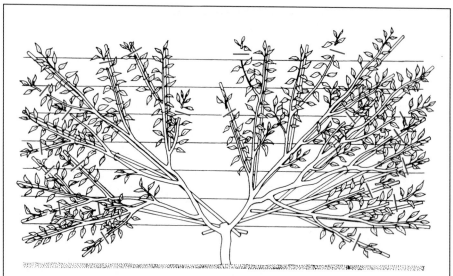

**FIG. 43**

*Towards the end of the summer, when those laterals selected have made 45cm (18in) of new growth they should have their growing points pinched out and then tied to canes supported on the wires. These are the laterals which carry the fruit next year.*

the extension lateral until it has made six leaves. They should then have their growing points pinched out. Shoots growing too close to a fruit should be pinched back to two good leaves. The remainder of unwanted shoots should be stopped at two leaves or removed entirely if they are crowded. Any subsequent growth from these shoots should be stopped at one leaf (see fig. 44).

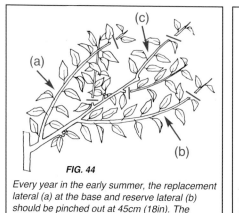

**FIG. 44**

*Every year in the early summer, the replacement lateral (a) at the base and reserve lateral (b) should be pinched out at 45cm (18in). The extension of the fruiting lateral (c) should be pinched out at six leaves.*

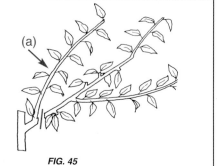

**FIG. 45**

*After harvesting, cut the fruited lateral back to its replacement (a) unless required as part of the framework.*

# PEACHES, NECTARINES & ALMONDS

After fruiting, the fruiting shoots are cut back to their replacement shoots unless they are required to extend the framework (see fig. 45).

## PROTECTION AGAINST PEACH LEAF CURL

Peach leaf curl is a serious fungal disease found on peaches, nectarines and sweet almonds. It is particularly troublesome in the U.K. climate but one that can be avoided (see page 187).

For fan trained trees, a clear polythene cover with the sides open and a gap of 30cm (1ft) at the bottom for ventilation, put on in December and removed in mid-May should prevent peach leaf curl. The polythene will exclude the rain, thereby denying the moisture the peach leaf curl spores need to germinate. The extra warmth will also protect the blossom from being damaged by frost as well as improving fruit set. Ideally the polythene needs to be supported on a timber framework. The cover will restrict access for pollinating insects, so hand pollination may be necessary.

*Polythene supported on a framework*

## FRUIT THINNING

Fruit thinning is necessary to produce large, good-quality fruit. If allowed to overcrop the fruits are small and dry and the tree over stressed. Fruit thinning is carried out in two stages:

1. When the fruits are the size of hazelnuts they should be thinned to 10cm (4in) apart, removing misshapen and poorly placed fruits.

2. When the fruits are the size of walnuts they should be thinned to 20cm (8in) apart leaving the best shaped, best presented fruits.

## MANURING

In early February each year the following fertilizers should be broadcast over the rooting area:

$35g/m^2$ (1¼oz/yd²) of sulphate of potash,
and $50g/m^2$ (1¾oz/yd²) of Nitro-Chalk (calcium ammonium nitrate)
or sulphate of ammonia;

and every third year:

> *70g/m² (2½oz/yd²) of superphosphate.*

Alternatively a compound fertilizer may be used annually following the manufacturer's recommendations.

## HARVESTING & STORAGE

Peaches and nectarines should be picked when fully coloured and ripe, at which stage they part easily from the tree. They should also be slightly soft at the stalk end when ripe. Peaches and nectarines will require picking over several times and should not be picked under-ripe if their full quality is to be appreciated. They will not keep for any length of time.

Almonds are usually harvested in early October at the stage when they fall of their own accord and the husks split open. The nuts are then taken from the husks and allowed to dry properly outdoors on a sunny day when there is some breeze about. The nuts should be kept off the ground by laying them on wire netting to permit air circulation. Alternatively they can be turned several times during the day. When they are thoroughly dry they should be stored in a cool area where there is no dampness. Squirrels can be a problem and then it is best to gather the nuts a little earlier and dry both the husk and nut to begin with before opening them.

## PESTS, DISEASES & DISORDERS

Some of the most troublesome pests, diseases and disorders are listed in the following table. See chapters on 'Common Fruiting Problems' and 'Pests & Diseases' for details.

| Symptoms | Possible problem | Symptoms | Possible problem |
|---|---|---|---|
| Leaf distortion/ marking on leaves | Aphids Peach leaf curl Silver leaf Spider mite | Discoloured/ cracking bark | Bacterial canker |
| | | Maggots in fruit | Plum fruit moth |
| Leaves/shoots/ branches dying off | Bacterial canker Frost damage Silver leaf | Marked/ distorted fruit | Aphids Brown rot |
| | | Fruit drop | Frost damage Incomplete pollination Plum fruit moth |
| Holes in leaves | Bacterial canker | | |

# CHERRIES

**S**weet cherries crop best under conditions of light rainfall (in areas of high rainfall they are prone to splitting). They do best on a deep, fertile, well-drained soil but will tolerate a range of soil types providing they are well drained and ideally 60cm (2ft) or more in depth. Cherries flower early and so require a sheltered position and may need protection against spring frosts. The biggest disadvantage of sweet cherries in the past has been that they make very large trees. However with the dwarfing rootstocks Gisela 5 and Tabel only a small tree is produced, around 2m (6ft 6in). Acid cherries do not grow as large as sweet cherries and are therefore suitable for small gardens.

## VARIETIES

The recent introduction of self-fertile cherries has been a great improvement as now only one need be grown, which is important where space is limited. These were first developed in Canada and several varieties are now available. ***A.G.M. signifies the Award of Garden Merit, the Royal Horticultural Society's most prestigious award.***

*Cherokee*

### *SWEET CHERRIES*

**CELESTE** — This new dark red dessert cherry is naturally very compact and therefore ideal for growing in pots and smaller gardens. The large fruits are firm and of excellent eating quality. Season: Mid-July. Self-fertile.

**CHEROKEE** — A high-quality dessert cherry with large dark red, almost black fruits of excellent flavour. Heavier yielding than Stella. Ideal for wet areas as the fruits are much less prone to splitting than most varieties. Season: Mid-July. Self-fertile.

*Merton Glory*

**MERTON GLORY** — This variety, raised in the 1940's, is one of the best sweet, white cherries. The fruit is very large and creamy-white with a red flush. Sweet and very juicy with an excellent flavour. Heavy cropping. Season: Mid-June. Requires a pollinator.

**PENNY** — This new late season black dessert cherry was bred in the U.K. and is a very regular cropper, even in years when fruit drop run-off has been severe in some of the Canadian self-fertile varieties. The dark red fruits are exceptionally large and firm, well flavoured and turn black when fully ripe. Penny is very precocious, cropping relatively early in its life. Season: Late July. Requires a pollinator.

*Penny*

*Sweetheart*

*Morello*

**STELLA** — This variety from Canada produces good quality dark red fruits and is less prone to bacterial canker than many other varieties. Season: Early July. Self-fertile. *A.G.M.*

**SUMMER SUN** — An excellent new dessert variety which is very suitable for the cooler areas of the U.K. as it holds its fruit well during poor summers. It is ideal for the amateur. Produces dark red fruits. Season: Mid-July. Self-fertile. *A.G.M.*

**SUNBURST** — This is a high quality dark red, almost black dessert cherry. The fruits are very large and will store very well for a short period after picking. Excellent flavour. Season: Mid-July. Self-fertile.

**SWEETHEART** — This new dark red dessert cherry is very heavy cropping and very late. The fruits ripen over a long period so even if heavy rain spoils some of the crop, there will be plenty more. Excellent eating quality. Season: Late August. Self-fertile.

*ACID CHERRIES*

**MORELLO** — This is the most common acid cherry. It is self-fertile and crops heavily and regularly. It is excellent for cooking but never sweet enough for dessert. The fruits are large, round and red. Season: August/September. *A.G.M.*

## TRAINING SYSTEMS

*SWEET CHERRIES*

Sweet cherries fruit on spurs on the older wood and at the base of the one year old laterals. Because of this they can be trained and pruned in the same way as plums (see pages 54-60). They can be grown as a Minarette, pyramid or bush in more favoured areas but in cool areas are best grown as a fan on a warm south, south-west or west facing wall or fence. Fans are, in any event, more easily protected from birds.

Cherries on Gisela 5 or Tabel can be spaced around 2.4-3m (8-10ft) apart for pyramids and 3-3.6m (10-12ft) apart for bushes; on Colt they should be spaced 3.6-4.5m (12-15ft) apart for pyramids and 4.5-5.4m (15-18ft) apart for bushes. Fans on Gisela 5 and Tabel need a space of at least 1.8m (6ft) high by 3.6m (12ft) wide (the size of two fence panels); on Colt, 2.4m (8ft) by 4.5m (15ft) is necessary.

# QUINCE & MEDLARS

Medlars, on the other hand, are best grown as a standard or half-standard to allow them to produce an attractive, somewhat weeping head. They should be spaced about 4.5-5.4m (15-18ft) apart. Pruning is carried out in the dormant season (November-March).

Initial pruning is similar to that for a bush apple or pear but pruning the main stem higher to about 1.35m (4ft 6in) for a half-standard and 1.8m (6ft) for a standard. A mature tree does not require regular pruning, but dead, diseased, crowding and crossing branches should be shortened or removed in the winter as necessary.

## MANURING

In early February each year broadcast over the rooting area:

> $25g/m^2$ (1oz/yd²) of sulphate of potash;

and in late February for medlars:

> $35g/m^2$ (1¼oz/yd²) of Nitro-Chalk (calcium ammonium nitrate) or sulphate of ammonia;

and for quince:

> $70g/m^2$ (2½oz/yd²) of Nitro-Chalk (calcium ammonium nitrate) or sulphate of ammonia;

and every third year:

> $70g/m^2$ (2½oz/yd²) of superphosphate.

Alternatively a compound fertilizer may be used annually following the manufacturer's recommendations.

If magnesium deficiency is a persistent problem, in early April each year apply:

> $50g/m^2$ (1¾oz/yd²) of magnesium sulphate (Epsom salts).

## HARVESTING

Quince should be left on the tree as long as possible until late October when they become golden coloured; they must however be harvested before the arrival of any air frosts. They can be stored under cool conditions until the end of the year but should be regularly inspected for rotting.

Medlars should be harvested in late October. The stalks should be dipped in a strong salt solution to prevent premature rotting and the fruits placed with their stalks upwards in a cool, dry place for two to three weeks until the flesh softens and turns brown.

# QUINCE & MEDLARS

## PESTS, DISEASES & DISORDERS

Medlars are usually trouble free but are occasionally attacked by caterpillars and affected by brown rot. Some of the most troublesome pests, diseases and disorders of quince are listed in the following table. See chapters on 'Common Fruiting Problems' and 'Pests & Diseases' for details.

| Symptoms | Possible problem | Symptoms | Possible problem |
|---|---|---|---|
| Leaf distortion/ marking on leaves | Aphids<br>Quince leaf blight<br>Spider mite | Maggots in fruit | Apple sawfly<br>Codling moth |
| Leaves/shoots dying off | Apple canker<br>Frost damage | Marked/ distorted fruit | Aphids<br>Apple sawfly<br>Brown rot<br>Green capsid bug |
| Holes in leaves | Green capsid bug | | |
| Disfigured/ cracking bark | Apple canker | Fruit drop | Apple sawfly<br>Codling moth<br>Frost damage<br>Incomplete pollination |
| Blossom damage | Apple blossom weevil | | |

# COBNUTS & FILBERTS

Cobnuts and filberts are related species of hazelnut *(Corylus)*. They are both small trees which bear separate male and female flowers on the same tree. The male flowers are the familiar catkins and the female flowers are small, red and unobtrusive. They are wind pollinated and two varieties are needed to ensure good cross-pollination and should be planted next to one another to aid this process.

The husk of the cobnut does not completely cover the nut, whereas the husk of the filbert completely envelops the nut which is longer and narrower than that of the cobnut. They are cultivated in the same way and will be referred to as cobnuts in the text.

## VARIETIES

**COSFORD** — This is a large, oblong cobnut with a short husk. It has bright yellow catkins and is a heavy cropper and good pollinator. It makes a vigorous tree. The flavour is good.

**KENTISH COB (LAMBERT'S FILBERT)** — Although called a cob, this is a filbert. It is a very long, large nut of good flavour. It has short, yellow/green catkins and is heavy cropping and moderately vigorous.

*Kentish Cob*

**RED FILBERT** — This filbert has striking long claret red catkins, rich purple foliage and delicious purple skinned fruits.

## SITE & SOIL

Cobnuts prefer a sheltered site and will grow on almost any well drained soil. They are lime tolerant and a pH of 7.5-8.0 is best. On acidic soils it may be necessary to apply lime to raise the pH. Poorer soils are preferable to rich soils which can lead to excessive growth.

*Red Filbert (foliage)*

## TREE FORM

In their natural form, Cobnuts are multi-stemmed bushes. However, in order to control the suckers, they are best grown as open-centred bushes with a short 30-38cm (12-15in) stem and then a framework of six to eight branches. The trees should be kept down to a height of 1.8-2.4m (6-8ft) and should be spaced 4.5m (15ft) apart. They should only require staking for the first few years.

## INITIAL TRAINING

If the bush comes from the nursery multi-stemmed, before planting, select a strong upright stem as the main leader and remove all other branches (see fig 46). The stem that has been selected will form the main trunk of the tree and should be cut back to a bud 30-38cm (12-15in) from ground level. In the second year, treat the bush as described below, (i.e. as if it has just come from the nursery as a single stem tree with branches coming off the main stem).

If the bush comes from the nursery as a single stem tree, with branches coming off the main stem, suitably placed leaders should be cut back by half to an outward facing bud after planting. Any laterals not required to form the framework should be cut back to three or four buds (see fig 47). This should be repeated each February for the first four or five years, aiming to produce six to eight good branches.

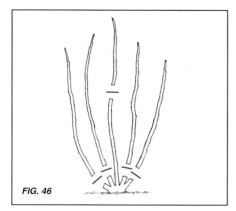

FIG. 46

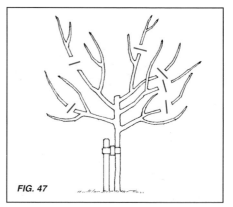

FIG. 47

## WINTER PRUNING OF THE ESTABLISHED TREE

This should be carried out at flowering time in late February to help shed the pollen and improve fruit set. Strong laterals should be pruned to three or four buds. Weak laterals carrying the female flowers should not be pruned. Leaders should be pruned by half to an outward facing bud and if necessary, branches should be cut back to a suitably placed lateral to maintain the height at 1.8-2.4m (6-8ft).

## SUMMER PRUNING

This is known as 'brutting' and should be carried out in August. Strong lateral shoots should be broken at about half their length and left hanging (see fig 48). This improves air circulation and light penetration, reduces vigour and encourages fruit bud formation. These brutted side shoots should be shortened back to two or three buds in late February (see fig 49).

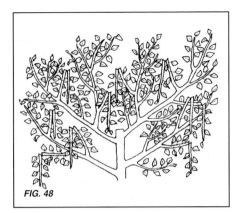

FIG. 48

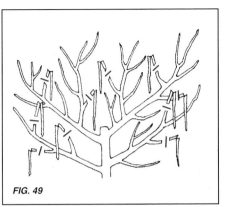

FIG. 49

## MANURING

In late January each year a compound fertilizer should be applied following the manufacturer's recommendations. The area to be covered should more or less equal that of the spread of the branches.

## HARVESTING & STORAGE

Cobnuts should be harvested when they are fully mature, usually in late September. The nuts should be picked when the husks start to turn yellow. They should be dried by spreading them out in a warm place and turning them every two or three days or by hanging them up in a net bag. When they are dry they should be de-husked and packed in earthenware jars or clay pots and stored in a cool, airy room or shed and protected against mice and squirrels.

## PESTS, DISEASES & DISORDERS

Squirrels are the most serious pest since they can quickly devour a whole crop. Netting is usually ineffective as they chew through it. Galvanised wire netting is effective but can lead to problems of zinc toxicity. The fruits can be attacked by nut gall mites, nut weevils and winter moth larvae. The trees are generally free from disease.

# SWEET CHESTNUTS & WALNUTS

**S**weet chestnuts (also known as Spanish chestnuts) are a native of southern Europe and are now grown widely throughout Europe. When grown as a standard they will grow to a height of about 10m (35ft) within twenty years and after this period will continue to grow even taller. They are therefore not suitable for small gardens unless planted in a root control bag. There are two types of chestnut, the marron and the domestic and it is the former which is grown for its nuts on account of their large size and sweet flavour.

The common English or Persian walnut *(Juglans regia)* is native to China, Iran and south-west Europe. The eastern black walnut *(Juglans nigra)* is grown in eastern and central U.S.A. Both species grow very tall, attaining a height of 25ft in 20 years and finally reaching 18-21m (60-70ft) unless planted into a root control bag.

**Marron de Lyon**

**Broadview**

## VARIETIES

### CHESTNUT

**MARRON DE LYON** — This is an old French variety, selected for its compact growth habit. The nuts are very large and of excellent flavour. Self-fertile.

### WALNUT

**BROADVIEW** — This compact variety originates from British Columbia. It is considered to be the best all-purpose walnut available. A slow grower but extremely precocious, usually bearing nuts three years after planting. Yields are medium to heavy and the size of the nuts are large. Suitable for planting nationwide. Self-fertile.

**MAJESTIC** — Originating from France, this variety produces exceptionally large nuts that are up to two inches in diameter. The tree itself is upright and vigorous. Heavy cropping. Self-fertile.

**RUBIS** — This French variety produces medium sized red nuts. The tree is moderately vigorous, reaching 6-7m in 10 years. Heavy cropping. Self-fertile.

## SITE & SOIL

Sweet chestnuts prefer to be grown in a light sandy soil where the pH is between 5.5 and 6.5. They will not succeed on a site which only has a shallow layer of top soil, is heavy clay and waterlogged in winter or in ground which is alkaline (pH above 7.0). They much prefer a site which is sunny for most of the day and sheltered from the prevailing wind. The tree will require staking and this is best done when it is first planted.

Walnuts will succeed on a wide range of soil types ranging from light sandy loams to heavy ones, provided they are well drained. The best soil for them is a heavy loam to a depth of at least 60cm (2ft) with limestone beneath and with a pH of 7.5 to 8.0. They prefer an open position provided they are given shelter from spring frosts during the flowering period. Temperatures below -2°C (27°F) will kill the majority of the female flowers and this should be taken into consideration when choosing a site to grow a walnut tree. Walnut trees do not transplant as easily as most fruit trees and need very careful treatment for the first few years. The ground within a radius of 3-4ft from the stem should be kept weed free and dug over in the winter annually until the tree has become well established.

## RESTRICTING THE SIZE OF THE TREE

By planting the tree in a Root Control Bag (R.C.B.), it is possible to limit the vigour of the tree. The R.C.B. restricts the tree roots, retaining the energy of the tree within. Only the white fibrous feeding roots find their way through the R.C.B. This prevents the tree from growing too tall and brings it into cropping earlier. The eventual height of the tree will of course depend on the fertility of the soil as well as many other factors.

## TREE FORM

Sweet chestnuts and walnuts are nearly always grown as standard trees with a central leader in position throughout their life. The height to which the main stem should be allowed to grow before allowing branches to form is optional but is usually 1.8m (6ft).

## PRUNING

The pruning of walnuts and sweet chestnuts is largely the same; the main difference is the time of pruning. Sweet chestnuts should be pruned when they are dormant (during the autumn or winter). Walnuts on the other hand should only be pruned between mid-summer and mid winter. Walnuts should not be pruned in the late winter or spring as the sap rises early and the pruning cuts will bleed profusely. Also, it is advisable to protect the pruning cuts on a walnut with a wound paint.

At the end of the first growing season and in subsequent years, any side shoots that have reached at least 20-30cm (8-12in) in length should be shortened back by half of their length. Any side shoots produced later in the season and situated near the top of the tree, should be left unpruned (see fig 50).

At the end of the second growing season and in subsequent years, the lower side shoots that had been pruned the previous season and are not required as part of the main framework should be cut back flush with the main stem (see fig 51).

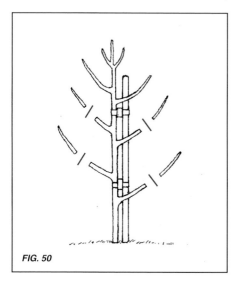

FIG. 50

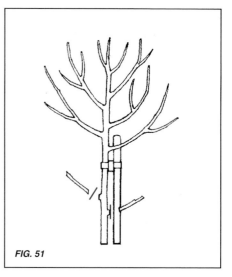

FIG. 51

This above pruning process should be followed through every year until the desired length of clear stem has been achieved. At this stage the topmost four or five laterals should be retained. These laterals will form the primary branch framework of the tree.

Pruning of the primary branches will consist of shortening them back by a half in order to double the amount of framework branches in the following year. Once the main branch system has been formed (this takes three to four years) little pruning is required other than the removal of crossing branches in the winter and any weak shoots in the late summer.

## HARVESTING & STORAGE

Sweet chestnuts and walnuts should be de-husked once they have fallen to the ground and have been collected. If this task is delayed for more than a few days the husks turn black and are then difficult to shell. Walnuts need to be brushed using a soft brush to remove the fibres present. The nuts should be spread out in a warm place to dry out, turning them two or three times a week. When absolutely dry they should be packed in barrels or earthenware jars. Walnuts should be packed with alternate layers of equal parts of dry peat and salt. Sweet chestnuts are best packed with alternate layers of sand. In this way they will keep for up to six months provided they are stored somewhere cool, dry, frost-free and away from vermin such as mice and squirrels.

## PESTS, DISEASES & DISORDERS

The Sweet Chestnut is relatively free from pests and diseases. Most pests of walnuts, including the Walnut Leaf Gall Mite, are not too serious and cause mostly cosmetic damage. Walnuts are susceptible to some diseases including Walnut Blight, Walnut Leaf Blotch, Honey Fungus and Grey Mould. See chapter on 'Pests & Diseases' for details.

# BLACK MULBERRIES

**B**lack mulberries *(Morus Nigra)* make attractive ornamental trees with compact growth and decorative leaves and bark, as well as being useful for the fruit they produce. The fruits resemble small loganberries and are almost black when fully ripe. They can be eaten fresh or cooked and used to make jelly and wine. The black mulberry should not be confused with the white mulberry, which is the species used to feed silkworms and not grown for fruit.

Mulberries will tolerate a range of soils, provided they are well drained. They do best in a warm sheltered situation where they can be grown as bush, standard or half-standard trees. In colder areas, espalier trained trees against south or southwest facing walls or fences are best. Mulberries are slow growing, taking about eight to ten years to come into cropping. A mature tree will reach 6-9m (20-30ft). There are only a few named varieties of the black mulberry. It is important to obtain plants propagated from cuttings rather than from seed which take longer to reach the fruiting stage and have unknown fruiting properties.

*Large Black*

## VARIETIES

**KING JAMES I** — This variety is actually derived from a tree that existed in Swan Walk — now known as the Chelsea Physic Garden — planted in the early 17th Century, during the reign of King James I. The fruit is unusually large and succulent, cropping early in its life. The flavour is intensely rich and second to none.

**LARGE BLACK** — This is a particularly good variety which ripens during August and September. Very juicy with a pleasant sub-acid flavour. A good ornamental tree with spreading branches and large leaves. *R.H.S. Award of Garden Merit.*

## PRUNING & TRAINING

In sheltered situations mulberries are best grown as bush or half-standard trees (or if a large tree is required, standard trees). The formative pruning is similar to that for a bush apple, pruning in the dormant season (November to March). Broken or crossing branches should be removed or shortened and any dead or diseased branches cut out. Also any branches which spoil the shape of the tree should be removed.

The formative training of espalier mulberries is similar to that for apples and pears. The pruning of fruiting laterals should be carried out in the summer to promote the formation of fruiting spurs. In late July or early August, side shoots should be shortened to four or five leaves.

# BLACK MULBERRIES

## MANURING

In late February each year, broadcast over the rooting area (approximately equal to the spread of the branches) a compound fertilizer as recommended for apples.

## HARVESTING

Mulberries should be eaten or preserved soon after harvesting. They ripen over a period of three to four weeks from mid-August. Fruit to be used for cooking should be picked when slightly under-ripe. Fruit for dessert should be picked when almost black, when it will part from the branch easily. Alternatively ripe fruit can be allowed to drop onto a clean surface such as a sheet of polythene or an old linen sheet (mulberry juice stains so do not use a good sheet!).

## PESTS, DISEASES & DISORDERS

The Black Mulberry is relatively free from pests and diseases. Ripening fruits should be protected against birds.

# FIGS

Figs are sub-tropical plants and need plenty of sun and warmth to grow and crop well outdoors in Britain. They can be grown outdoors in the south and west but further north need a very warm sheltered situation outdoors, otherwise they must be grown under glass. Root restriction should be provided to keep the tree compact and fruitful, as without it the fig is liable to grow rather large and remain vegetative.

## VARIETIES

*Brown Turkey*

**BROWN TURKEY** — Produces large oval fruits with very sweet, deep red flesh. It is the most reliable and widely grown variety. Heavy cropping. Ripens August to September. Self-fertile. *R.H.S. Award of Garden Merit.*

**BRUNSWICK** — A heavy cropping variety. Produces exceptionally large fruit with greenish white flesh that is pink in the centre. Self-fertile.

**WHITE MARSEILLES** — This early ripening fig produces large fruits with white, transparent flesh. Sweet and juicy with good flavour. Heavy cropping. Fairly hardy. Can be grown outdoors if given a sheltered position. Also very suitable for a cold greenhouse. Self-fertile.

## CROPPING HABIT

It is important to understand the cropping habit of the fig. The fig bears two to three crops each year but only one ripens in our climate. The figs are formed in the axils of the leaves near the tips of the young shoots. It is the small pea-sized embryo figs formed in the autumn that overwinter to produce a crop of figs the following summer (August/September). The crop of figs produced in the spring and early summer never ripen and should be removed in November.

The fig does not produce visible flowers; they are enclosed within the centre of the fruit. Varieties grown in the U.K. do not require pollination and the fruits are seedless.

## TREE FORMS

Figs need warmth and sun and so are best grown as fan-trained trees against south or south-west facing walls or fences. In very favourable areas they can be grown as free-standing bush trees. They are excellent for pot culture.

# FIGS

## PLANTING & ROOT RESTRICTION

The fig should be planted in an open-based box which should be constructed of 60cm x 60cm (2ft x 2ft) square paving slabs or something similar, set into the ground with the rim about 2.5cm (1in) above ground level. The base of the box should be packed with brick rubble or broken tiles to a depth of about 22cm (9in) to provide drainage and to prevent the roots escaping. The box should be filled with a loam-based potting compost such as John Innes No. 3. Alternatively a pot of 35-45cm (14-18in) diameter can be used and plunged into the ground, provided it has adequate drainage holes. Another option is to plant the fig in a Root Control Bag (RCB). If grown against a wall, plant approximately 25cm (10in) away from the wall.

## PRUNING & TRAINING A FAN

Figs are usually obtained from the nursery as two year old plants. They may have a single stem or two or more side shoots.

In March following planting, those plants with a single stem should be pruned back to about 38cm (15in). Plants with side shoots should have their central leaders removed and their side shoots shortened by a quarter to a third, to stimulate the production of further shoots. During the summer the side shoots are tied to wires, spaced 30cm (12 in) apart in a similar way to a peach.

## PRUNING THE ESTABLISHED FAN

To encourage the formation of compact short-joined shoots to carry the next year's figs, the growing points of every other shoot carried by the main framework branches should be removed once they have made four or five leaves, providing this is before the end of June. (see fig 52).

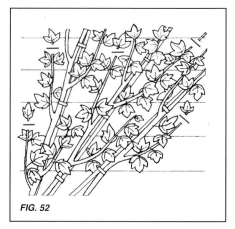

*FIG. 52*

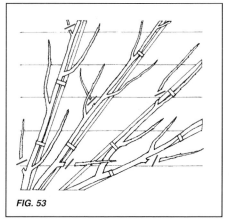

*FIG. 53*

# FIGS

In March or April after the worst frosts have passed, all dead, diseased and frost-damaged wood should be removed. Tie in the young shoots 15-30cm (6-12in) apart, cutting surplus shoots back to one bud.

In November, half the shoots that carried fruits during the summer should be pruned back to 2.5cm (1in). This will encourage new growth from the base the following spring. All the remaining shoots should be tied in parallel with the wall, approximately 20-30cm (9-12in) apart. Any growth in between should be cut back to source to avoid overcrowding. (see fig 53)

## GROWING FIGS IN CONTAINERS

Container grown figs are best grown as a bush on a short stem. It is best to select a plant with three or four branches coming from the stem around 38cm (15in) from the ground. Alternatively, cut back single stem plants to encourage branching. In the late winter cut back these branches by a half to develop a compact framework.

In the spring remove crossing and frost damaged shoots to maintain an open centre. Prune back over-long and bare branches where necessary to 5cm (2in) to encourage the formation of new shoots. In the summer pinch out any new shoots at 5 or 6 leaves to encourage fruit formation.

## MANURING

In March each year, broadcast over the rooting area a compound fertilizer as recommended for apples. When the tree is carrying a heavy crop, a liquid feed high in potash, such as a tomato fertilizer, should be applied every two weeks until the fruit begins to ripen.

Pot-grown trees should be fed weekly during the growing season, alternating a liquid feed high in potash, such as tomato fertilizer with a balanced feed.

## WINTER PROTECTION

In colder areas and in severe winters, the embryo figs can be damaged by frosts. Fig trees can be protected against frost by using a cover of bracken or straw held in place by a large mesh net. This should be put on in November and removed once growth starts in late April and May.

Pot-grown trees can be placed in a frost-free place such as a shed, garage or unheated greenhouse over winter. Alternatively, if this is not available, the container can be lagged with bubble wrap, sacking or some other suitable insulation and placed against a sheltered side of the house, away from the prevailing wind. Pack around the branches with straw and cover with hessian or horticultural fleece. Remove after the danger or frost is passed but before bud burst.

# FIGS

## HARVESTING

Figs are ready for harvesting when they become soft and hang downwards. Small splits develop in the skin and a drop of nectar may be exuded from the eye of the fruit. They should be inspected regularly, as ripe figs will soon rot on the tree. Once picked they will keep for 2-3 weeks if kept somewhere cool.

## PESTS, DISEASES & DISORDERS

Squirrels and birds are the most serious pests. The trees are generally free from disease but occasionally suffer from Coral Spot (dead twigs become covered in pink pustules). Diseased twigs should be cut back to a healthy bud and the prunings should be burned.

# BLACKBERRIES & HYBRID BERRIES

**A** selection of these fruits can provide fresh berries from early July until the first severe frosts occur in the autumn. They provide a variety of flavours ranging from that of the true blackberry to those arising from crosses between raspberry with blackberry and other *rubus* species. All these fruits will freeze well and make excellent jam. With good management and provided they remain free of virus infection, they will yield heavy crops for fifteen to twenty years.

*Black Butte*

*Boysenberry*

*Fantasia*

## VARIETIES

*A.G.M. signifies the Award of Garden Merit, the Royal Horticultural Society's most prestigious award.*

**BLACK BUTTE** — This new blackberry variety from America is notable for its exceptional fruit size. The giant berries are attractive, uniformly shaped and of very good flavour. The plants are winter hardy and the canes are thorny. The fruit is well presented on strong laterals. Ripens early July to mid August.

**BOYSENBERRY (THORNLESS)** — This American hybrid yields heavy crops of large, round oblong shaped berries which commence to ripen at the end of July to a dull, dark-red colour. The fruit has a characteristic bramble flavour. The canes are thin, numerous and moderately vigorous.

**BUCKINGHAM TAYBERRY** — Discovered in Buckingham, this is a natural thornless mutation of the Tayberry, which would appear to be identical to the Tayberry in all other respects.

**FANTASIA** — This is a relatively new variety of blackberry discovered growing on an allotment in Surrey and thought to be a cross between Merton Thornless and Himalayan Giant. The canes are very vigorous, thick and thorny and bear outstanding crops of extremely large blackberries, some even larger than a fifty pence coin. Berry size does not diminish noticeably throughout the cropping season which commences from early August onwards. Fantasia is much in demand by leading supermarkets on account of its excellent flavour and quality. It is the only variety to have the subtle flavour of the wild blackberry. *A.G.M.*

**HELEN** — A new early thornless blackberry raised by Medway fruits from a cross between Silvan and an unnamed selection. The fruits are large, firm, long and conical in shape and have a bright regular appearance. The flavour is excellent, rich and aromatic. Commences to ripen early to mid-July, providing the first supply of blackberries in the season. In trials, no serious diseases have been seen on this variety.

**JAPANESE WINEBERRY** — Also known as the Chinese Blackberry, this particularly decorative plant produces canes up to 2m (6ft 6in) in length, which are covered with soft red bristles. The berries are golden-yellow, turning wine red when fully ripe in August. The fruits all mature together, so that the whole sprig can be cut off and served with cream for dessert. The berries are sweet, juicy and refreshing to taste.

*Japanese Wineberry*

**LOCH NESS** — A relatively new thornless blackberry raised at the S.C.R.I., Scotland. Unlike other varieties with their trailing habit of growth, Loch Ness produces stout semi-erect canes which become more erect in well established bushes and require the minimum of support. In trials the canes have shown considerable winter hardiness, whilst the yields have exceeded those of Bedford Giant. Usually about half the crop ripens in late August and the remainder throughout September. The fruits are large and the flavour is good when fully ripe. *A.G.M.*

*Loch Ness*

**LOGANBERRY (THORNLESS)** — Raised in 1881, this remains the most popular of all hybrids. Ripening from the middle of July, the fruits are medium-sized, blunt conical in shape, dull dark red in colour and have quite a sharp flavour. The canes are only moderately vigorous. *A.G.M.*

**OLALLIEBERRY** — Raised in Oregon in 1935 from a cross between a loganberry and a youngberry, this hybrid fruit is grown extensively in California, where the fruit is very popular in pies. The fruits are glossy and resemble a large, elongated blackberry . They have a distinctive, sweet flavour that is more tangy than the boysenberry. It is delicious both fresh and cooked and is excellent for jam making. The plants are highly productive, vigorous and thorny. Ripens early July.

*Loganberry*

*Silvan*

*Tayberry*

*Veronique (in fruit and flower)*

**OREGON THORNLESS** — This variety yields light crops of firm, medium sized, shiny black berries that have a good sweet flavour. They ripen from late August onwards. The canes are moderately vigorous, whilst the foliage, being deeply indented, has an attractive bright green 'parsley-leaf' appearance which turns to bright autumn tints in the late season.

**SILVAN** — This relatively new blackberry was raised in western Australia. It is considered to be a variety of exceptional quality. The fruits, which are borne on canes with thorns, are larger than the Boysenberry (25mm [1in] diameter and 40mm [1½in] long) and the variety is more productive . It has displayed a high level of resistance to disease and is fairly tolerant to heavy soil, wind and drought. The fruit is ripe from early to mid-July onwards, providing the first supply of blackberries in the season, second only to Helen. *A.G.M.*

**TAYBERRY** — This comparatively new heavy yielding hybrid was raised at the S.C.R.I., Scotland. It has a long cropping period from early July to mid-August. The fruit is sweeter, much larger and more aromatic than that of the loganberry; blunt, chisel-shaped and dark red when fully ripe. The berries are borne on short laterals and are easy to pick. The canes are moderately vigorous and prickly. *A.G.M.*

**VERONIQUE** — A new compact pink-flowering, thornless blackberry derived from Loch Ness. Produces heavy crops of large fruit of good flavour. Freezes well. No official trial data is available yet but early indications suggest that it has similar characteristics to Loch Ness.

**WALDO** — This new early thornless blackberry from America, ripens mid to late July. The variety has good resistance to cane and leaf spot and does not appear susceptible to purple blotch. The thornless canes are semi-erect and moderately vigorous. However, the canes are rather brittle and can be damaged in exposed situations — they should be tied in early to avoid this from happening. The fruit is of superb quality, large and very firm with an intensely glossy black colour. They are also noted for the very small size of their seeds and hence make superb jam. The flavour is excellent.

## PLANTING DISTANCES

The minimum distances that these cane fruits should be spaced in the row on soils of average fertility should be as follows:

| | | | |
|---|---|---|---|
| Black Butte | 1.8m (6ft) | Loganberry | 2.4m (8ft) |
| Boysenberry | 2.4m (8ft) | Ollallieberry | 2.4m (8ft) |
| Buckingham Tayberry | 2.4m (8ft) | Oregon Thornless | 2.4m (8ft) |
| Fantasia | 4.5m (15ft) | Silvan | 4.5m (15ft) |
| Helen | 2.4m (8ft) | Tayberry | 2.4m (8ft) |
| Japanese Wineberry | 1.8m (6ft) | Veronique | 1.8m (6ft) |
| Loch Ness | 1.8m (6ft) | Waldo | 1.8m (6ft) |

If the above plants are planted in one row, the row should be 1.8-2.1m (6-7ft) away from other fruits.

## MANURING

With the exception of Fantasia, these fruits should be manured generously with a fertilizer containing nitrogen in order to encourage growth of the long lengths of cane required to cover the supporting wires. With Fantasia, the amount of nitrogen applied should be governed by the vigour of the canes. It may be advisable not to apply any at all in some years.

During March, or immediately following planting, whichever is the later, broadcast in a circle 45cm (18in) diameter round each plant:

*35g (1¼oz) Nitro-Chalk (calcium ammonium nitrate)*
*and 10g (¼oz) sulphate of potash.*

Similarly, at the end of May and June broadcast:

*20g (¾oz) Nitro-Chalk (calcium ammonium nitrate).*

In succeeding years each March, broadcast over a distance 90cm (3ft) on both sides of the rows or in a circle 90cm (3ft) around individual bushes:

*20g/m² (¾oz/yd²) Nitro-Chalk (calcium ammonium nitrate)*
*and 10g/m² (¼oz/yd²) sulphate of potash.*

Alternatively, a compound fertilizer may be used after planting and annually thereafter, following the manufacturer's recommendations.

## POST & WIRE SUPPORTS

These cane fruits are best grown on wires attached by vine eyes to a wall or fence or on a free standing framework of posts and wires. The wires should be 3.5mm (10 gauge). The end posts should be 10 x 10cm (4 x 4in) and 2.5m (8¼ft) in length, driven 75cm (30in) into the ground. Intermediate posts measuring 5 x 5cm (2 x 2in) should be positioned 3.9m (13ft) apart in the row. Four wires should be positioned at heights of 90, 120, 150 and 180cm (3, 4, 5 and 6ft respectively) loosely stapled to the intermediate posts and tightened around the end posts. An alternative method of supporting weaker growing varieties, such as Waldo or Loch Ness, is to tie their canes to a single, free standing stake 180 cm (6ft) out of the ground. The string used to loosely support the canes to the stake can be prevented from slipping down the stake by threading it through staples at 30cm (12in) intervals attached to the post.

## METHOD FOR TRAINING THE CANES

There are several ways that the new canes can be trained; the simplest is to divide them into two lots and train them in opposite directions on the ground below the fruiting canes. They are kept in position by means of wooden pegs or short lengths of wire pushed into the ground. At the end of the winter after the spent fruiting cane has been removed, the new cane should be picked up off the ground, disentangled and trained in their fruiting positions, using all the supporting wires.

There are several methods for training the new canes into their fruiting positions and the best one is to space full lengths of the canes out evenly across the wires. This method makes picking easy and gives the highest yield of fruit. The canes are tied onto the wires in a weaving pattern with thin string or 4in (10cm) twist ties (see fig. 54).

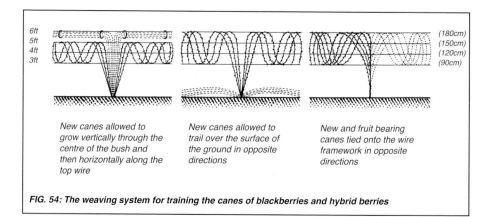

New canes allowed to grow vertically through the centre of the bush and then horizontally along the top wire

New canes allowed to trail over the surface of the ground in opposite directions

New and fruit bearing canes tied onto the wire framework in opposite directions

**FIG. 54: The weaving system for training the canes of blackberries and hybrid berries**

# BLACKBERRIES & HYBRID BERRIES

Some varieties, for example 'Loch Ness' produce semi-erect canes in the first year but become more erect as the stools become established in later years. They are too brittle to be tied on to the wires in a weaving pattern. They should be trained in a similar way to raspberries on two wires with supporting posts. To maximise yield, each new cane should have its growing point pinched out when it is 60cm (2ft) tall at the end of May. Each cane will then produce two to three secondary branches which will grow to a height of approximately 1.8m (6ft). When fruit picking is over, the old canes should be cut out at soil level and the new ones spread out in a fan shape and tied to the top and bottom wires. A space of 45cm (18in) in the centre of the stool should be left free from canes. In the following summer the new canes should then be trained and loosely tied into this space so as to separate the new canes from the fruiting canes and make fruiting easier (see fig. 55).

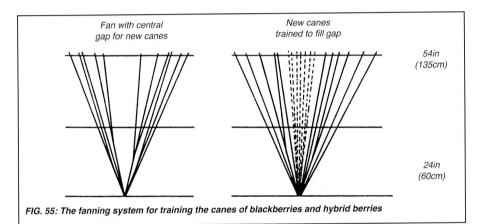

**FIG. 55: The fanning system for training the canes of blackberries and hybrid berries**

## PRUNING

The existing cane growth on bare root plants should be pruned back to 30cm (12in) before planting; in June when the new shoots are growing strongly, the old canes should be cut down to soil level to prevent flowering and fruit production. In subsequent years, pruning of the spent fruiting canes may be carried out at any convenient time after picking stops and before growth starts in early spring.

## CANE NUMBERS & THINNING

Some varieties produce large numbers of canes from the base of the plant, whilst other varieties produce few canes initially but secondary growth later on. To obtain high yields, as many canes as possible up to twenty four are required for each bush. In addition to these, a small number should be retained to allow for breakages. New canes in excess of these numbers should be removed in May and June whilst they are still short.

## THE BIENNIAL CROPPING SYSTEM

If there is sufficient space, it is worth considering planting two bushes and cropping them in alternate years. The advantages of biennial cropping are that the bushes are much easier to manage and to tie in, the fruit is easier to pick and pests and diseases can be controlled more effectively. The variety 'Fantasia' is so heavy cropping that it may not be necessary to plant two bushes, since the fruit harvested in its cropping year may be sufficient to stock the freezer for the family's consumption during its 'off' year.

Biennial cropping is achieved by cutting the fruiting canes out at ground level, once their crop has all been harvested (which is done in any case whether the intention is to crop the bush annually or biennially). At the same time, the young canes (next year's fruiting wood) produced during the summer months are cut out at ground level, though it is better to start cutting out these young canes from the time they emerge from the base of the bush in the spring and continuing to do so as they appear throughout the summer, rather than delaying the task until the fruit has all been picked. The bush will then be overwintering for the first time without any cane growth whatsoever. A new set of canes will appear in the spring from the base of the bush; these canes are tied in onto the supporting wires at intervals throughout the summer until the supporting structure or fence is completely covered. At this stage any further growth is pruned away; if an excessive number of canes are tied in it becomes counter-productive.

With the biennial cropping system, tying in is done during the summer months, usually once a fortnight and is completed by September. When blackberries are allowed to fruit every year, the tying in of the young canes is normally done during the autumn or winter months and involves separating the young canes from the fruiting canes as well as disentangling the young canes from one another.

With biennial cropping, there are no new canes growing up in front of the fruiting canes, making it difficult to pick the fruit. Furthermore, by pruning all the canes down to ground level in the autumn after harvest and burning them, the life cycle of pests and diseases will be interrupted.

## PESTS, DISEASES & DISORDERS

Some of the most troublesome pests, diseases and disorders are listed in the following table. See chapter on 'Pests & Diseases' for details.

| Symptoms | Possible problem | Symptoms | Possible problem |
|---|---|---|---|
| Leaf distortion/ marking on leaves | Aphids Cane spot Rust Spider mite | Maggots in fruit | Raspberry beetle |
| | | Marked/ distorted fruit | Cane spot Grey mould Redberry disease Stamen blight |
| Discoloured cane | Cane spot Purple blotch | | |
| Blossom damage | Stamen blight | | |

# RASPBERRIES

**R**aspberries will grow almost anywhere provided they are planted on well drained soil. They may grow less satisfactorily on heavy soils and on shallow, sandy or gravelly land and produce poor crops of small berries in dry summers, unless they are watered. Provided they do not become infected with virus, they may be expected to provide worthwhile crops for ten to twelve years, before needing to be replaced. It is essential to keep raspberries free from weeds and to spray with insecticide to control the larvae of the raspberry beetle which spoil the fruit.

## VARIETIES

If only one variety is to be grown, it is recommended that either 'Glen Prosen' or 'Redsetter' should be selected. Of the varieties listed, 'Malling Admiral', 'Octavia' and 'Tulameen' have the advantage of being the only summer fruiting varieties which come into fruit production after the June/July cropping strawberries finish fruiting. To provide fruit for the longest period possible, one could not do better than to include the varieties 'Redsetter', 'Glen Ample' and 'Tulameen' for cropping throughout the summer and 'Galante' for fruiting in the autumn.

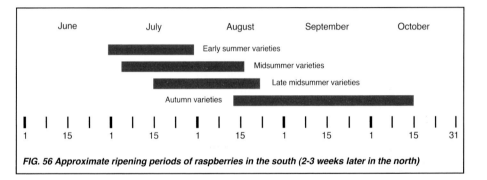

FIG. 56 Approximate ripening periods of raspberries in the south (2-3 weeks later in the north)

*Redsetter*

***A.G.M. signifies the Award of Garden Merit, the Royal Horticultural Society's most prestigious award.***

### *EARLY SUMMER*

**GLEN MOY\*\*** — This heavy cropping, early mid-season variety is resistant to aphid colonisation, with a compact growth habit and concentrated ripening period. The canes are spinefree and in southern counties of England bear a small autumn crop on the young canes in October, prior to producing their main crop the following summer. The berries are medium to large, well flavoured and suitable for all purposes. *A.G.M.*

95

*Glen Ample*

*Glen Prosen*

**MALLING JEWEL\*—** Jewel has been the standard raspberry variety for over fifty years because it is tolerant to virus infection and a consistent, although moderate cropper. It has a compact habit which is easy to manage. The firm, dark red, conical berries hang on the bushes for nearly a week without becoming over-ripe. The fruit ripens over a period of three to four weeks. To obtain maximum yields quickly, two canes should be planted at each planting position. The flavour is very good. *A.G.M.*

**REDSETTER —** This variety combine high yields, large fruit and good flavour. The fruiting laterals display the berries well. It is the first compact fruiting raspberry and has shown considerable resistance to raspberry dieback disease.

**VALENTINA\* —** This promising new variety produces heavy yields of very attractive bright apricot-coloured fruits with a slight pink glow. The fruits are medium to large and have a good flavour. The canes are tall and upright with only a few spines. Valentina has shown excellent resistance to raspberry dieback disease and good resistance to aphid colonisation, spur blight and cane spot.

## *MIDSUMMER*

**GLEN AMPLE\*\* —** This is a new, exceptionally heavy yielding mid-season variety with good levels of disease resistance. The canes are spine free, upright and of good vigour. Fruiting laterals are long and very upright with sparse leaf, resulting in excellent fruit presentation. The fruits are large, bright red and of good flavour. *A.G.M.*

**GLEN PROSEN\*\* —** This variety is similar to Glen Moy in many respects, excepting it is later ripening with an extended picking season and the fruit is exceptionally firm; it does not however, bear a second crop in the autumn. *A.G.M.*

## *LATE MIDSUMMER*

**MALLING ADMIRAL\* –** This is one of the best garden varieties as the fruits, which are suitable for all purposes, are large, conical in shape, dark red and have an excellent flavour. The canes are strong growing and resistant to disease infection. *A.G.M.*

*Glen Magna*

**OCTAVIA\*** – This new variety bridges the gap between the autumn fruiting varieties and the existing summer fruiting varieties, producing fruit well into August. The fruit is large and fleshy, is easily plugged and once picked, it stores very well. The flavour is excellent. It requires a well drained soil.

**Octavia**

**TULAMEEN** – This is an outstanding new variety that will crop heavily for an extremely long period of up to 50 days throughout July and August. The exceptionally large, bright, glossy berries are firm, very sweet and aromatic. Tulameen's exquisite flavour and juicy flesh has made it the supermarkets' favourite raspberry. The canes are virtually spine free and are therefore easy to pick and manage. They are also late to emerge in the spring which makes them less susceptible to frost damage and the variety has good winter hardiness. The fruits have a superior resistance to Botrytis (Grey Mould) and will stand adverse weather conditions.

## AUTUMN

**ALLGOLD** — This new yellow fruited variety has a similar season and cropping potential to Autumn Bliss. The fruit is strongly coloured and the flavour is distinct, sweeter and superior to Autumn Bliss.

**Tulameen**

**AUTUMN BLISS\*** — The first of the really heavy cropping autumn fruiting varieties. The berries ripen immediately after Tulameen & Octavia, the latest ripening summer varieties. The berries are large and have an attractive red colour, firm texture and good flavour. The canes are short and sturdy and in a sheltered garden may not need supporting. Resistant to raspberry dieback disease. A.G.M.

**GALANTE** — Bred in France, this variety produces very large fruits of excellent quality and superb flavour. The canes are short and erect with very small, non-prickly thorns. Will crop heavily twice a year — once in the autumn and again the following summer.

\*   Raised at the H.R.I., East Malling
\*\*  Raised at the S.C.R.I., Scotland

**Allgold**

# RASPBERRIES

## PLANTING DISTANCES

The best row width is 1.8m (6ft), particularly for autumn fruiting varieties and summer varieties such as Glen Magna that have very long laterals. Where space is limited, varieties such as Glen Moy, Glen Prosen, Malling Jewel and Redsetter that have short laterals may be planted as close as 1.5m (5ft).

The gardener has the choice of two types of training system — the Scottish stool system and the English hedgerow system. The Scottish stool system (which is always to be recommended) is easier to manage. Weeding and spraying is easier because the bushes are spread out and fruit quality is usually better because more light gets into the bushes and the air can circulate more freely. The English hedgerow system however remains the most popular and certainly makes sense where space is limited, since the plants can be planted closer. Fruit production per metre of row is greater under this system since the cane density is higher.

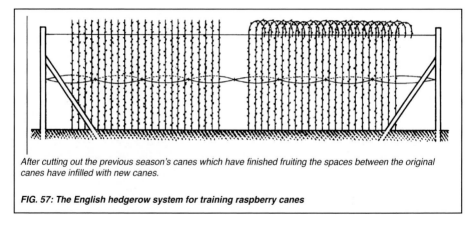

*After cutting out the previous season's canes which have finished fruiting the spaces between the original canes have infilled with new canes.*

**FIG. 57: The English hedgerow system for training raspberry canes**

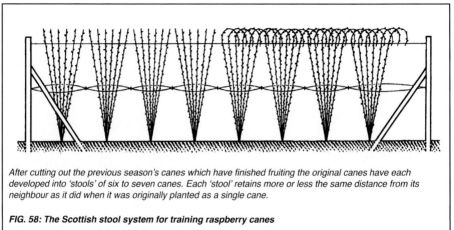

*After cutting out the previous season's canes which have finished fruiting the original canes have each developed into 'stools' of six to seven canes. Each 'stool' retains more or less the same distance from its neighbour as it did when it was originally planted as a single cane.*

**FIG. 58: The Scottish stool system for training raspberry canes**

# RASPBERRIES

When the bushes are to be grown on the Scottish stool system the canes should be planted 68cm (27in) apart in the row. To produce heavy crops quickly, 'Malling Jewel' , which is a poor cane producer, should have two canes planted at each planting position. It is not possible to grow autumn fruiting varieties on the Scottish stool system.

When the English hedgerow system is adopted, all varieties except 'Malling Jewel' and 'Leo' should have single canes planted 40cm (16in) apart in the row. Autumn fruiting varieties are always grown on the English hedgerow system and should be planted 40cm (16in) apart.

Fig. 57 and fig. 58 show both types of training system in an established row after cutting out the previous season's canes which have finished fruiting. Fig. 57 of the English hedgerow system illustrates where the spaces between the original canes have infilled with new canes. Fig. 58 of the Scottish stool system shows how the original canes have each developed into 'stools' of six to seven canes. Each 'stool' retains more or less the same distance from its neighbour as it did when it was originally planted as a single cane.

## PLANTING

If the soil is inclined to be heavy, the canes are best grown on a raised bed which can be made by digging trenches 45cm (18in) wide, 60cm (24in) from the proposed row of canes and spreading the soil over the bed allowing it to settle before planting. Alternatively, a planting ridge may be formed by digging the soil towards a centre line on which the canes are to be planted. The correct planting depth is essential if the canes are to make satisfactory growth in their first year. The uppermost roots should be positioned not more than 5cm (2in) below soil level and the white growth buds may be as high as at soil level. The soil should be well firmed over the roots.

If the canes have not already been cut back to approximately 15-22cm (6-9in) prior to planting, this should be done immediately afterwards. This will encourage new growth from beneath the soil level. The existing cane will normally (but not always) produce fresh growth in the spring but the new growth from beneath the soil level may not show until the early part of the summer.  When the new growth appears, the existing cane should be cut down to ground level to ensure the production of strong new canes.

## MANURING

Immediately after planting, or by the middle of March, whichever is the later, broadcast in a band 45cm (18in) wide along the row of canes:

> $35g/m^2$ $(1\frac{1}{4}oz/yd^2)$ Nitro-Chalk (calcium ammonium nitrate)
> and $10g/m^2$ $(\frac{1}{4}oz/yd^2)$ sulphate of potash.

Similarly at the end of May broadcast:

> $20g/m^2$ $(\frac{3}{4}oz/yd^2)$ Nitro-Chalk (calcium ammonium nitrate).

# RASPBERRIES

In the years following, in early March broadcast 90cm (3ft) both sides of the row:

*10g/m$^2$ (¼oz/yd$^2$) Nitro-Chalk (calcium ammonium nitrate) and 15g/m$^2$ (½oz/yd$^2$) sulphate of potash.*

Alternatively, a compound fertilizer may be used after planting and thereafter annually, following the manufacturer's recommendations.

## POSTS & WIRES

A supporting framework of posts and wires should be erected in the early winter following the first growing season and canes secured to the wires. The minimum size of the posts should be 5 x 7.5cm (2 x 3in) and 2m (6ft 6in) long, driven 52cm (1ft 9in) into the ground. The end posts should be strutted and if the rows are longer than 13.5m (15yd), intermediate posts 11m (12yd) apart will be required. No less than 12 gauge wire should be used to support the canes. Autumn fruiting varieties should not normally require a supporting framework in sheltered gardens because the canes are short and sturdy.

## CONTROL OF CANE NUMBERS

To obtain the maximum yield of fruit, it is essential that the number of new canes that are allowed to grow and bear fruit should be rigidly controlled. The number should be seven per stool for the Scottish stool system or ten per metre of row (nine per yard of row) for the hedgerow system — numbers in excess of this should be cut out or pulled out in early May and again in mid-June when they are 45cm (18in) tall. If there is still an excess number of canes present at the end of the summer, these should be dug or pulled up with their roots but not cut off at soil level.

## CANE VIGOUR CONTROL

Some varieties, for example 'Malling Jewel' produce canes that are too tall for the support system. This unwanted vigour should be reduced so that the fruit quality is improved, yield increased and picking made easier. This can be accomplished by pulling out or rubbing out every new cane before end of May when the average height is 10-20cm (4-8in). Within a fortnight a new set of canes will appear to take their place. They will not hide the fruit and their ultimate height will be much less.

# RASPBERRIES

## TRADITIONAL TRAINING SYSTEMS

The canes are secured between two bottom wires running parallel with each other at a height of 60cm (2ft) above ground level. The wires are tied or clipped together at intervals of 2.7m (3yd). The tops of the canes are either laced with a continuous piece of twine or individually tied to a single top wire positioned 1.2m (4ft) above the ground when the canes are fully grown.

## PRUNING & TYING-IN

### SUMMER FRUITING VARIETIES

Summer fruiting varieties produce fruit on the previous season's canes. They may be pruned at any time after picking has stopped and as late as the following February. However, it is an advantage to prune in August or September when the new canes are to be woven on the wires as the canes are more supple at this time. This method makes tying with string unnecessary.

The procedure should be to cut out with secateurs each spent fruiting cane, leaving the smallest stub possible. Then dig out or pull out by their roots all new canes that are growing away from the stools and in the case of the English hedgerow system, every cane that is situated at a distance of more than 15cm (6in) from the row. Next, cut off any spindly, short or damaged canes that are growing on the stools and in the hedgerow system similarly dig or pull out individual spindly, short or damaged canes. If after this there is still an excessive number of sound tall canes remaining in the row, the number should be reduced to a maximum of eight per stool, or nine per 90cm (1yd) of row. Once pruning has been completed, it is advisable that the canes should be secured to the wires to prevent them thrashing about in the wind and being damaged.

Raspberry canes frequently grow 2.1m-2.7m (7-9ft) tall and it is on the upper 60-90cm (2-3ft) that the better quality buds are borne. To avoid cutting off these buds, the canes should either be bowed over in a semi-circle and the cane tied a second time at its tip to the wire, or if this does not accommodate all the cane, a further measure should be to train the canes to the wires at an angle of 60°. The weaving of long canes along the upper wire makes pruning unnecessary but this method gives rise to a crowded mass of fruiting laterals that become drawn and easily broken. Whichever method of training is adopted, the final operation, in February, is to prune off the weak 15cm (6in) tip of each cane on which buds of poor quality are borne. Where canes grow to an excessive height in the following years, the application of fertilizer should be reduced or omitted and cane vigour control practiced in May.

### AUTUMN FRUITING VARIETIES

An autumn fruiting variety is one that **produces flowers on the top part of the current season's new canes,** the fruit of which ripens from mid-August onwards **but in addition produces fruit the following summer** on the lower part of the same canes.

# RASPBERRIES

In order to maximise the autumn crop, a bed of canes 60-90cm (2-3ft) wide is encouraged to grow and **each winter every cane is cut down to ground level.** The amount of autumn ripening fruit is maximised by the presence of a large number of new canes and not permitting any of the canes that have produced an autumn crop to overwinter and bear a second crop in the summer.

In order to produce two crops each year — the first crop in the autumn on the new cane growth and the second crop during the following summer on overwintered canes,  the following method should be adopted.

Instead of pruning all the current season's canes down to ground level each winter, a proportion of strong canes should be pruned just below that part of the cane which produced the autumn crop, and everything else should be cut out at ground level completely. The canes that have been retained will overwinter and crop the following summer, after which they are cut out at ground level.

There is a trade-off to producing two crops each season. The more canes that are left to overwinter, the poorer the autumn crop will be.

In the northern areas of the U.K. the canes may require some form of protection to ripen the later crop earlier. This could take the form of a polythene or glass structure.

## PESTS, DISEASES & DISORDERS

Some of the most troublesome pests, diseases and disorders are listed in the following table. See chapter on 'Common Fruiting Problems' and 'Pests & Diseases' for details.

| Symptoms | Possible problem | Symptoms | Possible problem |
|---|---|---|---|
| Leaf distortion/ marking on leaves | Aphids<br>Cane spot<br>Lime-induced chlorosis<br>Powdery mildew<br>Raspberry leaf & bud mite<br>Rust<br>Spider mite<br>Virus | Wilting shoots/ cane | Leatherjackets<br>Raspberry cane blight<br>Raspberry cane midge<br>Raspberry dieback<br>Raspberry spur blight<br>Wireworm |
| | | Blossom damage | Stamen blight |
| | | Maggots in fruit | Raspberry beetle |
| Discoloured cane | Cane spot<br>Grey mould<br>Purple blotch<br>Raspberry cane blight<br>Raspberry cane midge<br>Raspberry spur blight | Marked/ distorted fruit | Cane spot<br>Grey mould<br>Powdery mildew<br>Raspberry leaf & bud mite<br>Redberry disease<br>Stamen blight |

# BLACKCURRANTS & JOSTABERRY

**B**lackcurrants prefer a rich soil containing plenty of humus and a high nitrogen content. They have the reputation of doing well on heavier soils than would be suitable for red or white currants, but that does not mean that they can be grown on badly drained clay soils. Shelter from east winds at the time of blossoming is important because pollinating insects will fly freely only in a sheltered situation. The bushes start to bear fruit in the second year following planting; their length of life depends upon keeping them free from pests and diseases; if well managed, they should last eight years at least before needing to be replaced. The introduction of new blackcurrant varieties that are heavy yielding and resistant to frost and diseases now makes growing this fruit very worthwhile.

## VARIETIES

*A.G.M. signifies the Award of Garden Merit, the Royal Horticultural Society's most prestigious award.*

**BEN CONNAN** — A relatively new small bush variety particularly suitable for private gardens. It is early ripening and heavy cropping. The very large berries (up to 17mm in diameter) are very easy and economical to pick. Ben Connan is resistant to powdery mildew and the leaf curling midge. The leaves are uniformly green and the variety does not have yellow spotted leaves like those of Ben Sarek. The flavour is very good. *A.G.M.*

*Ben Connan*

**BEN HOPE** — A high resistance to the 'big bud' mite, rust, mildew and leaf spot makes this new variety particularly suitable for bio-friendly amateur gardeners. Heavy crops of medium sized berries are produced on long strigs. The fruit is of outstanding quality and ripens slightly later than Ben Lomond. The bush is tall, upright and vigorous.

**BEN LOMOND** — Ben Lomond is one of the most popular commercial varieties. It ripens its fruit during the last days of July. The bush is moderately vigorous, compact and requires the minimum of pruning. It is late flowering, resistant to frost but somewhat susceptible to infection by mildew. The flavour is good. *A.G.M.*

*Ben Hope*

**BEN SAREK** — This variety is particularly suitable for a small garden because it forms a small compact bush yet remains very high yielding. The branches are rather spreading and should be supported by link stakes or four canes with strings between them. The berries are unusually large and ripen at the same time as those of Ben Lomond. Ben Sarek is resistant to mildew and its blossom is frost resistant. The flavour is good. *A.G.M.*

*Ben Lomond*

**Jostaberry**

**TITANIA** — This new variety produces large fruits of excellent flavour. Crops heavily over a long period. Good mildew resistance.

**JOSTABERRY** — This comparatively new fruit was produced by crossing a blackcurrant x gooseberry hybrid with a blackcurrant x *R. divaricatum* hybrid. It is regarded as being a great improvement on the Worcesterberry. The bush is vigorous, upright and thornless and is resistant to American gooseberry mildew, blackcurrant leafspot and blackcurrant gall mite. The flowers, which can go unnoticed, are self-pollinating and unless protected, are easily damaged by severe frosts in spring. The berries resemble a large blackcurrant but are about twice their size, having a pleasant flavour, slightly different from both the blackcurrant and the gooseberry. The yield is heavy.

## TYPES OF BUSH

Blackcurrants should always be grown as a stool bush. For ease of management, the Jostaberry is best grown as a stool bush but can also be grown on a 75cm (2ft 6in) leg (but then needs to be staked) which will prevent the lower branches with a drooping habit from touching the soil.

## PLANTING DISTANCES

Bushes should be planted 1.5m (5ft) apart in the rows. However, the quantity of fruit can be doubled in the first four years by planting 75cm (30in) apart. The distance between the rows of blackcurrants and other soft fruits should be 1.5m (5ft) whilst 1.8m (6ft) is better for hoeing, spraying and picking. The dwarf varieties Ben Connan and Ben Sarek should be planted 1.2m (4ft) between bushes and 1.5m (5ft) between rows.

## PLANTING

A hole large enough for the roots to be spread out should be dug to a depth that positions the fork where the branches divide at soil level. On shallow soils it is better to plant the bush at an angle of 45° in a shallower hole where the soil will be more fertile. After planting, the soil should be well firmed over the roots.

## PRUNING

Although blackcurrants crop on the older wood, they bear the best fruit on the wood produced the previous summer. The objective is therefore to stimulate a constant succession of strong young shoots to carry fruit in the next season. This is achieved by fairly heavy pruning and by heavy feeding.

Immediately after planting, *each branch should be pruned back to within two buds or 2.5cm (1in) of ground level* (see fig. 59). Failure to do this is tantamount to mortgaging the future of the bush. It is best to select outward facing buds so the new growth does not cross over.

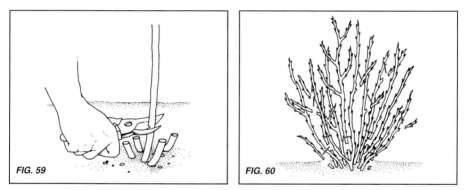

FIG. 59

FIG. 60

At the end of the first growing season, pruning should consist of cutting out any very thin, weak shoots (less than 30cm [12in]) and one strong shoot back to the base of the bush. In following winters, all branches that grow out at an angle of more than 45° from vertical should be cut out. Otherwise no attempt is made to limit the number of branches.

Blackcurrant bushes need constant renewal to ensure heavy crops. Older branches will bear fruit, but quantity and quality will decline with age. Therefore, when bushes are fully grown, three or four of the oldest branches should be cut back to strong new side shoots or, if there are none, to the base of the bush (see fig. 60). Any weak or very low growing shoots should also be removed completely. The Jostaberry should be pruned rather like a blackcurrant, removing some of the older wood each year. Pruning can be carried out when the fruit is being harvested or in the winter.

## MANURING

In mid-March, or after planting, whichever is latest, broadcast in a circle 45cm (18in) round each bush:

> *30g (1oz) Nitro-Chalk (calcium ammonium nitrate)*
> *and 10g (¼oz) sulphate of potash.*

In the years following, during early March, broadcast 90cm (3ft) round each bush:

*35g/m² (1¼oz/yd²) Nitro-Chalk (calcium ammonium nitrate)*
*and 10g/m² (¼oz/yd²) sulphate of potash.*

Alternatively, a compound fertilizer may be used after planting and annually thereafter following the manufacturer's recommendations.

When the bushes are fully grown, the amount of Nitro-Chalk and compound fertilizer should be reduced by two thirds.

## PESTS, DISEASES & DISORDERS

Some of the most troublesome pests, diseases and disorders are listed in the following table. See chapters on 'Common Fruiting Problems' and 'Pests & Diseases' for details.

| Symptoms | Possible problem | Symptoms | Possible problem |
|---|---|---|---|
| Leaf distortion/ marking on leaves | American gooseberry mildew<br>Aphids<br>Blackcurrant leaf curling midge<br>Leaf spot<br>Lime-induced chlorosis<br>'Reversion' virus | Marking on leaves | Rust<br>Spider mite |
| | | Holes in leaves | Gooseberry sawfly |
| | | Swollen buds/ discoloured flowers | Blackcurrant gall mite<br>'Reversion' virus |
| | | Marked/ distorted frui | American gooseberry tmildew<br>Grey mould |

# GOOSEBERRIES, RED & WHITE CURRANTS

The gooseberry is the first fruit of the season. The fruit should be thinned in late May and the thinnings used for cooking. The remainder should be left to swell near to full size and then used for pies, jamming and freezing. To appreciate a gooseberry as a fine dessert fruit a proportion should be left to ripen fully when they are sweet and richly flavoured. The requirements of gooseberries are similar to those of red and white currants and these two crops should be grouped together in any garden plan. Varieties of gooseberries differ widely in their performance depending on local soil conditions, for example the variety 'Whinham's Industry' does well on heavy soils which are generally unsatisfactory for gooseberries. Chalky, sandy and gravelly soils in particular require plentiful dressings of farmyard manure or garden compost before and after planting; they are usually more tolerant of alkaline conditions than most fruits.

## VARIETIES

*A.G.M. signifies the Award of Garden Merit, the Royal Horticultural Society's most prestigious award.*

*GOOSEBERRIES*

**CARELESS** — This variety is reliable and heavy cropping. The berries are large, smooth skinned and a green, milky-white colour when ripe. An excellent variety for cooking and jam making. Ripens mid-July. *A.G.M.*

*Careless*

**HINNONMAKI RED** – This dessert/culinary variety produces heavy crops of large red fruits. The flavour is excellent - the skin is tangy, the flesh is sweet. Resistant to American gooseberry mildew. Ripens mid July.

**HINNONMAKI YELLOW** – This new dessert variety produces heavy crops of very large yellow fruit. It has an excellent aromatic flavour with a hint of apricot. Resistant to American gooseberry mildew. Ripens mid July.

**INVICTA** — This is the most widely grown culinary variety. It is very heavy cropping, vigorous and resistant to mildew infection. The large, oval, pale green berries are smooth skinned and have a satisfactory flavour for a culinary variety. Ripens late July. *A.G.M.*

*Hinnonmaki Red*

**LEVELLER** — This variety has the reputation of having the best flavour of all gooseberries for dessert but is weak growing and requires a good soil and careful cultivation. The greenish/yellow oval shaped berries are smooth skinned and ripen mid-season. The bush has a drooping habit and is very susceptible to American gooseberry mildew. Ripens late July. *A.G.M.*

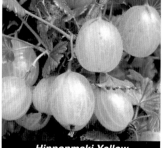
*Hinnonmaki Yellow*

*Whinham's Industry*

**PAX** — A new virtually spine-free dessert variety raised at Horticultural Research International, East Malling. Pax is moderately resistant to American gooseberry mildew and moderately resistant to leaf spot. Produces extremely heavy crops of large, slightly bristly, dark red fruit of moderate flavour. The canes are very vigorous and spreading but can be shaped by pruning. Ripens mid-July.

**REMARKA** — A new early ripening dessert/culinary variety. Produces large smooth dark red fruits of very good flavour. The plants are of good vigour. Resistant to American Gooseberry Mildew. Ripens mid-July.

**ROKULA** — This new, very early ripening dessert variety produces large dark red fruits of excellent flavour. The plants are of medium to weak vigour with a slightly drooping habit. Rokula is resistant to American gooseberry mildew on the fruit and plant. Ripens mid-July.

**WHINHAM'S INDUSTRY** — Whinham's is one of the most widely grown red dessert varieties of gooseberry as it is vigorous, does well on most soils and besides being well-flavoured when ripe, it is also suitable for culinary use whilst green. However, it is susceptible to American gooseberry mildew. The berries are medium to large in size, hairy and red, almost purple when ripe. Ripens late July. *A.G.M.*

*Jonkheer Van Tets*

## REDCURRANTS

**JONKHEER VAN TETS** — An early ripening Dutch variety that bears very heavy crops of large sized berries, ripening in early July. The attractive looking berries are borne on long trusses. Very good flavour. *A.G.M.*

**JUNIFER** — This new variety raised in France, is very early ripening and heavy yielding, outyielding all other existing varieties. It crops on both one year and two year old wood to give a good yield in the first season. The very high quality fruit is borne on long trusses. It has a high level of disease resistance.

**LAXTON'S NO.1** — This variety is early flowering and early ripening. It produces heavy yields of medium sized bright red berries which ripen in early July. The fruit is borne on long trusses. Moderately resistant to mildew. The flavour is good.

*Junifer*

*White Versailles*

**ROVADA** — A comparatively new, exceptionally heavy yielding, very late Dutch variety which commences to crop early August. The large berries are borne on long trusses. Good level of disease resistance. The flavour is good.

## *WHITE CURRANTS*

**WHITE VERSAILLES** — This is one of the few varieties of white currant available. The fruit is large, light yellow and sweet, ready for harvesting early July. It makes a fairly strong, vigorous, upright bush, cropping heavily.

## TYPES OF PLANT

Gooseberries, red and white currants can all be grown as a bush, stooled-bush, half-standard or upright cordon.

A bush with a leg should have a leg which is at least 20cm (8in) long with three or more equally spaced branches each 30cm (12in) in length. It should have at least six main roots 15cm (6in) or more long.

Bushes without a leg are called stool bushes and like a blackcurrant, their branches arise directly from the root system. The bush should have two to five shoots each over 30cm (12in) in length.

Half-standard forms (where the main stem length is approximately 60-90cm [2-3ft] in length) are now becoming very popular. They have several advantages over conventional low bush forms. They are more attractive looking and since they bear their fruit well above ground level, they are easier to manage and pick. They also take up less ground space, since the area beneath the bush can be utilised by low growing annuals. This is clearly an important consideration in a small garden.

Cordons should have a clear stem of 10-15cm (4-6in) and above that they should have plenty of side shoots.

*Half-standard gooseberry*

# GOOSEBERRIES, RED & WHITE CURRANTS

## PLANTING DISTANCES

Bush and half-standard forms should be planted 1.5-1.8m (5-6ft) between rows and 1.2-1.5m (4-5ft) between the plants. Invicta should be planted at the wider distances.

Cordons should be spaced 30-37cm (12-15in) apart for gooseberries and 37-45cm (15-18in) apart for redcurrants.

## PLANTING

Bushes grown on a leg should be carefully examined for dormant buds and small white shoots. These should be rubbed out to stop them from growing into unwanted suckers later on. Planting holes should be dug to a depth so that no more than one third of the stem is covered with soil. Any roots on the upper two thirds of the leg should be cut off. Stool bushes should be planted more deeply so that the bases of the shoots are at soil level.

Cordons should be planted and secured to a 1.5 or 1.8m (5 or 6ft) cane which should be secured to horizontal wires at 60cm (2ft) and 1.35m (4ft 6in).

## SUCKER CONTROL

Gooseberry and red and white currant bushes produce suckers throughout their lives. They should not be cut off but pulled off the stem or roots in June or July whilst they are still soft.

## PRUNING

### BUSH & HALF-STANDARD

The primary objectives are to grow a vase shaped bush which allows light and air to penetrate around all the branches to discourage disease infections and make spraying and picking easier. Following planting or at bud burst, whichever is the later, any branch that does not form part of this vase shape should be cut right out of the bush. The remaining branches should be cut back to a third of their original length to left and right facing buds (see fig. 61).

This treatment should be followed each year to increase the number of branches in the main framework of the bush and continued until the bush has occupied its allocated space (see fig. 62). At this stage the leading shoots that extend the main branches should be pruned back to half their length to downward facing buds for upright varieties and upward facing buds for drooping varieties. All lateral shoots on the main branches should be summer pruned to half their length at the end of June and further pruned back to two or three buds each winter. Strong shoots that grow into the centre of a bush in competition with the main branches or in any other unwanted place should be cut out from June onwards.

# GOOSEBERRIES,
# RED & WHITE CURRANTS

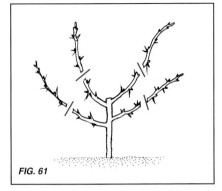

FIG. 61

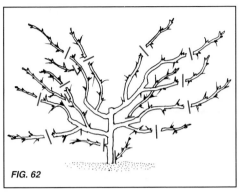

FIG. 62

## STOOLED BUSH

Stooled bushes should be pruned in a similar way to blackcurrants. After planting, cut back each shoot to two buds. In the years following, cut out all thin shoots and those that are likely to droop onto the ground. Then cut out to the base of the bush one third of the remaining shoots so that those left are equally spaced out. Any tips of shoots that are infected with mildew should be cut off and burned.

## CORDONS

Cordons should be pruned in the summer and winter. In June the young side shoots should be pruned to five leaves. The leading shoot should be tied to the cane during the summer (see fig. 63). In the dormant season (November-March) the side shoots should be pruned back to one or two buds. The leading shoot should be shortened by one third of the new growth each winter until it has reached the desired height. In following years the leader should be stopped at five leaves in June and pruned back to one or two buds in the winter (see fig. 64).

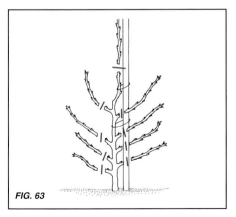

FIG. 63

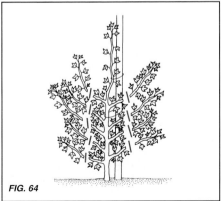

FIG. 64

# GOOSEBERRIES, RED & WHITE CURRANTS

## MANURING

To newly planted bushes in March, apply in a circle 60cm (24in) diameter around each bush:

*10g (¼oz) Nitro-Chalk (calcium ammonium nitrate)*
*and 15g (½oz) sulphate of potash.*

If by the middle of June extension growth is less than 22cm (9in) long, give a further application of 10g (¼oz) of Nitro-Chalk. In the two years following, apply similar amounts of fertilizer to each $m^2$ ($yd^2$) 90cm (3ft) round each bush.

When the bushes are fully grown and are cropping heavily, the rates of application should be increased to:

*35g/$m^2$ (1¼oz/$yd^2$) Nitro-Chalk (calcium ammonium nitrate)*
*and 15g/$m^2$ (½oz/$yd^2$) sulphate of potash.*

Every fifth year apply:

*70g/$m^2$ (2½oz/$yd^2$) superphosphate.*

Alternatively, a compound fertilizer may be used after planting and annually thereafter, following the manufacturer's recommendations.

## PESTS, DISEASES & DISORDERS

Some of the most troublesome pests, diseases and disorders are listed in the following table. See chapter on 'Common Fruiting Problems' and 'Pests & Diseases' for details.

| Symptoms | Possible problem | Symptoms | Possible problem |
|---|---|---|---|
| Leaf distortion/ marking on leaves | American gooseberry mildew Aphids Green capsid bug Leaf spot Lime-induced chlorosis Spider mite | Holes in leaves | Gooseberry sawfly Green capsid bug |
| | | Defoliation | Green capsid bug |
| | | Marked/ distorted fruit | American gooseberry mildew Green capsid bug Grey mould |

# BLUEBERRIES

**B**lueberries grow just as well as other fruits in the U.K. provided they are given the special acid conditions they require. If you do not have the appropriate soil, they should be grown in containers. Requirements as to site, shelter and exposure to the sun are similar to those for other soft fruits. Two varieties should usually be planted to improve pollination and ensure a good set of flowers under adverse weather conditions.

## VARIETIES

The Northern Highbush blueberries are the most widely grown and are bred for their heavy crops of large fruit. They will reach an average height of 1.5m (5ft) in 5 years and are very hardy and reliable countrywide. The Southern Highbush blueberries are recent hybrid introductions, bred for areas with high summer temperatures and little winter chill. They are mostly only suitable for gardens in the southern half of the U.K. and for sunny, dry south-facing positions in the north. They will reach an average height of 1m (3ft) in 5 years. Half highbush varieties are hybrids between the Northern Highbush blueberries and the low growing wild North American lowbush blueberries. They are exceptionally hardy and very compact, reaching no more than 1m (3ft) on maturity. They have a wild blueberry flavour and intense autumn colour, making them ideal ornamental fruiting plants.

### *NORTHERN HIGHBUSH*

**BLUECROP** — This popular variety should always be chosen for planting either by itself or in a collection of varieties. The bush grows vigorously with an upright habit. It bears heavy crops of light blue berries of good flavour. It is said to be more resistant to drought than other varieties. Ripens mid-season.

**EARLIBLUE** — This is the earliest ripening variety, two weeks before any of the others — in the third week of July in the south of England. The berries are large, light blue and of good flavour. The bushes are vigorous and upright, but only moderate yielding.

*Bluecrop*

**HERBERT** — This variety is considered the best flavoured of all. The berries are very large, medium-blue and ripening mid to late August. Herbert has a vigorous upright habit.

### *SOUTHERN HIGHBUSH*

**SUNSHINE BLUE** – This is one of the best southern highbush varieties for garden cultivation as it is reliable countrywide. The plant is bushy and compact, reaching about 3ft tall & 3ft wide. The flower buds are red and these are followed by bright pink flowers that fade to white. Heavy crops of medium sized berries. Excellent flavour. Ripens midseason. Self-fertile.

*Sunshine Blue*

# BLUEBERRIES

*Top Hat (in flower)*

### HALF HIGHBUSH

**BLUETTA** — A consistently heavy cropping variety with a good wild blueberry flavour. Reaches a maximum height and spread of 3-4ft.

**TOP HAT** – This dwarf variety is perfect as a border, rock garden or container plant on the patio. The mature bush reaches a maximum height and spread of just 16-24in. It produces heavy crops of medium sized fruits of outstanding flavour. The foliage turns a blazing crimson colour in the autumn. Self-fertile.

## SOIL CONDITIONS

Blueberries require a deep free-draining soil that has a gritty texture. Heavy soils that have a smooth feel and when turned over with a spade have a polished surface are unsuitable for blueberries. However, if they are high in organic matter and coarse grit is added, they can be brought into the right sort of condition that will support this crop. Blueberries must be grown in a soil with a pH of between 4.0 and 5.5. Soils overlying chalk or limestone and other soils that contain free lime cannot be brought into conditions that will grow blueberries. Soils that are otherwise suitable but have too high a pH can be acidified so that blueberries grow successfully. The pH of such soils should be measured with an electronic meter or chemical testing kit. Each bush should be treated in accordance with the following table with either flowers of sulphur, peat or sawdust, to bring the pH down to 4.0.

| pH | Flowers of sulphur | | | | Peat | | | | Sawdust | | | |
| | light soil | | medium soil | | light soil | | medium soil | | light soil | | medium soil | |
| | $m^2$ | $yd^2$ | $m^2$ | $yd^2$ | $m^2$ | $yd^2$ | $m^2$ | $yd^2$ | $m^2$ | $yd^2$ | $m^2$ | $yd^2$ |
| 5.5 | 34g | 1oz | 68g | 2oz | 10cm | 4in | 20cm | 8in | 10cm | 4in | 10cm | 8in |
| 6.5 | 68g | 2oz | 136g | 4oz | 20cm | 8in | 40cm | 16in | 20cm | 8in | 20cm | 16in |
| 7.5 | 102g | 3oz | 204g | 6oz | 30cm | 12in | 60cm | 24in | 30cm | 12in | 30cm | 24in |

The chosen material should be applied twelve months before planting and thoroughly worked into the soil as deeply as possible with a fork or rotavator. Applications of 30cm (12in) or more of sawdust could lead to problems; by substituting some of the sawdust with sulphur or peat, these can be avoided. If planting cannot be delayed for a year, 2 litres (½gal) of peat should be mixed with the soil in the planting hole.

# BLUEBERRIES

Blueberries can also be grown in containers using an ericaceous compost mixed with an equal volume of sharp sand or grit.

## PLANTING DISTANCES

Bushes should be planted 1.2-1.5m (4-5ft) apart and 1.5-1.8m (5-6ft) from other fruits.

## MANURING

Blueberries should not be given fertilizers containing lime or calcium. The best fertilizers to use are sulphate of potash and sulphate of ammonia. Before planting, fork into the soil:

*35g/m² (1¼oz/yd ²) super-phosphate and 20g/m² (¾oz/yd ²) sulphate of potash;*

followed by a similar application at the end of March of:

*15g/m² (½oz/yd ²) of sulphate of ammonia.*

Each March in the years following, broadcast over the soil 10in (25cm) beyond the spread of the branches:

*15g/m² (½oz/yd ²) sulphate of ammonia*
*and 10g/m² (¼oz/yd ²) sulphate of potash*

.
Alternatively, a lime or calcium free compound fertilizer specially formulated for ericaceous plants (e.g Chempak ericaceous fertilizer) may be used following the manufacturer's recommendations.

If the bushes do not grow sufficiently well and produce new shoots 30-45cm (12-18in) long, the sulphate of ammonia should be increased by a half or more. If the bushes grow so strongly that new shoots are broken or diseased, the amount should be reduced.

## PRUNING

During the two winters after planting, pruning consists only of cutting out diseased or damaged shoots and branches. To encourage the production of strong new shoots, any fat round fruit buds should be rubbed out to prevent the setting of any fruit. In later years, pruning consists of cutting out any new branches that are likely to be borne onto the ground by the weight of crop. The clusters of thin bushy wood that accumulate on the older branches should be cut back to ground level or to strong side branches; this will remove about 20% of the older branches and encourage the production of new growth.

then be covered with lime-free stones or brickbats over 2.5cm (1in) in diameter to a depth of 7.5cm (3in). These should be covered with a sheet of polythene mesh to prevent the compost or peat, with which the bed will be filled, from clogging up the drainage material. For this purpose old polythene compost bags in which numerous drainage holes have been made, would be suitable. The bed should be filled with either horticultural peat or two parts of peat and one part of soil, or three parts of peat and one part of coarse sand. Heavy clay soils should not be used as they are almost impossible to mix with the peat satisfactorily.

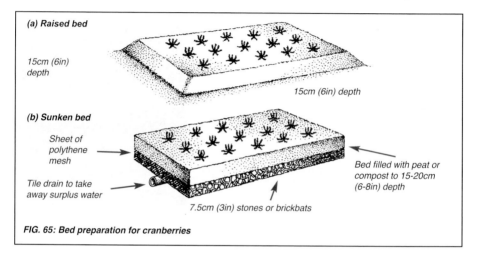

**(a) Raised bed**

15cm (6in) depth

15cm (6in) depth

**(b) Sunken bed**

Sheet of polythene mesh

Tile drain to take away surplus water

Bed filled with peat or compost to 15-20cm (6-8in) depth

7.5cm (3in) stones or brickbats

*FIG. 65: Bed preparation for cranberries*

## PLANTING

Plants grown in pots are likely to be the only type of stock available for purchase. These should be planted into peat or compost at any time during the winter.

After planting, the bed should be covered with 2.5cm (1in) of coarse lime-free sand. This is not absolutely necessary but it prevents the surface of the peat from drying out; it gives some weed control, as fewer weeds germinate in sand than do in peat, and it provides a medium in which the cuttings root easily. The bed should be watered with lime free water using the gentle spray from a watering can until the peat is saturated.

## MANURING A NEWLY PLANTED BED

During the first year the objective should be to obtain rapid growth by the judicious application of fertilizer, to get a good cover of the bed with new shoots. Harm could be done by exceeding the following rate of application. Broadcast over the bed:

# CRANBERRIES

In April:

        *20g/m² (½oz/yd²) Phostrogen.*

In May:

        *10g/m² (¼oz/yd²) Phostrogen.*

In June:

        *10g/m² (¼oz/yd²) sulphate of ammonia.*

In July:

        *10g/m² (¼oz/yd²) sulphate of ammonia.*

Alternatively, a lime or calcium free compound fertilizer specially formulated for ericaceous plants (e.g Chempak ericaceous fertilizer) may be used following the manufacturer's recommendations.

Any fertilizer that has lodged on the plants should be washed off with a quick sprinkling of water.

## ANNUAL CULTURE

Vines are the horizontal shoots that creep over the surface and extend the area of the bed. Upright shoots grow from the vines. These are 5-7.5cm (2-3in) long, they flower during June and bear fruit in September/October. Pruning should be carried out after harvest, cutting off any vines that have been pulled to the top of the bed and any upright shoots that have been damaged during picking. When the bed is fully established and covered with shoots, pruning carried out in March should firstly consist of judiciously thinning out vines and upright shoots that are overcrowded and secondly, trimming the edges of the bed. Three to five months elapse before the plants fully cover the surface of the bed.

## SANDING

Every four years 1cm (½in) depth of sand should be applied to the bed in early winter. This is not absolutely necessary but it can be beneficial by encouraging the vines and uprights to form more roots, and when necessary grow more vigorously.

## MANURING AN ESTABLISHED BED

If, at the end of March, the peat in the bed has not been saturated by winter rainfall, the bed should be watered until the peat is saturated. During April, broadcast over the bed the same fertilizers, at the same rate as advocated for the first year.

# CRANBERRIES

## WATERING

The amount of water that a bed requires depends upon the natural rainfall that occurs. It would be better to err on the side of over-watering provided that the bed had good drainage when it was first made. Beds in gardens situated in the wetter northern and western districts of the U.K. will require less additional water than those situated in the drier districts of central and south-east England.

It would be unlikely for beds made up with a large proportion of peat to require an application before the middle of June. If after that, a period of two to three weeks drought occurs, the bed should be saturated with lime free water, using gentle spray from a watering can. If using tap water, it is best to use it in conjunction with Chempak ericaceous fertilizer which will neutralise the lime in the water

In large beds, mains water free from lime should be available for application to the bed using a garden sprinkler. A hosepipe should not be used as it would disturb the sand and peat too much.

## HARVESTING & STORAGE

In southern England, the berries ripen from late September onwards. Although they can be picked over by hand when the first ripening berries develop their full colour, it is probably better to wait until all the crop is ready for picking as it is a back breaking task, even worse than picking blackcurrants singly! In America, the berries are combed off the plants with a scoop shaped container that has set on its lower lip a comb-like arrangement, the teeth of which are set wide enough apart to pull the berries off the shoots but to allow the shoots to pass through with a minimum of damage. It should be possible to make a similar gadget from a plastic dustpan or other plastic container of suitable size and thickness. The bed should always be combed in the same direction so that the stems are disturbed as little as possible. Providing all damaged fruits are removed, cranberries will keep for two to three weeks at moderate room temperatures, for two to three months in a refrigerator at 2-4°C and almost indefinitely deep frozen. They require no preparation apart from being dry and being placed in sealed polythene containers.

# GRAPES

The highly productive grape vine in your garden will become a focal point of beauty. Grapes are very hardy and the breeding and selection of varieties has progressed so far in the last ten years, that it is now possible to plant a range of varieties suitable for growing outdoors throughout the U.K., both for dessert and wine production. They will give the best results if planted and trained against a south facing wall; they will also do well when trained onto a horizontal wire support away from any wall. When grown under glass, vines can be planted outside the house and brought in through the wall or planted inside the glasshouse border. Vines should be spaced 1.2-1.5m (4-5ft) apart.

## VARIETIES

*INDOOR*

**BLACK HAMBURGH** — This early dessert grape was at one time the most widely grown grape in Britain. The famous Hampton Court vine is of this variety. The berries are medium to large, roundish or slightly oval, dark purplish red or purplish black, with heavy bloom, juicy and sweet but without a muscat flavour. The bunch is of medium size and compact. The vine is of good to moderate vigour and does best in a hot house. It will ripen in a cool house but then the quality may only be fair.

*Black Hamburgh*

**FLAME** — This red seedless grape will ripen in a cold greenhouse in most U.K. areas. It produces crunchy red grapes as sold in supermarkets but they are better flavoured when home grown and fully ripe.

**LAKEMONT** — This new seedless grape is a big improvement on Thompson's Seedless. The fruits will ripen in a cold greenhouse throughout the U.K. and it can be grown outdoors on a warm wall in southern areas. Good mildew resistance. Produces large bunches of yellow oval grapes with a good muscat flavour.

**MUSCAT HAMBURGH** — Often considered the best flavoured black dessert grape. It can be grown in an unheated greenhouse in much of the U.K., though it benefits from a little early heat in cooler areas. Crops heavily. The fruit is large and sweet with a fine muscat flavour. Excellent for dessert and very good for wine-making. Ripens  mid-season.

*Muscat Hamburgh*

**MUSCAT OF ALEXANDRIA** — The finest flavoured white dessert grape grown in the U.K. Cropping is variable. It will benefit from hand pollination. Will grow to a good size and ripen in a cool house but requires a warm house to bring it to perfection. Berries are large and very attractive. Excellent musky aromatic flavour.

*Muscat of Alexandria*

# GRAPES

*Mueller-Thurgau*

*Rondo*

*Siegerrebe*

**LEON MILLOT** — Mid-season, black wine grape, also suitable for dessert. Berries are small-medium size, juicy and of excellent flavour. Bunches are of medium size. Very vigorous vine, cropping heavily. Useful for covering walls. Very hardy. Good resistance to mildew. Crops early October.

**MUELLER-THURGAU (RIESLING SYLVANER)** — Mid-season, white wine grape, also suitable for dessert. The most widely planted variety in the U.K. Berries are medium, pale green, sweet and juicy. Makes a wine with an attractive bouquet and a low acid content. The vine is vigorous, cropping prolifically and consistently. Requires warm, sunny conditions during the pollination period. Crops mid-October.

**PERLETTE** — This early ripening French variety produces heavy crops of golden-green seedless grapes. The vine is vigorous and can be grown outdoors on a warm wall in southern England and Wales.

**PHOENIX** — This early/midseason dessert/wine variety can be grown outdoors throughout most of the U.K. The vine has very good disease resistance and is very suitable for organic growers. Produces compact bunches of large pale green grapes with a slightly muscat flavour.

**POLO MUSCAT** — This modern dessert/wine variety will ripen outdoors throughout most parts of the U.K. It produces heavy yields of early ripening yellow/green fruit with a a light muscat aroma and a good balance of sweetness and acidity. Good disease resistance.

**REGENT** — A high quality modern wine variety that can also be used as a dessert grape. The very large blue-black grapes have a sweet flavour. The leaves turn a beautiful red colour in the autumn. Very disease resistant.

**RONDO** — One of the latest hybrids bred in Germany. This variety is very hardy as well as disease resistant. It flowers early and produces blue/black grapes for quality wine. In the autumn the leaves turn an attractive red colour.

**SIEGERREBE** — Very early German white grape. Considered one of the best dual-purpose varieties. Berries are of medium sized, round, deep golden-tawny colour, juicy, sweet and of excellent flavour. Makes an excellent dessert wine. The vine is of moderate vigour. Does not do very well on an alkaline soil and requires a sheltered site. Crops late August to early September.

# GRAPES

## PLANTING

This can be done anytime between late October and March. Before planting, the top growth must be cut back to 5-7cm (2-3in) from the main stock and the roots trimmed to 15cm (6in) or less. The vine should be planted about 15cm (6in) away from the wall, in a hole 10-15cm (4-6in) deep, and the roots trodden in very firmly. About 15cm (6in) of litter or compost should be laid on the surface of the soil above the root area to protect the roots from being damaged by frost. Where more than one vine is grown, they should be spaced 1.2-1.5m (4-5ft) apart. The young vine should be lightly tied to a stake and not attached to the wall or fence to which it is to be trained for at least a month after planting. Indoor vines can be planted outside the glasshouse or inside in a prepared border which should be well drained and made up of a loam-based compost such as John Innes No.3.

## TRAINING SYSTEMS

Grapes are flexible climbers with strong growth and tendrills. There are many ways to grow a grape — as a single cordon (rod and spur system), a multi-cordon or in the single or double Guyot system. A cordon system is suitable for all varieties and is normally chosen when grown under glass or in a restricted area. The double Guyot system is normally used for grapes growing outdoors.

## TRAINING & PRUNING THE SINGLE ROD

Unless a large glasshouse is available, one grape should be grown as a single cordon (rod). In a small house, it should be planted at the gable end and trained parallel with the ridge towards the door. It should be tied to wires fixed 38cm (15in) from the glass, spaced 30cm (12in) apart. In larger houses rods can be spaced 1.2m (4ft) apart and trained parallel to the glass and 38cm (15in) away from it. The aim is to produce a strong rod with fruiting laterals (spurs) every 30cm (12in).

### FIRST YEAR

Following planting in November/December, the young vine should be shortened by two thirds of its length, pruning to a bud.

In the first spring after planting, one shoot should be chosen to become the leader and this should be trained to canes fixed to the wires. The shoot must be trained on the underside of the wires. Laterals produced from the leading shoot should be stopped at five or six leaves and any sub-laterals produced, stopped at one leaf. Any flowers or tendrils produced should be removed.

### SECOND YEAR

The strongest laterals should be selected at 30cm (12in) intervals and these should be stopped at five or six leaves as in the first year. The leader should be trained on as in the first year.

# GRAPES

This is the same as in year one and in subsequent years the leader should be shortened by two thirds of the previous summer's growth until the vine has reached its allocated length. After that the leader is treated in the same way as the other laterals.


## TRAINING & PRUNING THE DOUBLE GUYOT SYSTEM


*FIRST YEAR*

To train a grape in the double Guyot system takes two seasons. In the first season the rod should be cut down to about 15cm (6in) above ground level or 15cm (6in) above the graft union in the case of a grafted plant. Only one strong stem should be allowed to grow during the summer. Any side shoots are stopped at one leaf (see fig. 66). In November or December the leading rod is cut back to the topmost of three good buds below the bottom supporting wire (see fig. 67).

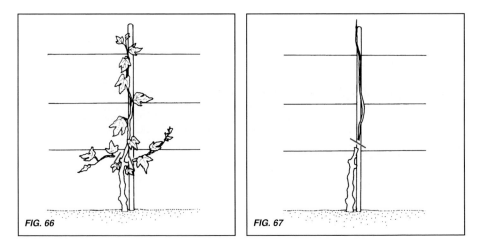

FIG. 66

FIG. 67


*SECOND YEAR*

In the second summer three strong stems should be allowed to grow vertically, pinching back any other shoots to one leaf as they grow (see fig. 68). As soon as the leaves fall (normally in November or December), two stems should be tied down gently (referred to as replacement shoots in the subsequent seasons) to the bottom wire, one on each side. Prune off the immature wood, leaving 60-75cm (2-2½ft) each side. Cut the third (middle) stem back to three or four good buds to provide replacement shoots for the following season (see fig. 69).

# GRAPES

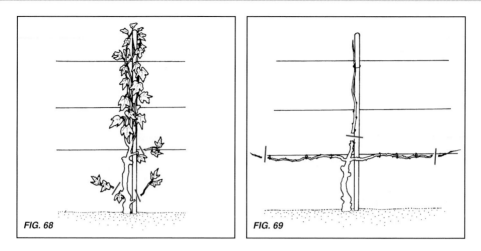

FIG. 68

FIG. 69

## THIRD YEAR ONWARD

In the third summer and subsequent seasons, three strong replacement shoots should be trained vertically from the centre (see fig. 70). Any side shoots are pinched back to one leaf and the flowers removed. The fruiting shoots grown from two horizontal arms on both sides are trained vertically, pinching out the growing points when they reach the top wire. The vertical shoots should be tied onto the supporting wires, allowing 15cm (6in) between shoots. During the growing season, pinch back or shorten unwanted side shoots that are growing along the fruiting shoots. Thin out the foliage to expose the fruit trusses if necessary.

At the end of the season (November), completely remove the horizontal arms together with their fruited shoots and tie down two replacement shoots onto the bottom wire. The third replacement shoot should be cut down to three or four good buds (see fig. 71). This completes the renewal circle.

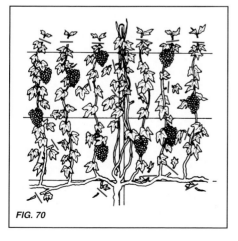

FIG. 70

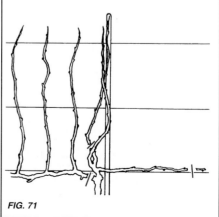

FIG. 71

## MANURING

With outdoor grapes, care must be taken to ensure that the soil is not too rich at any time; the application of rotted manure should be restricted to really poor soils and even then in very small amounts.

A vine grown inside a glasshouse requires much more care in feeding and watering than one grown outside, but there is more control over the plant.

In March each year apply a compound fertilizer according to the manufacturer's recommendation.

From four weeks after starting into growth until the fruit begins to ripen, a liquid feed high in potash, such as a tomato fertilizer, should be applied every two weeks according to the manufacturer's instructions.

## CROPPING & HARVESTING

The vine should not be allowed to fruit in the first two summers but in the third summer, three or four bunches can be allowed and thereafter building up to one bunch per lateral. A vine will crop heavily from the fourth year onwards and should continue cropping for fifty years or more. Grape vines are one of the heaviest yielding soft fruits.

Grapes should be harvested when fully ripe; this is often a while after they are fully coloured. They should be cut with a 'handle' of 5cm (2in) of stem both sides of the bunch. This way they can be carried without touching the fruit.

## PESTS, DISEASES & DISORDERS

The most troublesome pest is spider mite, particularly on vines grown under glass. The most serious diseases are powdery mildew and brown rot. See chapter on 'Pests & Diseases' for details.

# KIWI FRUIT

The Kiwi Fruit *(Actinidia deliciosa)* and the closely related Hardy Kiwi Fruit *(Actinidia arguta)* are very hardy twining climbers and can be cropped outdoors wherever grapes grow. The bush requires very good shelter from prevailing winds, otherwise tender young shoots will be broken off and damage at any time to the leaves will reduce the yield. Bushes are excellent for covering old walls and should be planted at least 5.5m (18ft) apart.

## VARIETIES

The Kiwi Fruit *(Actinidia deliciosa)* is the kiwi that you see in the grocery store. The fruits are approximately the size of a hen's egg with a hairy, brown, skin finish. The lesser known Hardy Kiwi Fruit *(Actinidia arguta)* produces fruits that look quite different from the Kiwi fruit. They are considerable smaller (approximately 1 inch long), They are borne in clusters and have smooth edible skins so they can be eaten just like grapes. They have a much sweeter and more aromatic flavour than the Kiwi Fruit. As implied by the name, this plant can tolerate extremely cold conditions and are hardy to approximately -25°F (-30°C)

### KIWI FRUIT

**HAYWARD** — Probably the best variety to grow in England because it is very late flowering, its fruits are larger, are better flavoured and keep longer than other varieties. The fruits are light greenish-brown, covered on the outside with fine silky hairs. Hayward is self-sterile and it is therefore necessary to plant a male plant (such as Tomouri) close by to provide pollen for the female plant.

**JENNY** – The only self-fertile variety in cultivation. Strong growing with large attractive leaves and well-flavoured fruit.

**TOMOURI** — Late flowering male plant. One male is sufficient to pollinate up to eight female plants.

*Hayward*

### HARDY KIWI FRUIT

**ISSAI** — This variety produces fruit of excellent flavour and appearance. It is heavy cropping and precocious, often bearing fruit after the first year. It will set some fruit without pollination, but is best planted with a male plant.

*Issai*

# KIWI FRUIT

## CLIMATIC CONDITIONS & ASPECT

Kiwi fruits are most likely to succeed south of a line drawn from the Wash to Shrewsbury, provided they are grown against a south facing wall. Ideally the site should have a southerly or south-westerly aspect with maximum shelter from the prevailing winds and away from low lying ground which can attract spring frosts.

## SOIL CONDITIONS

The vines of kiwi fruits grow best on deep fertile soils which will retain moisture. The soil should be slightly acid (pH 6.5) and the manure requirements of the bushes are similar to those of blackberries.

## PLANTING DISTANCES

The kiwi fruit is a very vigorous climber and should be planted at least 5.4m (18ft) apart. Under garden conditions where space is limited, one male and one female plant can be planted in the same hole, and their vines trained along the supporting framework in opposite directions.

## ESPALIER SPUR PRUNING SYSTEM

Kiwi fruit can be grown on a similar type of support as required by blackberries, excepting the wires should be 45cm (18in) apart. Vines trained in this way have to be spur pruned.

A 2.1m (7ft) long bamboo cane should be pushed into the soil next to the vine and tied to the wires. The vine should be cut back at the height of the lowest wire. The three strongest shoots that grow should be selected and any others pinched out. The upper one, as it grows, should be trained and tied to the bamboo cane but should not be allowed to twist itself round the cane or its growth could be restricted. The remaining shoots should be trained in opposite directions along the wire. The procedure should be repeated as the centre vine reaches each wire.

The laterals should have their growing points pinched out when they have grown 90cm (3ft) long. This encourages the production of side shoots and these should be pinched back to five leaves to form fruiting spurs; subsequent sub-laterals should be removed as they appear. This procedure encourages the formation of fruit buds. When spurs bear fruit, vegetative shoots should be regularly pinched back to seven leaves. During winter, fruiting spurs should be cut back to two buds beyond where the fruit was borne in the preceding season.

# KIWI FRUIT

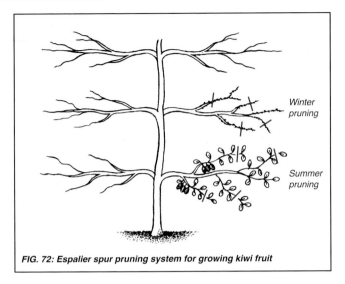

Winter
pruning

Summer
pruning

**FIG. 72: Espalier spur pruning system for growing kiwi fruit**

## WINTER PRUNING

Winter pruning should be left until the end of the winter so that any shoots that have been killed by frost can be removed. Any fruit spurs should be pruned back to two buds beyond where the last fruits were borne. The arms that bore fruit in the previous year should be cut back to their replacement shoots. Approximately three fruiting laterals with plump, closely-spaced buds should remain on each fruiting arm to bear fruit. Those in excess of this number and have flat widely-spaced buds, should be cut out. Bleeding from the wounds might occur but this is harmless and will soon cease.

## MANURING

In April, May and June following planting, each plant should have broadcast in a 1m (3ft) diameter circle around its base:

10g (¼oz) Nitro-Chalk (calcium ammonium nitrate).

In the years following, in March, broadcast either side of the row a compound fertilizer following the manufacturer's recommendations.

# KIWI FRUIT

## PROTECTION FROM SPRING FROSTS

The flowers and young growth can be severely damaged by spring frosts; it is therefore advisable to protect the young growth and flowers during this period by covering with fleece or heavy gauge polythene but keeping the ends open. This may also help to give protection from the prevailing winds which can damage the tender growth.

## POLLINATION

In order to obtain a good set of fruit, the female flowers should be hand pollinated by gently brushing the anthers of the male flowers in a circular motion over the stigmas of the female flowers. There is sufficient pollen on one male flower to fertilize eight female flowers. The pollination should be done no more than three times — when one third, one half and all the flowers are open.

## HARVESTING & STORAGE

The fruit is ready for picking when a slight depression can be made in the surface of the fruit if pressed hard with the thumb. The largest fruits should be gathered first, allowing the smaller ones to swell a bit more. All the fruit should be harvested as soon as there is a risk of night frost occurring. Stored in a cool place, the fruit will keep for up to three months.

## YIELDS

It will take up to five years for the vines of the kiwi fruit to bear any appreciable amount of fruit; under glass the time taken is much less. It takes eight to nine years to achieve full production outdoors and at this stage yields of 13.5kg (30lb) or more of fruit can be expected.

## PESTS, DISEASES & DISORDERS

In the U.K, kiwi plants are largely trouble free and can be grown organically very successfully.

# STRAWBERRIES

The attractions of strawberries are many; the cost of planting stock is small, and they produce fruit even when given the minimum attention and expense, though under these conditions the crop will vary in size considerably from year to year. The berries have a more attractive colour than any other fruit, are sweet and well flavoured, enabling them to be eaten when picked direct from the bush. Their one fault is that they do not freeze very well and this provides every incentive to prolong the ripening season for as long as possible by various means.

## VARIETIES

There are more than sixty varieties of strawberry under cultivation in Europe. These cannot all be worth growing in the United Kingdom and a selection has been made of those that have stood the test of time and in addition, a selection of new varieties that have been bred in the U.K. as well as on the Continent and in North America, which are considered worthy of trial and could replace some of the older varieties.

For anyone who is contemplating growing strawberries for the first time, the choice could be Elsanta because of its proven record. To extend the season further, one could not do better than to include the varieties Honeoye and Florence for cropping throughout the summer and Mara des Bois for fruiting in the autumn. These remontant, or 'perpetual' fruiting varieties as they are often referred to, continue to be grown in increasing numbers for their seasonal appeal. Their quality and flavour leaves nothing to be desired and they are at their best when the mid-season varieties have all but disappeared from the shops.

*A.G.M. signifies the Award of Garden Merit, the Royal Horticultural Society's most prestigious award.*

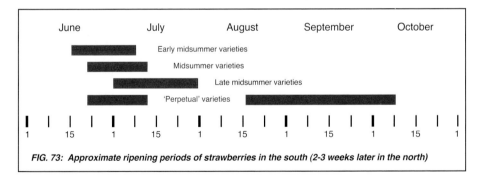

**FIG. 73:** *Approximate ripening periods of strawberries in the south (2-3 weeks later in the north)*

*EARLY MIDSUMMER*

**ELVIRA** (Netherlands) — A relatively new early mid-season variety which replaces Cambridge Vigour. The fruits are larger and firmer, the yield is heavier, and the variety is a little less susceptible to powdery mildew. Elvira is particularly recommended for growing under glass or plastic tunnels because it makes a low open plant. Very good flavour.

*Gariguette*

*Rosie*

*Cambridge Favourite*

**GARIGUETTE** (France) — This variety dates back to the 1930's and is considered to be the French equivalent to Royal Sovereign on account of its pleasing fragrance and sugar-sweet flavour. The elongated fruits are a brilliant vermilion-red. The flesh is delicate, soft and particularly juicy. Excellent flavour.

**HONEOYE** (U.S.A.) — This relatively new, very early variety, bears heavy crops of large, attractive, round-shaped berries. The fruit is bright red, very firm and of good quality. It is excellent for freezing. Honeoye is susceptible to verticillium wilt. Good flavour. *A.G.M.*

**MAE\*** (U.K.) — The most promising early variety to have emerged in recent years. Mae is superior to Honeoye in all aspects of fruit quality, producing heavy crops of large, firm, glossy, bright red fruits. Susceptible to powdery mildew, verticillium wilt and crown rot on some soils. Excellent flavour.

**ROSIE\*** (U.K.) — This new heavy cropping variety is predicted to take over from Honeoye as the leading early commercial variety, on account of its superior quality and flavour. The firm, dark red berries are very attractive, with a glossy finish. Recommended for growing under glass or plastic tunnels. Susceptible to powdery mildew, verticillium wilt and crown rot on some soils. Very good flavour.

## *MIDSUMMER*

**CAMBRIDGE FAVOURITE** (U.K.) — This was once the most widely grown variety by commercial growers and private gardeners because it could be relied upon to crop well under a wide range of conditions. Furthermore, the fruits can be left to 'hang' on the plants for a long period without getting over-ripe or going rotten. The berries are round to conical in shape and pale red in colour with white flesh. They are medium in size and this size is maintained throughout the season. It is very susceptible to infestations by spider mite but is resistant to infection by powdery mildew. Good flavour. *A.G.M.*

**CAMBRIDGE LATE PINE** (U.K.) — One of many varieties raised at Cambridge University Horticultural Research Station shortly after the Second World War; Cambridge Late Pine ceased being of commercial importance in the mid-fifties, as Cambridge Favourite, with its ability to remain on the plant for a long time without going soft, became nationally popular with commercial growers. The fruits are medium sized, roundish and dark crimson. The flesh is fairly firm, juicy and very sweet. By modern standards it is a comparatively light cropper. It is susceptible to powdery mildew in some seasons when a suitable fungicide has not been applied to control this disease. Excellent flavour.

**ELSANTA** (Netherlands) — This is the most widely grown variety and is favoured by the supermarkets because of its remarkably long shelf life once picked. It is a few days later than Cambridge Favourite and bears heavy crops of large, firm, attractive looking berries. It is susceptible to powdery mildew and verticillium wilt and therefore should definitely not be grown on land following potatoes. Powdery mildew can be controlled by spraying the leaves with a suitable fungicide. Very good flavour.

*Cambridge Late Pine*

**EROS\*** (U.K.) — This new variety has a similar yield to Elsanta and is at least as firm. The berries however are larger and less prone to malformation. They are very attractive with a mid-red colour and glossy skin. Eros has shown some resistance to red core and the plant's open habit means that grey mould should not be too much of a problem. It is however moderately susceptible to powdery mildew and verticillium wilt. Very good flavour.

**HAPIL** (Belgium) — This variety gives high yields of large, firm, conical, bright red fruits and is one of the leading commercial varieties for the 'pick your own' trade as well as being an extremely popular garden variety. It crops well on light soils and under dry conditions but on some soils is susceptible to verticillium wilt and spider mite. Excellent flavour. *A.G.M.*

*Elsanta*

**KORONA** (Netherlands) — This heavy cropping variety ripens about the same time as Cambridge Favourite but has much larger fruits which are firm, juicy and red right through to the centre. Good resistance to verticillium wilt, red core and grey mould. Some resistance to powdery mildew. Excellent flavour.

**PEGASUS\*** (U.K.) — This variety is a good alternative to Elsanta, commencing to crop about three to seven days later. It produces a similar yield and fruit size which is maintained well into the second cropping year. The appearance of the berries is superior, with a more regular shape and a brighter skin finish and no tendency to produce distorted skin tips. It is not quite as firm as Elsanta, a characteristic which can be a disadvantage in

*Hapil*

*Pegasus*

*Tenira*

*Florence*

hot summers. The open habit of the plant allows the free movement of air around the foliage and fruit, thereby reducing the incidence of grey mould. It is moderately susceptible to verticillium wilt. Good flavour. *A.G.M.*

**SONATA** (Netherlands) — This new variety is a cross between Elsanta and Polka. It is predicted to become a major commercial variety on account of its high percentage of top quality fruit. Compared to Elsanta, it produces a much lower incidence of misshapen fruit, the berry size is generally bigger and the fruit is sweeter. It appears to be able to stand up to very hot spells of weather and periods of heavy rain. Very good flavour.

**TENIRA** (Netherlands) — Tenira has the reputation of being one of the best flavoured varieties. It also makes a very high quality jam. The medium sized, conical shaped fruits are bright crimson. The flesh is red and has a moderately firm texture. Tenira is capable of bearing heavy crops of fruit when moisture and soil conditions are ideal. In its maiden year it can outyield Cambridge Favourite but in succeeding years crops may be much less. It is best grown for two years only and then replanted. Excellent flavour.

## LATE SUMMER

**ALICE\*** (U.K) — This is a new heavy cropping variety with good disease resistance. The bright red fruits are attractive with a glossy finish and are consistently sweet and juicy. The average berry size is larger than Elsanta. Alice appears to have good resistance to crown rot and verticillium wilt and is a little less susceptible to powdery mildew than Elsanta. Very good flavour.

**CHELSEA PENSIONER** (U.K.) — This new variety will produce heavy crops of large bright red fruits. From early observations, it appears to have significant disease resistance. Excellent flavour.

**FLORENCE\*** (U.K.) — This new variety offers an exciting combination of quality fruit and good disease resistance. Heavy crops of large, firm, dark red fruits. The fruit should be picked when fully coloured to achieve the best flavour. Florence appears to be resistant to verticillium wilt, crown rot and vine weevil colonisation and is moderately resistant to powdery mildew. Does well on all soils. Very good flavour.

**JUDIBELL*** (U.K.) — This new variety is so late, it sets a new standard for 'late summer'. It commences to crop after the last fruits of Alice have finished ripening. The fruits are large. Initial trials have shown the variety to be resistant to Verticillium Wilt and Crown Rot with some resistance to Powdery Mildew. Good flavour.

**MAXIM** (Netherlands) — This variety will produce extra-large, single wedge-shaped, medium-red, juicy fruits that are as big or bigger than one of its parents, Grandee. An excellent variety for exhibition purposes. Very heavy cropping and resistant to drought. Good flavour.

*Maxim*

**SYMPHONY**** (U.K) — A promising new variety with similar fruit characteristics to Elsanta. It bears good yields of very firm, juicy, medium-large sized berries which have a very bright-red glossy appearance and are regular in shape. Unlike Elsanta, Symphony is not prone to malformation and production of green tip fruits. Symphony is resistant to red core and is said to be resistant to vine weevil colonisation. However, this variety is prone to powdery mildew. Good flavour. *A.G.M.*

## 'PERPETUAL'

**CHALLENGER** (U.K.) — This new heavy cropping variety is highly recommended for the amateur gardener to grow on account of its superior flavour and resistance to powdery mildew. Excellent flavour.

*Flamenco*

**FLAMENCO*** (U.K.) — This new variety combines heavy crops with exceptional fruit quality and is predicted to become a major commercial variety. The large glossy berries are very sweet. The fruit hangs on the plant well allowing for less frequent picking. It has good resistance to Powdery Mildew. Excellent flavour.

**MARA DES BOIS**** (France) — This is the only cultivated strawberry to combine the flavour of the woodland strawberry with the size of English summer varieties. When fully ripe, the fruit colour is intensely red and it is at this stage that it develops the characteristic flavour and aroma of the woodland strawberry. It is resistant to powdery mildew and crops well. Excellent, aromatic flavour.

.
\* *Raised by H.R.I., East Malling.*
\*\* *Raised by S.C.R.I., Scotland.*
\*\*\* *Raised by J.Marionnet, France.*

*Mara des Bois*

# STRAWBERRIES

## SITE & SOIL

Strawberries will grow on all kinds of soils, ranging from light sands and gravels to heavy clays. However, it should be borne in mind that on the former there will be a reduction in crop if the bed cannot be watered in times of drought. On heavy soils, poor drainage can lead to disease infection and rotting of the roots. On chalky soils, strawberries may suffer from deficiencies of iron and manganese, making it necessary to apply these elements in the form of chelated compounds.

Strawberries grow best on a site sheltered from the prevailing wind; they should not be planted in the shade of trees, nor on the north side of a wall or house. It should also be noted that if they are planted against a south facing wall they will require frequent watering.

## ROTATIONS

With rotations, the most important rule is to allow the longest period of years possible to pass before replanting strawberries in ground where they had grown previously. If possible, they should follow crops such as turnips, cauliflowers or cabbages that had received an application of bulky organic manure, and which tended to suppress weed growth. Where bulky organic manure has not been applied, peas and broad beans are a suitable preceding crop because they are harvested in midsummer and allow the strawberries to be planted early.

There are few reasons why strawberries cannot be planted directly after other fruit crops such as blackcurrants or raspberries, provided the soil is free from perennial weed, but it would be easier to prepare the soil for planting if a whole year were to elapse between grubbing and replanting.

Strawberries should not follow potatoes because the latter can infect the soil with verticillium wilt, a disease that seriously affects the growth of, or kills strawberries. Potatoes left in the ground can also be a problem and getting rid of them may interfere with the roots of the strawberry plants.

## SOIL PREPARATION & MANURING

The strawberry plot should be carefully prepared to enable the plants to crop satisfactorily for three or four years. The soil should be dug with a spade or fork to a depth of 25cm (10in) and the bottom of the trench forked over in order to break up any hard layers of soil and improve drainage. Ideally this should be done several weeks beforehand to allow the ground time to resettle. At the same time, the roots of any perennial weeds should be picked out of the soil as they are impossible to remove after the strawberries are planted. Best of all, an application of organic matter at the rate of a barrowload to 5m$^2$ (6yd$^2$) in the form of well rotted farmyard manure or spent mushroom or garden compost should be spread on the soil after digging and forked into a depth of 15cm (6in). Poultry manure should not be regarded as an organic manure but a substitute for fertilizer and should only be applied to strawberries in limited quantities; for instance, 140-270g/m$^2$ (4-8oz/yd$^2$).

## APPLYING LIME & SULPHUR

Strawberries grow best on soil that is very slightly acid (pH 6.5), for at this level all the plant nutrients will be available to the roots. Therefore, it is advisable to check the pH of the soil with a soil testing kit or pH meter.

If the soil is too acid (i.e. the pH reading is lower than 6.5) then ground chalk or carboniferous limestone should be applied according to the manufacturer's instructions. The lime should be forked or rotavated into the ground. A pH of 5.5 may not appear to be very serious but is ten times more acid than one of 6.5.

When a pH meter indicates that a soil is too alkaline and provided there are no particles of chalk or lime in the soil, the pH may be reduced by the application of flowers of sulphur (obtainable from Ken Muir Ltd, tel: 01255-830181). An application of 70g/m$^2$ (2½oz/yd$^2$), forked or rotavated into the soil, will reduce the alkalinity or increase the acidity by a pH of one. The sulphur should be forked or rotavated into the soil.

## APPLYING FERTILIZERS

New gardens are likely to be deficient in potash and phosphate. The soil should therefore be given a broadcast application of:

*35g/m$^2$ (1¼oz/yd$^2$) of sulphate of potash*
*and 15g/m$^2$ (½oz/yd$^2$) of super-phosphate.*

In addition to these amounts of fertilizer recommended, established and new gardens should have raked into their soil before planting, a compound fertilizer suitable for strawberries, at the rate recommended by the manufacturer.

## RAISED BEDS

Strawberries can be cultivated on raised beds which have the following advantages over conventional growing:

(1) They reduce the risk of waterlogging and soil-borne diseases.
(2) They increase the available rooting depth on shallow soils.
(3) They warm up quickly and so produce early crops.

These advantages in turn lead to higher yields.

Raised beds are covered with a polythene mulch (usually black or other opaque colours) and have some form of trickle irrigation laid beneath the polythene (see page 139). The polythene suppresses weeds, prevents runners rooting near the plants and keeps the berries clean.

# STRAWBERRIES

## CONSTRUCTION & PLANTING OF A RAISED BED

A raised ridge 7.5cm-10cm (3-4in) high in the centre after firming down and 60cm (2ft) wide should be constructed. The ridge should have an even curve and the soil broken down to a fine tilth so that the polythene fits well without any bumps or hollows.

The drip line should be laid along the top of the ridge slightly off centre. Black polythene 1m (3ft 3in) wide and at least 50 microns (200 gauge) should be stretched across the raised bed and the surplus polythene on either side should be pushed vertically into the soil using a spade.

The runners should be planted through cross slits cut in the polythene. The size of slit is an important consideration — too small and crown growth will be restricted — too large and weeds can be a problem. An 8cm (3in) diameter hole is a good compromise for most planting material. Plants should be spaced 30-40cm (12-16in) apart. Rows should be spaced 75-90cm (30-36in) apart leaving a 15-30cm (6-12in) gap between the rows for water to penetrate.

The majority of polythene covered raised beds constructed by commercial strawberry growers carry two rows of plants, 30-40 cm apart (12-16in), with plants 40-45 cm (16-18in) apart within the row. In these circumstances the distance from centre bed to centre bed is 1.5m (60in).

## POLYTHENE MULCHES

Various types and colours are available, but whichever type is chosen, it is essential to select the correct width and thickness to last the life of the crop. Using polythene mulches (except white), results in soil warming, depending on the type used and the time of the year. All types will conserve soil moisture by reducing evaporation from the soil surface. All types except clear and white types suppress weed growth and thereby remove the need for herbicides, eliminating any associated growth checks. Since runners cannot root through plastic, polythene mulches provide a useful way of maintaining discrete plants.

Clear polythene gives the greatest soil warming effect, as radiation passes through to the soil producing a 'glasshouse' effect which can advance cropping by up to a week. However it will not suppress weed growth and can only be used after a residual herbicide is applied prior to laying the polythene. White polythene has similar limitations.

White on black polythene laid white side up is useful for delaying cropping. The white side reflects light and heat, keeping the soil and therefore the roots cool, whilst the black side suppresses weed growth.

*Black polythene mulch*

# STRAWBERRIES

Black polythene is probably the most widely used type at present. It suppresses weed growth and warms the soil by conduction and radiation, and so advances cropping by several days. However, in very hot sunny weather, fruit resting on the black polythene can be damaged and straw is therefore sometimes used to protect the berries from 'cooking'.

Certain pests, in particular vine weevil, find the microclimate beneath the polythene very attractive and numbers can build up rapidly.

## IRRIGATION

Although polythene mulches will conserve moisture in the soil by reducing surface evaporation, irrigation is still essential to sustain plant growth and cropping throughout the season. The best method of supplying water on most soil types is by trickle irrigation tubing, laid beneath the polythene. Generally, a single line of tubing laid down the centre of each bed will provide adequate water but on some drought prone soils two lines should be used, one for each row of plants. Various types of trickle tubing are available, with different flow rates, orifice sizes and durability. Uneven watering will quickly be reflected by uneven growth, so careful consideration should be given to irrigation layout prior to planting.

In most cases, overhead watering alone will not supply adequate water to the rooting zone (particularly as the crowns increase in size and fill the planting hole) and will cause 'puddling' in the alleyways. Strawberries planted through polythene without irrigation lines will, in times of drought, need to be watered individually using a watering can or hose.

## PLANTING

### TYPES OF PLANT AVAILABLE

Two types of strawberry runners are available:

(1) October-November: Open ground runners that have been newly dug before being sold.
(2) March-July: Cold-stored plants. These are open ground runners that were dug in January and kept in cold storage until required for sale before the end of July.

Runners, when received, should have a minimum of twelve primary roots that are not less than 10cm (4in) in length when measured from the base of the crown. This is particularly important when autumn planting is contemplated outdoors but less so when planted out in the spring. There are a few varieties, notably the 'perpetual' fruiting ones and some of the classics, which do not produce runners which meet the above specification; the 'perpetual' fruiting varieties nevertheless, grow into large plants by the time they are ready to fruit in the early autumn.

## IMPORTANCE OF SPEEDY HANDLING

Freshly lifted strawberry runners should be unpacked immediately they are received and soaked in water for a few minutes only. If it is not possible to plant them in their permanent quarters straight away, they should be potted up or heeled into a tray of damp compost and watered so that they are kept moist. **Coldstored runners should always be planted out or potted on within twenty-four hours of receipt and thoroughly watered in.** If for any reason this is not possible, they may be kept wrapped in polythene for a few days in an ordinary domestic refrigerator, **but not frozen.** The roots should be lightly sprayed with water if they look dry.

## EFFECT OF DIFFERENT PLANTING DATES ON YIELD

Time of planting has an important bearing on the amount of fruit that will be produced in the first full cropping year. Early planting with coldstored runners in July (or better still May or June), will give the heaviest yields; from as much as 450g (1lb) per plant or 1.4kg/m (2½lb/yd) of matted row, depending on the variety. The later planting is carried out in the autumn, the less the maiden crop may be. The yields of fruit in succeeding years will not be affected.

Runners that are planted outdoors in their permanent quarters between the end of November (end of October in the north) and the end of February will not root well in cold soil and can be heaved out of the soil by the frost and possibly killed. Runners obtained during the winter months are therefore best potted up or heeled into a tray of damp compost and kept in a coldframe or greenhouse. The compost should just be kept barely damp during the winter period. Alternatively the runners can be firmly 'heeled in' outdoors 5cm (2in) apart into a shallow trench until the spring. If severe frosts should ease them out of the ground, they need to be pushed or better still planted back into the trench. A covering of loose bark chippings 10cm (4in) deep over the top of the heeled in runners will greatly assist in preventing severe frosts from lifting them out of the ground.

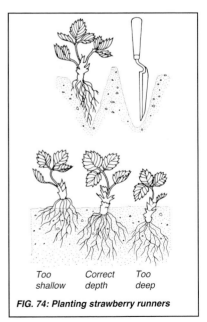

## FINAL PREPARATION OF THE SOIL & PLANTING

The soil should be finally prepared for planting by consecutively raking and rolling or treading until it is as firm as a seed bed prepared for the sowing of small seeds. The distance between the rows should be 75-90cm (30-36in) and the distance between the plants should be 30-40cm (12-16in).

| Too shallow | Correct depth | Too deep |

**FIG. 74: Planting strawberry runners**

# STRAWBERRIES

Planting should be carried out with a trowel or small spade which should be used to open a 'V' shaped slit 15cm (6in) deep in the soil (see fig. 74). The base of the crown of the runner should be placed on the edge of the slit with the roots hanging in the slit to their fullest extent without curling upwards. If the roots are too long for ease of planting, they may be shortened back to not less than 10cm (4in) in length, using a knife or pair of scissors. The soil should be eased back onto the roots with the trowel or spade after which the soil should be well firmed with the sole of the boot. It is important that the strawberry runners are planted at the correct depth; if the crown is buried or the roots left exposed, the plants will not thrive and may eventually die. A test for correct firmness is to attempt to gently pull a plant out of the soil by one of its leaves (or the crown of the plant in the case of coldstored runners). If the plant moves before the leaf tears, the planting has not been firm enough.

## ANNUAL CULTURE & MAINTENANCE

### DE-BLOSSOMING IN THE MAIDEN YEAR

Flowers will appear in May on plants grown out of doors, or in the case of coldstored runners, 2-4 weeks after planting (depending on when they are planted). Provided the plants are growing strongly, they may be left to bear a crop of fruit. However, if for any reason the growth of the plants is poor, the flower trusses should be cut off with scissors so that the plants may devote their resources to building up strong crowns that will produce the following year's crop.

### WEED CONTROL

A strawberry bed may be kept free from weeds by hand-hoeing throughout its life but this is tedious work and during periods of wet weather, difficult to do properly. This work should be done with a dutch or swan-necked draw hoe taking care not to draw soil away from the crowns or allow the weeds to grow past the seedling stage. Once they have grown past this stage it becomes more difficult to control them without damaging the strawberry plants.

Alternatively, subject to availability, herbicides can be used, remembering of course that it is extremely important to read the manufacturer's instructions beforehand and to follow them precisely.

### TREATMENT OF THE NEW RUNNERS

From June onwards, runners will start appearing and a decision will have to be made whether to have a bed of single plants or matted rows. Single plants are easier to keep free from weeds and the fruit is well displayed for picking. Furthermore, a higher proportion of large sized fruit may be expected than from matted rows which, though more difficult to keep free from weeds, bear a heavier crop of fruit within the same sized plot.

By repeatedly cutting off the stolons as soon as they appear and well before the runners start to root, strong single plants consisting of many crowns will be formed round the original plants. To form a matted row, the runners should be trained to root into a strip of soil 35-45cm (14-18in) wide along the originally planted rows. For every original plant, between six and nine runners should be allowed to root. Any runners in excess of this number that appear should be cut off so that a clear pathway 35-45cm (14-18in) wide is left for walking between the matted rows. It is not possible to form a matted row having planted strawberries under polythene, because the runner crowns do not have the necessary contact with the surface of the soil to be able to root.

*Removing runners after harvest*

## FROST

The yield of strawberries can be seriously reduced by spring radiation frost that can occur during the month of May when strawberries are in flower. Frost damage can be prevented by covering the plants with either fleece, straw, sheets of polythene or hessian on frosty nights. Whatever form of protection is used should be removed during the daytime and if necessary replaced in the evening. The television meteorologists forecast very accurately when damaging frosts are likely to occur and when these precautions should be taken.

## STRAWING & NETTING

At the beginning of June, straw should be placed in the rows and around the plants under the fruit trusses, to keep the fruit clean and provide a clean walking surface. Barley straw is best because it is soft and pliable. If straw is difficult to obtain, polythene sheeting is a satisfactory alternative. Strawberry mats are not recommended as they are seldom large enough for their purpose.

A net should be placed over the plants after the last spray for grey mould has been applied as there are few gardens in which the ripening fruit will not be attacked by blackbirds and other bird species.

## HARVESTING

Strawberries are ready for picking when the fruits have coloured to that shade of red which is characteristic of that particular variety. For example, Cambridge Favourite will be a paler shade of red when picked than the darker coloured Florence. At this stage of development, the fruits will have developed their full flavour, sweetness and aroma.

They are best picked at this stage for eating fresh, freezing and making into jam; they will keep very satisfactorily for forty-eight hours in a domestic refrigerator at a temperature of 2°C (35°F). When necessary — for instance, if the family is going away for a few days, the fruit may be picked when two thirds of the berry has turned to pink. They should be stored in a refrigerator at 2°C (35°F) where they will remain in a satisfactory condition for up to ten days, during which period they will gradually ripen, though the quality and flavour will not equal that of fruit that ripens on the plant.

Strawberries should always be picked with the green calyx in place and without bruising the flesh. The stalk of each berry should be taken between the thumb and forefinger and severed by the nails pressing each side. A little practice soon enables this to be done so that the berries can be placed in the picking container without the actual fruit being touched or bruised. Fruit should only be picked into shallow containers, because by using deeper ones, the lower fruits will be bruised by the weight of fruit above pressing down on them.

## FEEDING

If a strawberry bed has established well in its maiden year on weed free soil, little work will be required in its fruiting years. Strawberries require a minimum of fertilizer or manure and a bed that was established with healthy plants that grew without check should only have broadcast over the bed each February:

$15g/m^2$ (½oz/yd²) of sulphate of potash.

Strawberries produce a maximum crop when the colour of their leaves is pale green; thus a bed should not be given nitrogenous fertilizer until it is seen that the vigour of the plants is declining; then the application of sulphate of potash should be replaced by a compound fertilizer suitable for strawberries, following the manufacturer's recommendations.

## SPRING CLEANING

At the end of March, the bed should be weeded, cutting off any dead leaves and loose runners that had not rooted. For the following three months, the bed should be examined weekly for the presence of greenfly, spider mite, capsid bugs and powdery mildew and if an infestation is severe enough, sprayed with the appropriate insecticide or fungicide, following the manufacturer's instructions. (See pages 166-193 — Pests & Diseases).

## WATERING

A bed should only be watered *after* flowering if the plants are grown on light soil or drought conditions are experienced. Then a water sprinkler should be used once every two weeks to apply 50-75 litres of water per m² (11-17 gal/yd²) or the equivalent of 50-75mm (2-3in) of rain. This may be measured by placing two straight sided tins under the sprinkler and these will give an approximation of the amount of water that has been put on the bed.

Water applied too early in the year encourages leafy, rank growth and a meagre set of fruit which will develop poorly.

# STRAWBERRIES

## *DEFOLIATION*

It is not generally realised that the immature flower parts from which the next year's crop develops are formed in the crowns during July and August. Therefore the new leaves that appear at this time should be given every encouragement to grow rapidly. The bed should be thoroughly weeded, any straw removed and on all vigorously growing varieties, the old leaves should be cut off with a pair of shears or short knife without cutting into the crowns. All this dead plant material should be collected and put on the compost heap, or burned. This operation must be carried out as soon as picking finishes and not delayed, otherwise next year's crop could be reduced. If the soil is very dry, the bed should be watered, applying 50 litres per m$^2$ (11gal/yd$^2$).

The new set of leaves grows rapidly and provided they are fully exposed to the light, they will effectively manufacture food material for flower initiation. Any further runners that single plants produce and those that grow into the pathways from matted rows should be cut off as they appear.

## 'PERPETUAL' FRUITING STRAWBERRIES

These varieties commence flowering and fruiting at the same time as midsummer varieties and following a short interval of two to three weeks continue to produce a succession of flowers and ripe fruit for the remainder of the year, until cold weather in October prevents further ripening. The total crop and the size of the fruits will be greater than that of 'Elsanta'.

As the main reason for growing 'perpetual' varieties is to provide fruit from July onwards, it is recommended that flowers appearing before the end of May should be cut off with scissors so that all the energies of the plants are directed towards bearing the maximum weight of fruit from July onwards. De-blossoming reduces the overall yield but increases the yield of late fruit.

'Perpetual' fruiting varieties are cultivated in the same way as standard varieties with two major exceptions. They produce few runners but any that are produced flower immediately and crop. These runners should be allowed to root and increase the yield from what are otherwise only moderately yielding varieties. The plants are not defoliated in August but the major weeding and removal of old leaves and rubbish is carried out in late winter just before growth recommences.

In August the fruit should be protected from birds. Polythene or glass cloches are better for this purpose as they hasten the ripening and increase the overall yield of fruit. As wasps also attack the ripening fruit, a jar of sugar solution should be placed in the bed.

From the end of August onwards, when ripening proceeds very slowly, the fruits are very liable to infection by grey mould. Spraying should therefore be carried out according to the manufacturer's instructions from the period of early flowering until ripening commences.

'Perpetual' fruiting strawberries are sometimes offered for sale as 'climbing', 'elevated' or 'trellis' strawberries. Neither 'perpetual' or any other kind of strawberry is able to climb. If grown in this way, stolons and runners of a 'perpetual' variety have to be trained and tied to a specially erected framework. This is not successful because the parent plant does not have a root system sufficiently large to support its own fruit as well as that of the rootless runners. It is better to allow the runners to root in the soil and support their own fruits.

# STRAWBERRIES

## REPLACING THE OLD STRAWBERRY BED

The useful cropping life of a strawberry bed depends upon the variety and inherent fertility of the soil, how well it is managed, and not least, the strawberry plants remaining comparatively free from virus diseases.

Normally a bed ought to give two or three good crops, but it could go on cropping satisfactorily for as long as five or six years, though the berries are likely to be small at the end of this period. In most circumstances, a bed should have a useful life of three full cropping years. A replacement bed should therefore be planted before the last cropping year, to ensure a succession of fruit from year to year.

An alternative plan is to decide how much of the garden can be devoted to strawberries and plant a quarter of the area every year — this method reduces the risk of a sudden crop failure and allows new varieties to be tried more quickly.

## DEEP STRAWING (DELAYING PRODUCTION)

Deep strawing can be used to delay the cropping of late June bearing varieties such as Florence and Symphony. It is usually only practiced in the final year of cropping since it tends to weaken the plants. Plants covered with 15cm (6in) of straw in January (preferably when the ground is frozen) and uncovered in early to mid-May should crop at least five days later than normal — up to two weeks later in some instances. Sometimes plants are simply left to grow through the straw covering, or alternatively, only part of the straw is raked into the alleys. Deep strawing may result in yields being reduced by 10-15%.

## PRODUCTION UNDER CLOCHES, POLYTHENE TUNNELS & COLD FRAMES

The basic cultural practices used in outdoor bed production apply to early protected crops of strawberries.

For early production, coldstored runners must be planted by the end of July and no later. Open ground runners are too variable in quality at this time of the year to be recommended for this purpose.

Planting distances for low barn cloches or a 50cm (20in) wide polythene tunnel should be 25cm (10in) between twin rows, with plants 23cm (9in) apart and staggered in rows. The distance between rows of cloches or tunnels should be 37cm (15in).

At the end of February (by which time the plants should be large and well established), the soil should be weeded and hoed, and any dead leaves removed. The plants should be checked for greenfly and sprayed if necessary. Cloches or polythene tunnels should then be placed over the plants.

When the flowers open, on sunny days the glass cloches or frames should be opened and the sides or the polythene raised so that the bees may enter and pollinate the flowers, otherwise fruit set is likely to be poor.

Strawberries grown in this way require more watering, and at least two applications of water, equivalent to 50mm (2in) of rain — 50 litres per square metre (9 gal/yd$^2$) should be given. The first application of water should be made after flowering and the second before the berries begin to ripen. On warm, sunny days when the temperature rises above 18°C (65°F), adequate ventilation should be provided. With a cloche or cold frame this may involve removing some of the panels or opening the vents. With a polythene tunnel ventilation can be achieved by raising the polythene sides. The cover should be replaced or the vents closed in mid-afternoon. When ventilation has to be given during cropping, the gaps should be covered with netting to prevent birds eating the fruit.

Picking from under glass cloches or frames usually commences towards the end of May and from under polythene fourteen days later and continues for four weeks. The yield should be between 100-300g (¼-¾lb) per plant, depending on the time of planting and the variety being grown.

*Strawberries growing under a cloche*

Strawberries that have been covered may be retained to crop in later years, either in the open or to be covered again. If they are covered in the second year, one of each twin rows should be removed, otherwise the cloches will be filled with leaves that will smother the flowers and give rise to a very poor set of fruit. For the same reason, no nitrogenous fertilizer should be applied to these plants. In either case, as soon as picking stops, the cloches or polythene should be removed and the bed cleaned up in the usual way, removing the old leaves to allow the newly emerging leaves access to full sunlight. In particular, any pests or diseases that may be present should be controlled and if the soil is dry, a thorough watering should be given to aid the initiation of flower buds for the succeeding year's crop

## FLOATING POLYTHENE MULCHES

Clear, perforated polythene laid directly over the top of established plants in the second or third week of February and removed at first flower (or shortly afterwards), will advance cropping by about two weeks. If removal is delayed for too long, although additional protection will be given to the crop, full pollination may not occur and fruit may be misshapen. Polythene bags containing soil can be used to anchor the sheet in place around the edges. If the sheet is carefully removed it can be re-used several times. This technique should only be used on carefully selected sites since there is a danger of frost damage to the flowers once the polythene has been removed.

# STRAWBERRIES

## INDOOR FORCING OF STRAWBERRIES

For the earliest crops, strawberries must be grown indoors, either in a heated or unheated greenhouse. They may be grown in either 15cm (6in) pots, growbags or self-watering Towerpots, which will save space.

The pots are best planted in June or July with coldstored runners, using a proprietory soil-less compost such as Arthur Bowers or Levington. 'Perpetual' varieties can be planted later, or even in the early spring with freshly lifted plants, and still bear a heavy crop of fruit within twelve months.

Following planting, the pots should be given one good watering and afterwards not over-watered. They should be placed outdoors in a sunny sheltered position, where they should remain until the late autumn. They then need to be housed under cover in an unheated greenhouse, garage or garden shed until the end of February (unless they are to be grown on in a heated greenhouse). The compost must be kept moist at all times and not be allowed to dry out; neither should it be excessively wet, especially with plants grown in Towerpots where the system relies on capillary uptake of water and there is no free drainage to take away excess water. (See page 149 — Watering Plants in Containers).

When the strawberries are to be grown in a heated greenhouse, provided the minimum temperature is not allowed to fall below 13°C (55°F), the pots may be brought into the greenhouse at any time after the beginning of January.

When the plants are brought into the greenhouse, all the dead leaves and any stolons that may have previously grown should be removed. The leaves should be kept under close observation, in particular for powdery mildew, greenfly and spider mites and if found, sprayed with the appropriate pesticide recommended for the outdoor crop, according to the manufacturer's instructions. (See pages 166-193 — Pests & Diseases).

### WATERING & VENTILATION

It is important not to allow the plants to get too soft and rank in their growth. Up to the time when the flowers set their fruits, watering should be done sparingly, so that the compost is not always saturated with water. At the same time, the vents should be opened when the temperature rises above 13°C (55°F). When the fruits are swelling, the plants are large and leafy, the sun is shining and temperatures are high, the plants should be watered more frequently — often twice a day. As far as the vents and doors allow, a temperature of 18°C (65°F) should be aimed for. Shading of the glass will assist greatly in preventing the temperature inside the greenhouse from rising too high. Far larger fruit will be obtained when the temperature (during the day) is kept to a maximum of 18°C (65°F) and the fruit ripens more slowly. Grey mould can become a serious problem, even under glass, so it will be necessary to spray the plants with a suitable fungicide at least three times during the flowering period.

### POLLINATION

One of the troubles that besets early strawberry production is poor pollination, which gives rise to flower abortion or distorted berries. To facilitate pollination, either a rabbit's tail or a camel-haired brush should be passed daily over the flowers that have not set their fruits.

# STRABERRIES

*FEEDING*

Strawberries growing in pots are more susceptible to deficiencies in plant foods, particularly potash, than plants growing in the open ground. The reason for this is simply that the roots have only a limited amount of compost from which they can take up their food requirements, and the available nutrients are likely to be depleted through being leached out of the compost by rain during the winter months or as a result of being watered copiously after flowering. With a view to maintaining healthy foliage and avoiding any risk of potash deficiency, the leaves of the plants should be examined twice weekly from the flowering period onwards. If the general colour of the leaves becomes excessively pale, or the leaf margins lose their colour, the pots should be watered once each week with a liquid fertilizer that is high in potash, thoroughly wetting the compost. (See pages 150 — Feeding Plants in Containers).

## CONTAINER GROWING

Of all the popular summer fruits, strawberries are one of the easiest to grow in containers on the patio. Container growing is particularly advisable where ground space is limited, or where the soil or situation would otherwise prove to be unsatisfactory for the growing of strawberries. However, heavier yields per plant can be obtained at far less cost and effort by growing the crop in the traditional way outdoors.

There are many different types of container available which vary considerably in shape, size, price and design. The most popular containers include strawberry barrels, Self-Watering Towerpots and hanging baskets. Basically any container will suffice so long as there is sufficient room for the roots and it has adequate drainage holes. Traditional terracotta pots are not to be recommended as they dry out very quickly and usually have very small planting holes.

The best position for strawberry plants growing in containers is in full sunlight, but sheltered from the prevailing winds. Barrels should be stood upon bricks for drainage purposes and turned occasionally so that all the plants receive a share of sunlight.

*Strawberries in a Plant-A-Tower*

*PLANTING*

Choosing the correct compost is fundamental to success. Disappointing results will follow from the use of unsatisfactory mixtures. The ideal compost is one that retains water and nutrients for a long period but does not become waterlogged through over-watering. For small to medium sized containers such as Self-Watering Towerpots or hanging baskets best results will be obtained by using a proprietary peat based potting compost. However, with large containers (such as a strawberry barrel) better drainage will be required. This is achieved by mixing the compost with vermiculite or perlite in the appropriate ratio. (See page 151-152 — Filling the Barrel and Planting). It is important that the compost mixture is moistened with a **moderate** amount of water **before** planting.

When planting the base of the crown of the runner should be positioned at soil level with the roots hanging to their fullest extent without curling upwards. If the roots are too long for ease of planting, they may be shortened back to not less than 10cm (4in) in length, using a knife or pair of scissors. It is important that the strawberry runners are planted at the correct depth; if the crown is buried or the roots left exposed, the plants will not thrive and may eventually die. A test for correct firmness is to attempt to gently pull a plant out of the soil by one of its leaves (or the crown of the plant in the case of coldstored runners). If the plant moves before the leaf tears, the planting has not been firm enough. The plants should be lightly sprinkled with water immediately after watering.

## *WATERING PLANTS IN CONTAINERS*

Overwatering is the most common cause of failure of strawberry plants grown in containers. No hard and fast instructions can be given for watering because plants require very limited amounts of water when they are small, temperatures are low and under dull light conditions. Frequent watering is required when temperatures are high, the sun is shining, the plants are large and the fruits are swelling.

Strawberry plants have a fine fibrous root system and for this reason will not survive for very long if they are allowed to grow in compost which is too wet. More mature plants are better able to cope with this situation because they have a large root system and plenty of leaves to remove excess moisture but even they will die in time if this is allowed to carry on. Very young plants will be affected much more quickly because they are unable to remove excess water quickly enough. They should therefore be grown in a compost that is damp to begin with. The moisture content can be increased as the plants expand and the temperature rises but not to the extent of allowing the compost to become saturated. Too frequent over-watering will also remove nutrients from the compost.

A test to ascertain whether the compost is too wet is to take some in the hand and squeeze it. If the compost is saturated, any excess water will drain out between your fingers. If this happens then you will know that the compost is saturated and if allowed to continue the plants will die. The first sign of distress in the plants will be wilting of the foliage. The roots will be black in colour and such plants will not revive.

Do not allow the compost to dry out completely. If this should happen then it should be remoistened quickly, taking care not to saturate the compost. If the plants have already started flagging as a result of drying out, the containers should be temporarily shaded, to allow the plants to recover.

## FEEDING PLANTS IN CONTAINERS

The nutrients in fresh compost should be sufficient to provide satisfactory growth until the plants come into flower. At this stage, a liquid feed high in potash and low in nitrates (e.g. Ken Muir Strawberry Feed or tomato fertilizer) should be given once a week until the fruits start turning colour.

Like over-watering, the regular application of a fertilizer high in nitrates can adversely affect the cropping. Strawberries will crop best if they have the appearance of suffering from a slight deficiency of nitrogen resulting in the leaves having a pale green colour. A rather too yellow-green leaf colour is an indication that the plants need feeding.

A compound fertilizer should be applied after the plants have finished fruiting, when the old foliage has been cut back. This will encourage new growth and flower initiation for the following year. After the end of September, plain water only should be used. Reduce watering to a bare minimum after about four weeks when growth shows signs of slowing down; this is usually when the leaves begin to show autumn tints. The compost should be kept slightly damp throughout the winter. The plants should not be fed again until the following spring unless the leaves appear pale green.

## ANNUAL CULTURE & MAINTENANCE
## OF CONTAINER GROWN STRAWBERRIES

### DE-BLOSSOMING & RUNNER CONTROL

Containers that have been planted in late summer or early spring and have strongly growing plants in them should be allowed to flower and fruit in their first year. If for any reason, the plants are growing weakly, the flowers should be cut off to enable the strength of the crowns to be built up for the following year's crop. From June onwards the plants will start producing stolons on which runners will form. These stolons should be cut off as soon as they appear.

### DEFOLIATION

The strawberry produces two sets of leaves each year — a spring set that supports the fruit and an autumn set which builds up new crowns for the following year's crop. Immediately after the plants have ceased fruiting, all the leaves should be cut off as close to the crown as possible so that new leaves are fully exposed to the light as soon as they appear. In late winter the set of leaves that carried the plants through the autumn should be cut off. The leaves of 'perpetual' fruiting varieties should not be cut off in midsummer, other than any diseased or dead ones.

### REPOTTING

The original plants should crop for two or three years if they are looked after carefully. Most plants will benefit from repotting with fresh compost once a year. This is best done during the early spring when the plants first start showing signs of growth. Remove the plants from the pots, comb out as much of the old compost as possible, prune away 10% of the root system and replant with fresh compost. If the plants are growing in a large barrel it would be impractical to change the compost each year. In the second and third year, success will therefore depend upon maintaining the nutrients in the compost at a satisfactory level. To achieve this, liquid feed should be added to each watering to maintain a moderate fresh green colour and size of leaf. If the leaves turn dark green and grow too large, the addition of feed to the water should stop.

## STRAWBERRIES IN BARRELS

There are a number of different makes and sizes of plastic barrels available. They will accommodate from thirty to fifty plants in a very small space. Very cheap products are not likely to have a useful life of more than a year or so. The better models have large planting cups and a central watering system. (See fig. 75).

Problems can arise with water not reaching the roots of plants at the base of the barrel if it does not have a central watering tube. This difficulty can usually be overcome by placing a drainpipe, or if not available, three lengths of wood set to form a triangle, in the middle of the barrel, vertically on top of the first layer of soil. This centre piece is then filled with rubble or crocks whilst continuing to fill the barrel with the compost and strawberry plants, until the planting is completed. The drainpipe or triangular frame should then be extracted.

*Strawberries in a Victorian style plastic barrel*

### *FILLING THE BARREL & PLANTING*

The mixture should consist of two thirds by volume of a proprietary soil-less general purpose potting compost to one third of vermiculite, perlite or coarse grit. There should be little deviation from this mixture otherwise there could be plant failures, particularly if the plants are overwatered. The incorporation of garden soil or home made compost must never be considered. It is important that the compost mixture is moistened with a **moderate** amount of water **before** planting.

Before filling the barrel with compost, the top of the watering tube should be blocked with kitchen paper or cloth to prevent the tube from filling up with compost. The barrel should be filled with compost to a level of 5cm (2in) above the lowest ring of holes. The compost should then be consolidated, particularly near the planting holes, to prevent the whole mixture from sinking when watered. The level of the compost should fall just below the tops of the holes. If it does not, the necessary amount of compost should be added or taken away. The roots of each strawberry plant should be inserted from the outside through the hole, so that the base of each crown is in line with the side of the barrel at the top of the hole and the roots spread out over the compost. Further layers of compost should be added and compressed so that the holes can be planted and the tub finally filled and consolidated with compost to within one inch of the rim. Strawberry plants should also be planted in an upright position at the top of the barrel.

Finally, if you are using a 'leaky pipe' as a watering tube down the centre of the barrel, it is advisable to fill the bottom half of the pipe with shingle or small stones to slow down the rate of water flow (otherwise the water tends to gush straight out of the bottom of the barrel).

## *WATERING*

After planting and for the first two weeks a small amount of water should be lightly sprinkled over each plant in the sides and the top of the barrel. It is not advisable to use the central watering tube at this early stage because if the compost gets saturated with water, you will drown the roots of the young plants. (See page 149 — Watering Plants in Containers).

After this initial period, the central watering tube can be used to evenly distribute the water, but take care not to overwater. To ensure that the top plants receive an equal amount of water to the sides, the planter should continue to be sprinkled with water from above.

As the plants develop more leaves and temperatures rise, the frequency of watering should increase until under sunny weather conditions the barrel may have to be watered daily.

**FIG. 75: Cross section of a strawberry tub, planted with strawberry runners and showing the central watering tube**

## SELF-WATERING TOWERPOTS

Self-Watering Towerpots are elegantly designed stackable pot systems. A set of Self-Watering Towerpots comprising of four stacking modules will accommodate twelve or twenty-four plants (depending on the size of the runners) in a vertical arrangement, occupying less than 30cm$^2$ (1ft$^2$) of ground space. Each module has three large planting pockets and its own built in reservoir to ensure even distribution of water throughout the column.

## *PLANTING*

To plant the Towerpots, separate the modules and spread them out on a work surface. Best results will be obtained by using a proprietary soil-less potting compost. Ensure the compost is moist before planting.

With young single crowned plants, two plants can be planted in each planting position (i.e. six plants in each module). If the plants are multi-crowned, only one plant should be planted in each planting position. The roots of each plant should be trimmed back to about 4 inches. The plants should be positioned at a slight angle, with the roots pointing towards the reservoir.

## *WATERING*

To assist the plants to become established, lightly sprinkle each level from above after planting, taking care not to overwater. Ideally, the modules should be left spread out on a greenhouse bench or on the patio for approximately 2-3 weeks or until the plants really start growing well. You can continue to water lightly from above during this period. After this initial period, the modules can be stacked together and the reservoirs can be used for watering.

Water the plants as necessary, but do not overwater them, otherwise you may drown their roots. (See page 149 — Watering Plants in Containers). You should allow the reservoirs to empty themselves between waterings so that the compost remains moist but not fully saturated. Each Towerpot is designed so that as long as there is only some water in the reservoir, the capillary wick will transfer it to the compost until saturation point is reached and the compost cannot absorb any more.

## *POSITIONING YOUR TOWERPOTS*

Towerpots can be kept outdoors throughout the summer but make sure that they do not get waterlogged. Continuous rain can cause the compost to become over wet causing the reservoirs to fill with water. If this should happen, tip the pots on their sides to empty them.

*Strawberries in Towerpots*

To avoid waterlogging during the winter months, it is advisable to keep Towerpots under cover in a garage, garden shed or unheated greenhouse between November and early March. The plants can be without light during this period because they are in a dormant state. Keep an eye on the Towerpots throughout the winter to ensure the compost doesn't dry out completely - it should remain just damp throughout the winter. In early March the pots should be moved into the light, either outdoors or into an unheated greenhouse.

## *REPOTTING*

In the early spring when the first signs of growth are seen, remove all the plants and compost from each module and separate them. Select just three plants for each module and repot using a fresh soil-less compost. Make sure the compost you are using is at least damp and not too dry. Place each of the three selected plants, one to each planting pocket, in each module. Any surplus plants can be planted in the ground outdoors or in another container. (See pages 150-151 — Repotting).

# STRAWBERRIES

## TABLE-TOP PRODUCTION

Commercial strawberry growers are beginning to move away from the traditional practice of planting directly into the open ground over to what is termed 'table-top' growing. This method involves planting directly into containers or bags of compost which are supported about 90cm (3ft) off the ground (table-top height). This new approach has many advantages over conventional methods whether the plants are to be raised outdoors in the open or protected under glass or polythene. Its great advantages are that cropping is much heavier, picking is a lot easier because there is no bending down, the fruit cannot be splashed with mud, there is no need for strawing, it doesn't depend on having a suitable patch of soil and there will be much less trouble (if any) from slugs, vine weevils, soil-borne diseases and weeds.

Purpose made Table-Tops are available. Alternatively, the growbags can be laid on planks supported on concrete blocks, plastic crates or wooden boxes (preferably rot-proofed). They could even be laid directly on upturned crates!

Some gardeners have tried large gutters or home-made troughs filled with compost and supported off the ground. In this case however, the disadvantage is that they cannot be easily removed onto the ground for overwintering.

*Strawberries growing on a Double-Decker Table-Top*

*PLANTING*

Use any good quality growbag that is recommended for growing tomatoes. Growbags are best planted in the spring and summer with coldstored runners or potted plants. These plants will carry a small maiden crop of large fruit later on in the year. It is not recommended to put more than ten plants in a 1m bag.

New bags are often very firm and compressed when purchased. Fluffing up the compost by bashing the bag sideways on a hard surface will ensure the compost is loosened up but it is important to make sure the bag remains evenly filled along its length. To facilitate drainage, cut a 5cm (2in) horizontal slit just below the seam at each end of the bag and spike some small holes along the bottom where it overhangs the support.

A staggered double row of ten planting holes should be cut in the top side of the growbag (See fig. 76). For bare-rooted plants an X-shaped cut 5cm x 5cm (2in x 2in) should be made with a sharp knife. The centres of the holes should be 7.5cm (3in) from the edge of the bag, about 19cm (7½in) apart and there should be a 10cm (4in) gap between the rows. It is advisable to mark up the growbag prior to cutting the polythene, in case of any miscalculations! Fold the cut flaps under.

# STRAWBERRIES

Use a narrow trowel, a kitchen fork or a T-tool (specially designed for planting strawberry runners into growbags) to insert the plant into the compost so that its roots are as straight as possible and fully buried in the compost. The base of the crown of the plant, where the leaves are attached, should be resting on the surface of the compost.

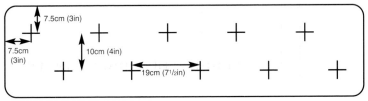

*FIG. 76: The positions of the planting holes in a growbag*

Pot grown plants will need a larger X-shaped cut in order to make a big enough planting hole. Fold the cut flaps under and make a hole in the compost with your fingers or a narrow trowel, planting so that the plant ends up at the same depth as when in the pot.


## *WATERING*

The secret to watering plants in growbags is little and often. Commercial growers use drip irrigation. If you have a similar system available, allow at least two drippers per bag.

Using a watering can to water growbags is relatively easy if there are large enough planting holes. However, once the growbag is planted, it is impossible to pour water in through the small planting holes described above. You can use a Speedfeed Irrigator. This consists of a long piece of perforated tube which is inserted into the length of the bag and a watering pot at one end where you pour the water or liquid feed. A good alternative is to make a crude funnel out of cut off bottle tops to facilitate easier watering. Cut two round holes, 7-10cm (3-4in) in diameter in the centre of the bag between the rows of planting holes, 30cm (12in) apart. Bury the cut off tops of plastic bottles into these holes and pour the water in.

Take great care not to allow the compost to become saturated with water, especially with very young plants having little or no leaf. If you allow this to happen, more often than not it will result in the death of the plants. Too frequent overwatering will also remove nutrients from the compost. (See page 149 — Watering Plants in Containers).

After planting or after moving bags with established plants in them (which can disrupt the roots if not done carefully), the bags should be thoroughly watered to settle the compost around the roots. After flowering, as the fruit starts to swell and ripen, the growbags will require watering twice a day, especially during sunny weather; at this stage you should bear in mind that when it rains most of the rain will run off the bags, making little or no contribution towards wetting the compost.

The water takes a while to soak in so it is advisable to go around the bags several times with the watering can until water begins to drip from the drainage hole. Bags that dry out are very difficult to re-wet; should this happen, light watering at frequent intervals would be the best way of re-wetting the compost.

# STRAWBERRIES

## FEEDING

New growbags will usually have enough nutrients to last the first three to four weeks before they need to be replenished. Used bags will often have a lot of nutrients left from the previous crop. After these first weeks (or from the start of growth where plants are overwintered from the previous year) a liquid feed should be added on each occasion that the growbags are watered.

Use a liquid feed that contains a high level of potassium, e.g. Ken Muir Strawberry Feed (15:15:30), Phostrogen (14:10:27), Levington Tomorite (4:4.5:8) or Bio Tomato Food (6:5:9). Ratios shown in the brackets are the percentage of nitrogen, phosphorus and potassium contained in the compound fertilizers.

A compound fertilizer should be applied after the plants have finished fruiting, when the old foliage has been cut back. This will encourage new growth and flower initiation for the following year. After the end of September, plain water only should be used. Reduce watering to a bare minimum after about four weeks when growth shows signs of slowing down; this is usually when the leaves begin to show autumn tints. The compost should be kept slightly damp throughout the winter. The plants should not be fed again until the following spring unless the leaves appear pale green.

## FROST PROTECTION

The yield of strawberries can be seriously reduced by spring radiation frosts that can occur during the month of May when strawberries are in flower. Frost damage can be prevented by covering the plants with fleece, sheets of polythene or hessian on frosty nights. This should be removed during the day if the plants are in flower to allow pollination to take place. The television meteorologists forecast very accurately when damaging frosts are likely to occur and therefore when these precautions should be taken.

## BIRD PROTECTION

To achieve maximum yields, ripening fruit should be protected against birds with a net which should be supported away from the fruit.

## RAIN PROTECTION

Heavy rain at the time of fruiting can seriously damage the strawberry crop. To avoid this happening, the Table-Top should be covered with polythene during prolonged periods of heavy rain. Do not cover the ends as ventilation must be provided. It is important to remove the polythene as soon as the weather changes.

## RUNNER CONTROL

Strawberry plants start producing runners in June following flowering. These should be removed as they appear, using a sharp knife or secateurs.

# STRAWBERRIES

## OVERWINTERING

The bags should be left on the Table-Top support after picking has finished and fed and watered as described. When the leaves begin to die off in late November the old dying leaves and the remains of fruit trusses should be cut off; this should leave a central rosette of short stemmed green leaves.

The bags should be carefully lifted down from the tables so as not to damage the root systems of the plants and placed on the ground in a sheltered spot. If left on top of the Table-Top over winter the rooting system of the plants can be damaged if the bags are frozen solid in severe weather.

In very cold districts the bags should be covered with one or two layers of horticultural fleece to keep out icy winds. In early March, the growbags should be returned to their Table-Top, at the same time trimming away any further dead leaves. If two people lift each bag or if a thin rigid board is slipped under each bag before lifting, the compost and the roots are less likely to be disturbed.

The strawberry plants in the growbags should be capable of yielding three crops before fruit size gets too small as the plants get more crowded.

## PESTS, DISEASES & DISORDERS

Some of the most troublesome pests, diseases and disorders are listed in the following table. See chapters on 'Common Fruiting Problems' and 'Pests & Diseases' for details.

| Symptoms | Possible problem | Symptoms | Possible problem |
|---|---|---|---|
| Leaf distortion/ marking on leaves | Aphids<br>Eelworm<br>Green capsid bug<br>Lime-induced chlorosis<br>Powdery mildew<br>Spider mite | Stunted growth | Eelworm<br>Leather jackets<br>Spider mite<br>Strawberry tarsonemid mite<br>Vine weevil |
| Holes in leaves | Green capsid bug | Flower damage | Strawberry blossom weevil |
| Wilt | Chafer beetle<br>Clay coloured weevil<br>Crown rot<br>Leatherjackets<br>Overwatering<br>Redcore<br>Verticillium wilt<br>Vine weevil<br>Wireworm | Marked/ distorted fruit | Grey mould<br>Powdery mildew<br>Slugs & snails<br>Strawberry seed beetle<br>Tortrix moth |

# RHUBARB

Although rhubarb is classified as a vegetable, it is eaten as a dessert and it would therefore seem appropriate to refer to it here. Rhubarb is grown from 'sets' obtained by dividing the crowns of three year old plants. A crown should have one or more buds and the rootstock should be about the size of one's fist.

*Strawberry Rhubarb*

## VARIETIES

**STRAWBERRY RHUBARB** — This is a late variety of moderate vigour from the U.S.A. which can be harvested through until September. The stalks are a deep-red colour which is retained after cooking — hence its name. The yield is approximately three quarters that of Timperley Early; the flavour is excellent.

**TIMPERLEY EARLY** — This is the earliest and best all round variety for both forcing and outdoor cultivation, producing large sticks of satisfactory colour and good flavour from early March to late-August.

## PLANTING

Planting should be undertaken when the plants are dormant (between late November and late March). The divisions should be planted 90cm (3ft) apart each way with the crowns slightly above ground level.

In order to avoid Crown Rot problems (particularly when the soil is inclined to be slightly heavy or over wet), it is advisable to establish the plant in a container, before transferring to the open ground in the spring. Each crown can be individually planted in a 20cm (8in) container, using a multi-purpose compost. The container should be positioned in a cold greenhouse, garage or garden shed and the compost should be kept slightly damp at all times. The plant can then be transferred to the open ground in April when the weather and soil conditions are more suitable.

## MANURING

Rhubarb will respond to annual surface dressings of farmyard manure or compost covering the plant. In addition, immediately after planting or at the end of March, whichever is the later, each crown should have broadcast in a circle 45cm (18in) diameter around it:

*25g (1oz) Nitro-Chalk (calcium ammonium nitrate)*
*and 10g (¼oz) sulphate of potash.*

At the end of May and June broadcast:

*20g (¾oz) Nitro-Chalk (calcium ammonium nitrate).*

In subsequent years in March, broadcast on each m$^2$ (yd$^2$) in a circle 90cm (3ft) diameter:

*20g (¾oz) Nitro-Chalk (calcium ammonium nitrate)*
*and 10g (¼oz) sulphate of potash.*

Alternatively, a compound fertilizer may be used following the manufacturer's recommendations.

## CROPPING PERIOD

Depending upon the variety, sticks may be harvested from April until September. No sticks should be pulled in the year of planting but in the following year a small number may be harvested; in the third year, a good crop should be forthcoming. With good management, rhubarb should produce worthwhile crops for six or seven years before the stems get thin and there is a need to divide the crowns and replant.

## REPLANTING

If space permits, it is worthwhile planting a few new crown divisions each year, so that the oldest plants can be removed before they become unproductive; where possible, a fresh site should be chosen for the new plantings.

# COMMON FRUITING PROBLEMS

T his chapter deals with some of the most common fruiting problems not necessarily connected with either pests or diseases but which are just as important. These problems are of a physiological nature and stem from a great number of different variables which are intimately and intricately co-related with one another and may vary from one year to another.

## BLOSSOM DROP

There are two main reasons for a tree which was in full blossom losing its flowers without setting fruit. Either the flowers were not pollinated or the weather conditions were poor when the tree was in flower.

### *POLLINATION*

If blossom drop happens year after year, the most likely cause is the absence of a pollination partner. If the variety is not self-fertile, it will not set fruit unless another variety with compatible pollen is growing nearby (pages 17-18).

### *POOR WEATHER*

If blossom drop only occurs occasionally then poor weather at flowering time is the most probable reason. Frost damage is a common problem on cold, exposed plots. Very dry air can result in poor pollination and a wet, cold spring reduces the activity of bees.

It is important to protect early flowering fruits against spring frosts if a worthwhile crop is to be obtained. The television meteorologists forecast very accurately when damaging frosts are likely to occur and therefore when precautions should be taken. Some frost protection during the flowering period can be provided by putting a top net over a fruit cage.

Wall fruit can be protected by rolling down a cover of fleece, hessian or thick netting at night when frost is likely and rolling it up during the day. This should be supported away from the plants by bamboo canes. Alternatively a clear polythene cover with the sides open and a gap of 30cm (1ft) at the bottom for ventilation, can be used and left on during the day but this restricts access for pollinating insects, so hand pollination may be necessary. Ideally the polythene needs to be supported on a timber framework (see page11).

Small free-standing trees can be protected against frost by making a temporary framework of bamboo canes and draping this with a cover of fleece, hessian or thick netting.

# COMMON FRUITING PROBLEMS

## FRUIT DROP

The major shedding of healthy fruitlets of apples and pears during June and July is known as the 'June Drop'. This is usually beneficial as a heavy set must be thinned anyway to discourage biennial bearing. However, in some years the 'June drop' is unusually heavy with only a sparse crop remaining.

There are several reasons for a large 'June drop'. Newly planted trees will often shed most of their fruit in this way — it is nature's way of making sure the young tree is not overburdened. Some varieties, such as 'Cox's Orange Pippin' are notorious for shedding large amounts of fruit in the 'June drop'. Frost damage, irregular water supplies, starvation and overcrowding can also cause an exceptionally large 'June drop'.

Fruits can also be shed before the 'June drop'. The first drop of apples and pears occurs when the fruitlets are pea sized. This is usually the result of incomplete pollination due to a cold wet spring.

Fruits can also fall as a result of pest damage. It is therefore important to look for grubs in fallen apples, pears and plums and if a problem is identified, take the necessary steps to prevent an infestation the following year. The larvae of the apple sawfly, pear midge and plum sawfly are all common pests that will cause fruits to fall to the ground before maturity.

## CHERRY FRUIT DROP (CHERRY RUN-OFF)

In the U.K. the most common type of fruit to suffer crop failure by fruit drop is the sweet cherry. The problem is known as cherry run off and can be severe in some years. It varies between different varieties and between geographical locations.

Recent research suggests that one of the main factors affecting the extent of cherry run off is the weather. Fruit drop appears to be more severe following a wet and cold autumn. Furthermore, if the light levels are particularly low during the blossom period (as a result of bad weather) and temperatures are more cold than usual during the early stages of fruit development, there will be a higher incidence of cherry run off. For this reason, cherries grown in northern areas of the U.K. are more likely to be affected than those grown in the south. When the leaves send insufficient photosynthetic products (food) to the fruit it causes an imbalance in the hormones within the fruit which results in fruit drop.

Any measure that maximises light to the leaves, thereby increasing the photosynthetic rate is likely to reduce cherry run-off. Unfortunately, nothing can be done about the weather, but trees can be pruned to allow the light levels to penetrate. Trees are best grown in a sunny position, preferably against a south facing wall and light reflective mulches such as pale woodchips can also be used beneath the tree.

Some of the new varieties bred in the U.K. such as 'Summer Sun' and 'Penny' seem to be less prone to Fruit drop than the Canadian self-fertile varieties.

# COMMON FRUITING PROBLEMS

## THE OVER-VIGOROUS, UNFRUITFUL TREE

The most common cause of failure to produce any flowers after two years is over-vigorous growth, signified by lush and extensive leaf and stem growth. More often than not, lack of flower bud is due to over-zealous winter pruning or applying nitrogenous fertilizer in excessive amounts. Summer pruning of restricted forms (i.e. Minarettes, cordons, espaliers & fans) will on the other hand restrict growth. With apples and pears, it is usually only necessary to do this once during the summer but with stone fruits it may be necessary to carry it out several times.

The first step is to control the vigour of the tree by reducing the supply of nitrogenous fertilizer and switching to a fertilizer high in potash. If this does not work, the more drastic methods of festooning, bark-ringing or root-pruning may be necessary. Stone fruits should not be bark-ringed because of the risk of silver leaf disease. Mature trees should not be root pruned because they have less resilience than young trees.

### FESTOONING

Festooning is a training technique which can be used to reduce the vegetative growth of a vigorous tree and stimulate fruiting growth. It involves tying down branches to a horizontal or downward position with strings, or hanging clothes pegs on the ends of branches during the growing season. This method is less drastic than bark-ringing or root-pruning and should therefore be considered the first option.

### BARK-RINGING

Bark-ringing is an operation which should not be performed unless really necessary. Bark-ringing should only be undertaken in the spring between the pink bud stage of the blossom and petal fall when the sap is running freely and callus soon heals the cut edges of the bark.

Bark-ringing consists of the removal of two semi-circles of bark 12mm (¾in) wide from opposite sides of the tree trunk, the two semi-circles being vertically separated from one another by a 10cm (4in) space. This method interrupts the flow of sap without the risk of being stopped altogether, which would result in the death of the tree (see fig. 77). The rings should be covered with surgical tape as soon as the bark is removed, to prevent the exposed wood from drying out. Young trees which are growing too vigorously are best ringed by drawing a knife twice concentrically round the main stem but only making the one ring, immediately covering it with surgical tape.

It is not advisable to bark-ring stone fruits, although it can be done but not without risk to the tree; by tying tarred string tightly around the stem of a plum tree it is

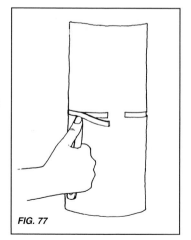

**FIG. 77**

possible to induce profuse amounts of fruit bud. Care however must be taken to remove the string in the event of the tree showing any signs of distress. Trees which have been bark-ringed should produce fruit bud later in the year and crop the following year.

## ROOT-PRUNING

Root removal is thought to lead to more carbohydrates in shoots, which induces flower bud formation. In November or December, dig up the tree and prune back the thick roots with a pruning saw. Retain the thinner fibrous roots and spread them back into the trench. Cover the soil and firm the ground. Mulch the root area with well-rotted manure or compost. Water well during the summer.

## THE STUNTED, UNFRUITFUL TREE

Sometimes a tree will fail to produce fruit because growth is poor, resulting from a weakening by pests and diseases or lack of water or vital nutrients.

The first step is to check for any signs of pests and diseases with the aid of a 20x lens. If a problem is apparent, it should be identified and dealt with immediately.

If there are no signs of pests and diseases, the growing conditions should be questioned. Sandy, gravelly or shallow soils over chalk, all of which tend to dry out quickly, are unsatisfactory; they can be improved by various means such as increasing the depth of shallow soil, the incorporation of bulky organic manure to increase water retention or regular mulching and irrigation when necessary. Water-logged land should be drained. If the tree is planted in an exposed site or sunless spot, it would be advisable to look for an alternative position. The tree should however, only be moved in the late autumn, when it is dormant.

## BIENNIAL BEARING

Biennial bearing (cropping heavily one season and then very lightly the next) is a common problem with apples and pears. Certain varieties such as 'Bramley's Seedling', 'Blenheim Orange', 'Egremont Russet' and 'Rev. W. Wilks' are prone to it. However, nearly all varieties can fall into this habit if not watered, fed or thinned. Frost destroying the blossom one spring can also sometimes initiate biennial bearing.

Once a tree gets into the rhythm of biennial bearing, it is difficult to correct, although certain methods can be adopted to try and improve the situation.

In early spring before an expected heavy crop, half to three-quarters of the fruit buds should be rubbed off the spurs, leaving one or two per spur. This reduces the burden of too heavy a crop in that year, and should enable the tree to develop fruit buds for the next year. At the same time, a policy of more generous feeding and watering must be adopted.

# COMMON FRUITING PROBLEMS

If bud rubbing fails to work, an alternative technique is to induce the tree to crop biennially over half the tree by removing half the blossom. Alternate branches are selected — half are chosen to crop in the even years and half in the odd years. Each spring, those branches selected not to crop in that particular year should be de-blossomed. After the third or fourth year the branches should accept this alternate pattern and little blossom removal will be necessary.  As with bud rubbing, generous feeding and watering is recommended.

## SPLITTING OF THE FRUIT

Splitting of the fruit is a common problem with apples, plums, gages, damsons and cherries, particularly following an erratic supply of water. The splitting occurs when the tree puts on a sudden spurt of growth, when moisture becomes available after a period of drought.

On apples, shallow cracks appear on the skin of the fruit, slightly penetrating into the flesh and usually running around the stalk end of the fruit. The cracks are usually single but occasionally several may appear on the same fruit. These cracks may dry up and heal over, allowing the formation of a corky layer. However, if the fruit is more mature it may be invaded by secondary organisms such as brown rot.

With stone fruits, the cracks usually run longitudinally. They may dry up and heal over or they may succumb to secondary organisms.

Growing conditions can be improved by regular watering and feeding. This is particularly important with container grown trees, where the compost is more prone to drying out. A mulch consisting of straw or bark spread around the base of the tree will help prevent the soil from drying out completely.

Damaged fruits that are fully ripe should be harvested and consumed immediately, before they are infected by secondary organisms. Any split fruits that are left on the tree should be checked at regular intervals for signs of fungal infections which will spread to healthy fruits if not removed.

## LIME-INDUCED CHLOROSIS

Fruit trees and bushes growing on alkaline soils, especially shallow soils with a pH of 7.0 or above, may suffer from lime-induced chlorosis caused by deficiencies of iron or manganese or both. They can be distinguished by the fact that iron deficiency shows first by yellowing of the new leaves, whilst manganese deficiency shows first as a yellowing of the older basal leaves.

Lime-induced chlorosis can be corrected by the application and thorough working into the soil of ground sulphur (Flowers of Sulphur) to reduce the pH to 6.5 in accordance with the following table. Further applications may be necessary from time to time.

# COMMON FRUITING PROBLEMS

| pH | Light sandy soil $g/m^2$ | $oz/yd^2$ | Sandy loam $g/m^2$ | $oz/yd^2$ | Heavy clay soil $g/m^2$ | $oz/yd^2$ |
|---|---|---|---|---|---|---|
| 8.0 to 6.5 | 100 | 3 | 200 | 6 | 300 | 9 |
| 7.5 to 6.5 | 70 | 2 | 140 | 4 | 200 | 6 |
| 7.0 to 6.5 | 36 | 1 | 70 | 2 | 100 | 3 |

It would be too expensive to acidify a soil in which free lime or chalk is present. Flowers of Sulphur can be obtained from Ken Muir Ltd. It cannot usually be obtained from garden centres.

*Manganese deficiency in raspberry*

*Iron deficiency in raspberry*

# PESTS & DISEASES

I t is important to be vigilant, checking once a week throughout the spring and summer with the aid of a 20x lens for pests and diseases, especially the undersurface of the leaves. The various important pests and diseases that cause loss of yield and occur most frequently are described in this section. In addition, there are a number of others that only occasionally give trouble but when they do occur, can be serious. As it is easier to prevent than cure a severe infestation during the summer, a constant look-out should be kept for these less important troubles. Apart from Ken Muir advisory service, assistance is also available from other various sources in identifying and obtaining recommendations for their control:

*Royal Horticultural Society, Wisley, Surrey GU23 6GB*
*(A free service to members only but also available to the general public at RHS shows. For details please go to www.rhs.org.uk/advice/advisory_service.asp)*

*County Council Horticultural and Agricultural Colleges*

*Gardening magazine advisory departments.*

## INTEGRATED PEST MANAGEMENT

'Integrated Pest Management' (I.P.M.) is the term used to describe a balanced approach to pest and disease control. A combination of pest and disease resistant varieties and biological and cultural control methods are used to minimise the use of agrochemicals. It requires planning and vigilance and involves the whole garden environment and does not simply involve treating symptoms.

### GENERAL CONSIDERATIONS

(1) Plants and habitats which attract and provide a refuge for beneficial insects that feed on pests should be encouraged

(2) Only the most appropriate insecticide or fungicide should be used to control insects or diseases that get out of hand.

(3) A sensible spraying procedure should be adopted which includes following pack instructions carefully and spraying before the pests and diseases build up and cause damage. Spray in the late evening, when bees are less active and treat only the infested parts of the plant to avoid wasteful run-off.

(4) Pruning will allow good air circulation and light penetration The free air movement will help to keep the incidence of disease to a low level.

(5) Plants under water stress are far more likely to suffer from diseases such as mildew. The use of surface mulches and drip or trickle irrigation will help reduce water stress.

(6) The removal and burning of dead and diseased material, dead plants, prunings, etc is always important in reducing pest and disease levels in the garden. This should be undertaken as frequently as possible.

# PESTS & DISEASES

(7) It is important to choose varieties with a good pest and disease resistance and those best suited to the site. For example, in high rainfall areas such as the south-west, it is important to choose apple varieties with some scab resistance and in the drier east of the country, those with some mildew resistance. Ministry certified plants should be obtained wherever possible as these are less likely to be sources of infection for other plants.

## BIOLOGICAL CONTROL

This can involve encouraging natural predators to control pests: for example, *Typhlodromus pyri* — a predatory mite which feeds on fruit tree red spider mite; or ladybirds and lacewings to control aphids. Alternatively, predators can be introduced, for example, the predatory mite *Phytoseiulus persimilis* to control the two-spotted spider mite, a troublesome pest of strawberries, peaches and raspberries in particular, a problem outdoors as well as under glass. Predators are available from Defenders, Ashford, Kent, (tel: 01233-813121).

Pheromone traps should be used for codling moth and plum moth monitoring and control. These traps catch male moths, resulting in fewer fertilized females and so fewer larvae and reduced damage. Insect barrier glue should be used to prevent winter moths climbing up trees and laying eggs.

## CHEMICAL CONTROL

Chemicals are not cheap, so it is important to make the best use of them. Spraying is more effective than dusting and the kinds of dust available are more limited than the kinds of sprays; however, an effective general purpose spraying machine will cost between £50 and £100.

Before using any chemicals, note any limitations such as the type of plants on which the product can be used. Chemicals should only be applied according to the manufacturer's instructions. An accurate weighing machine and measuring cylinder should be obtained — chemicals can be wasted by making concentrations unnecessarily strong or by making them too weak and ineffective. If chemicals are too strong they may cause damage to the foliage.

At the time of going to press, the various chemicals recommended in this chapter could be readily obtained from garden centres. However, from time to time, products are withdrawn and others take their place. Where chemicals have been recommended, the active ingredient has been given rather than the trade name, which varies according to the manufacturer. Whilst every care has been taken to ensure that the information given is both accurate and up-to-date, the author does not accept any liability to any party for loss or damage incurred by reliance placed on the information contained in this book or through omission or errors, howsoever caused.

Chemicals should only be applied when there are significant levels of pests present. Where possible, chemicals should be chosen which do not harm naturally occurring or introduced predators and beneficial insects such as bees. Chemicals particularly harmful to predators include many broad spectrum insecticides, in particular the pyrethroids such as permethryn. Some fungicides are also harmful to beneficial insects.

# PESTS & DISEASES

## PESTS

**APHIDS (GREENFLY)** — Aphids (blackflies, greenflies etc.) occur in both winged and wingless forms. They can be found clustered together in large numbers on leaves and shoots of all fruit stocks. Aphids feed on sap, causing leaf distortion, stunting of the new shoots and premature fruit drop in currants, gooseberries and blueberries. Some species may infect the bushes with virus disease. Many species secrete an abundance of honeydew, much sought after by ants and other insects; 'sooty' type moulds then form on the leaves, shoots and fruits. Action should be taken as soon as attacks are diagnosed and before excessive damage is caused. Aphids are best dealt with by spraying with bifenthrin in the spring after they have

*Aphid damage*

hatched out (but not during the flowering period). However, this chemical can only be used on certain fruits. Rotenone is an effective organic insecticide. In a greenhouse or conservatory, natural predators can be used. *Aphidoletes aphidmyza* is a gall midge which lives exclusively on aphids, controlling virtually all species. Lacewing larvae and ladybirds also feed on aphids. These populations can be increased substantially if a lacewing chamber and/or ladybird house is installed in the garden.

*Apple blossom weevil damage*

**APPLE BLOSSOM WEEVIL** — This pest is most commonly found on apple trees but pear, quince and sometimes medlars are also attacked. Eggs are laid singly in the side of the bud from bud burst onwards. The young larvae feed on the developing anthers and styles and then attack the petals to form the characteristic brown 'capped' blossom. There is no recommended method of chemical control available to the amateur gardener.

**APPLE LEAF MINER** — The apple leaf miner is a fairly common pest, frequently found on apples and sometimes cherries and other fruit stocks. The damage caused by this pest is rarely of significant importance. The adult moth deposits eggs singly in the underside of the leaf in May. After hatching out, each larvae commences to mine towards the upper surface of the leaf, feeding as they go. A single mine is usually very long, widening gradually throughout its length. The tissue surrounding the mines become discoloured. If several mines are present, an infested leaf may eventually shrivel up and die. It is rarely necessary to carry out control measures against this pest, which is just as well since its method of feeding makes it very difficult to tackle. The pest is usually automatically kept in check by routine pre-blossom sprays for winter moth. Removal and destruction of infested leaves may be worthwhile with small infestations, in order to prevent a secondary generation from appearing.

*Apple leaf miner damage*

**APPLE SAWFLY** — Apples are often affected by this pest and fruit losses are often severe. Other top fruits can also be attacked by related species of sawfly but generally to a lesser extent. The apple sawfly attacks earlier in the season than the codling moth. It lays its eggs in the fruitlets at flowering time. After hatching, the larvae burrow into the fruitlets and tunnels just beneath the skin before making their way to the core. Affected fruitlets drop off in June and July and when fully fed the larvae leave the fruit, creating an exit hole and burrow into the soil to pupate. The exit hole will be filled with masses of wet, black sticky frass. Further migration to other fruitlets may occur, either before or after infested ones have dropped to the ground. If the larvae dies before it can bore into the core, the fruit will reach maturity. Early feeding beneath the skin will however produce a broad, corky, ribbon-like scar on the fruit surface, often running from the eye end to the middle of the fruit. As a precautionary measure, apple trees should be sprayed with bifenthrin one week after 80% petal fall. If signs of maggot damage are seen, pick off and burn infested fruitlets before the larvae escape into the soil.

**BLACKCURRANT GALL MITE** — The blackcurrant gall mite or 'big bud' mite, as it is often called, is an important and widespread pest of blackcurrants. The mites, which are invisible to the naked eye, live and breed within blackcurrant buds, causing a condition known as 'big bud'. There may be several thousand mites within a single bud. Attacked buds soon become noticeably round and distorted and are very conspicuous after leaf fall. In the following spring, they swell further and although opening they do not usually produce leaves or flowers. The swollen buds measure up to 15mm across and remain on the bushes until June or July when they eventually dry out and die. Heavy infestations of buds and shoots affects bush development and reduces cropping. More importantly, if a bush develops even a single 'big bud' it is doomed to eventually get 'reversion' virus, for which there is no cure (see pages 191). There are no chemicals available to amateur gardeners to control this pest. Removing and burning shoots with 'big bud' from lightly infested bushes in late winter will limit infestations, although it will only be a matter of time before the bush shows the first signs of 'reversion' virus. Badly affected bushes should be removed and burned immediately after fruiting.

*Apple sawfly larva*

*Blackcurrant gall mite damage*

**BLACKCURRANT LEAF CURLING MIDGE** — This can often be a serious pest of blackcurrants. The varieties 'Ben Connan' and 'Ben Sarek' are however, resistant. The adult midges emerge from the soil in late April and lay eggs in the unfolded leaves. The minute, white, legless grubs, feeding on the surface of the leaves, stop them 'unfolding' and they remain twisted and necrotic and eventually turn black. A severe infestation stunts the new growth. There is no recommended method of chemical control available to the amateur gardener. Cultivating the soil around the bushes during dry weather in the summer will destroy many pupae by exposing them to drying conditions.

*Blackcurrant leaf midge damage*

**CATERPILLARS** — There are a great number of species of caterpillars that feed on the leaves and fruit of fruit stocks. Some of the most important are the larvae of the apple sawfly, codling moth, gooseberry sawfly, plum fruit moth, tortrix moth and winter moth. For further information see the relevant sections in this chapter.

**CHAFER BEETLE** — The grubs feed upon the roots of all fruit stocks but it is newly planted and established strawberries that they seriously damage. They are particularly common in light, well-drained soil. The larvae are white bodied with brown legs and are up to 40mm long. They feed on the roots of plants, making them wilt and sometimes die. When fully grown, they pupate in the soil and emerge as adult beetles between late spring and early summer. There is no recommended method of chemical control available to the amateur gardener. Where infestations are light (and this is often the case in the vegetable garden), it is usually feasible to search for the grubs in the soil near plants that have suddenly wilted.

**CLAY COLOURED WEEVIL** — This pest feeds on all soft fruits. It is rarely seen, as it feeds at night and hides in the soil during the daytime. The weevil is the same colour as the soil and has a large body, small head and long snout. It should be looked for with a torch after dark. Attacks commence during April and continue for six to eight weeks. The adult weevil feeds on the leaves and fruiting laterals, notching the veins and flower stalks so that wilting and dead tissue can be found hanging on the bushes. In a serious attack, a bush can be denuded of every piece of green leaf and stalk. There is no recommended method of chemical control available to the amateur gardener.

*Chafer beetle larva*

**CODLING MOTH** — This is a very serious pest of apples. It also attacks pears and occasionally plums, damsons and quince. The adult moths lay their eggs on developing fruitlets and on foliage. The larva forms a small cavity just below the fruit skin and burrows down to the core, leaving a conspicuous, red-ringed entry hole in the side or near the eye, characteristically blocked by dry frass. On cutting an affected fruit open, the small pinkish maggot, approximately 18-20mm long, may be seen amongst the internal damage. After about four weeks, the fully grown larvae vacate the fruit which may or may not have dropped to the ground. The removal of broken stakes, rough supporting ties and loose bark, will greatly reduce the number of suitable overwintering sites for the larvae. Infested fruits should be collected and destroyed before the maggots escape. Codling Moth pheromone traps should be installed soon after the middle of May. The traps use the 'pheromone' scent of the female moth to attract and catch male moths thereby reducing the females' mating success and egg laying. Trees should also be sprayed with bifenthrin in June and July after petal fall. More accurate timing of spray applications can be achieved by using the traps to monitor moth activity.

*Clay coloured weevil damage*

*Codling moth larva*

**Leaf eelworm damage**

**Stem eelworm damage**

**EELWORMS (NEMATODES)** — There are several different species of eelworms which affect soft fruits. The **leaf eelworm** feeds in the buds and between the unfolded leaflets of strawberry plants. The fully expanded leaves are distorted and puckered and rough-grey or silver-coloured feeding areas are present near the veins. Fruiting is affected because the main crown is killed and replaced by a number of weak secondary crowns. Leaf eelworm can also be found on blackcurrant, chrysanthemum and many other plants. The **stem eelworm** infests parsnip, rhubarb, beans, onions and strawberries. It persists in the soil and will attack these crops if they follow each other on the same ground. Symptoms on strawberries are thickening and shortening of the leaf and flower stalks; the leaf blades have a typical crumpled and ridged appearance and the plants are severely dwarfed. The **dagger and needle eelworm** are soil inhabiting and feed on the roots of strawberries, other bush fruits and weeds. More seriously, they transmit certain virus diseases. Even when virus is not present the feeding of large numbers of eelworms on the roots will reduce the vigour of the shoots and branches. The best safeguard is to plant Ministry certified stock to ensure that the plants are healthy in the first place. Keeping fruit plots absolutely free from weeds reduces eelworm numbers and the risk of infection. Many of the eelworms, except stem eelworm, are unlikely to survive if the soil is kept absolutely free from weeds for four months between planting susceptible crops.

**GOOSEBERRY SAWFLY** — The gooseberry sawfly is a common pest of gooseberries, red and white currants. A related species attacks blackcurrants. The adult sawfly lays its eggs in the centres of gooseberry bushes. The larvae are up to 20mm long, green with black spots and black heads and are usually noticed after fruit-set towards the end of May. Damage commences mid to late spring. The larvae feed on the foliage throughout the bushes. If control measures are not implemented, the bushes can be completely defoliated and the berries do not swell. There can be two or three generations, so further damage may occur later in the season. Plants should be checked regularly for sawfly and larvae can be picked off by hand. Affected plants should be sprayed with rotenone or pyrethrum (pyrethrins).

**Gooseberry sawfly larva**

**GREEN CAPSID BUG** — This pest infests all fruit stocks. It is widespread and often abundant. The adults are approximately 6mm long, bright green in colour, similar to greenfly, but can be distinguished from the latter because they run quickly over the leaves and cause severe damage to the leaves and shoots. On soft fruits, capsid bugs appear on the plants in early May when they feed between the unopened leaves at the tips of the shoots and canes. They cause brown, necrotic spots and these later turn into holes when the leaves are fully expanded. When severe infestations occur, crop yields can be reduced considerably and the shoots and canes can cease growing altogether or branch out with secondary growth. On gooseberries, fruits become cracked and scarred and frequently drop prematurely. On strawberries the pest also feeds on the flowers and developing fruits, causing distortion of the flesh, sometimes described as cat-faced fruits. On apples, pears, plums and cherries, the capsid bug feeds on the leaves, causing brown spots to develop which later turn into holes. Corky, pitted scars may also form on attacked fruits which can be severely disfigured. As soon as signs of the presence of this pest are seen, spray the plants with bifenthrin. However, this chemical can only be used on certain fruits.

*Green capsid bug damage*

*Leatherjacket*

**LEATHERJACKETS** — The larvae of the crane fly ('daddy-long-legs') can devastate strawberry, raspberry and blackberry crops. Attacks are worse on recently dug grassed areas and less severe on light, dry soils and in hot, dry years. The legless, fat earth-coloured grubs are up to 45mm long, without obvious heads. They feed below soil level on the shoots of newly planted raspberry canes and the crowns of strawberry plants. Damage is most evident in the spring when infested plants make poor growth and may begin to wilt. Leatherjackets can be controlled by broadcasting slug pellets around the base of fruit bushes and strawberry plants. Slug pellets can kill cats and dogs, so care should be taken in their use.

Leatherjackets can be collected by covering small areas of the ground with black polythene overnight after heavy rain or irrigation. The grubs will come up to the surface and can be removed the next morning when the polythene is lifted. The natural predator *Steinernema carpocasae* can be used against older larvae when the soil is moist and warm.

**NUT WEEVIL** — The nut weevil is a common pest of hazelnuts, cobnuts and filberts. The nut weevil bores a small hole in the shell of the immature fruit and lays its eggs. These hatch into small, white maggots that feed on the kernel. There is usually only one larvae per nut. In August the fully grown larvae exits the shell through the now much enlarged hole and drops down and pupates in the soil. Usually only a small proportion of the crop is attacked. No method of chemical control is available. Cultivating the soil around the trees during the winter will destroy many overwintering larvae and thereby reduce infestation levels the following spring.

*Nut weevil damage*

**PEAR LEAF BLISTER MITE** — The pear leaf blister mite is a common pest of pear and occasionally apple. The damage is largely cosmetic. It gives the tree an unhealthy appearance but has little effect on the tree's ability to produce fruit. The microscopic gall mite lives within the leaves of pear trees. During May, as it feeds on the foliage, it secretes a chemical causing blistering of the tissue. As the mite gains access to the inside of the leaf, 'pocket like' galls are formed and breeding occurs within. In spring, the galls are evident as soon as the leaves unfurl. They first appear as greenish raised pustules and quickly turn yellow and eventually pink. By midsummer the blisters darken and eventually turn black. Severe attacks can cause premature leaf drop. There is no satisfactory method of chemical control available to the amateur gardener. If there is a light infestation, affected leaves should be picked off and destroyed in the summer. If the infestation is heavy, the pest just has to be tolerated.

*Pear leaf blister mite damage*

*Pear leaf midge damage*

**PEAR LEAF MIDGE** — This is a common pest of pear trees. Adults appear from mid-April onwards but are most numerous in August and September. The larvae are approximately 2mm long and whitish and can be found within the tightly rolled pear leaves. There are usually three generations in one season. Adults lay their eggs within the rolled margins of young pear leaves. They hatch within a few days and the larvae then feed on the leaves, preventing the leaf margins from unrolling. Leaves are badly distorted in severe attacks and their margins remain tightly rolled. The foliage turns red and finally blackens and dies. The damage caused by this pest can easily be confused with frost damage which is very common during the spring. There are no effective insecticides approved for use by amateur gardeners, but when the attack is slight, all infected leaves should be removed and burned.

**PEAR MIDGE** — An attack of this pest is readily diagnosed soon after the fruit has set. For an initial period of about two weeks, infested fruitlets grow more rapidly than healthy ones and become either noticeably rounded or malformed. However, they cease to develop when they reach 15-20mm in diameter and then usually shrivel, crack and decay and finally drop to the ground. The centres of such fruits will be found to consist of wet, black debris together with a number of small yellowish-white maggots, 4-5mm long. Even healthy fruitlets may drop, following competition for assimilates from rapidly growing infested fruitlets in the same cluster. The maggots escape by burrowing into the soil when the attacked fruits fall to the ground. They pupate in the soil and emerge as small, inconspicuous midges the following April, ready to lay eggs in the pear blossom. Some protection against attack from the adult midges before they lay their eggs can be made by spraying with bifenthrin when the blossom is at the white bud stage, but before the flowers open. It is important to spray the trunks and undersides of the branches since the adult midges rest in such places. Collection and destruction of infested fruitlets will reduce the number of maggots carried over from one season to the next. Hoeing the ground very thoroughly around the trunks of affected trees each week from the second week of June until the end of July will also help control this pest.

*Pear midge damage*

**PLUM FRUIT MOTH** — The plum fruit moth is a common pest attacking plum, gage, damson and occasionally peach. The female lays her eggs at the base of the fruit stalk and the larvae hatches out ten days later and immediately enters the fruit and burrows towards the stone. The larvae are 10-12mm long, reddish with a dark brown head. The damage caused to the fruits by the red plum maggot is very similar to that caused by the plum fruit sawfly but it occurs much later in the season. The red plum maggot feeds within relatively large fruitlets. It makes a hole at the base of the plum and bores into the fruit. On entering the flesh, the young larva forms a narrow winding mine. The mine soon turns brown and is then clearly visible through the skin. From near the stalk the mine is extended to the centre of the fruit and as the

*Plum fruit moth larva*

larva grows the flesh around the stone is eaten and replaced by wet, brown frass. When fully fed the larva escapes through the side of the fruit, leaving a small circular hole in the skin. Attacked fruits ripen early and are easily recognised amongst the developing crop. Plum Fruit Moth pheromone traps should be installed soon after the end of May. The traps use the 'pheromone' scent of the female moth to attract and catch male moths thereby reducing the females' mating success and egg laying. There are no chemical controls approved for use for amateur gardeners. Applications of rotenone before blossom and again after petal fall may give some protection. More accurate timing of spray applications can be achieved by using the traps to monitor moth activity.

*Raspberry beetle larva*

**RASPBERRY BEETLE** — The raspberry beetle is a serious pest of blackberries, raspberries and hybrid berries (Tayberries, loganberries etc.). The larva are 6-8mm long, creamy white, with brown markings on their upper surface. They can often be seen crawling around the punnet after the fruits have been picked. The adult beetle can cause extensive damage if large numbers attack raspberries or hybrid berries before blossom time. Buds can be destroyed completely, open blossoms are also injured, the stamens and nectaries being bitten and destroyed. Ultimately, there will be many small malformed fruits and heavy crop losses. The damage caused by the larvae is even more important. The adult lays its eggs on the flowers during early and midsummer. One female may lay one hundred or more eggs, usually one per flower. Eggs hatch out after about ten days, usually from the green fruit to early pink fruit stages. The larvae initially feed at the base of the berries but later feed in the inner core or plug. Attacked drupelets turn brown and hard, particularly at the stalk end of the berry. The presence of the grub inside the fruit renders (for most people) the fruit inedible. There are no label approved chemicals available to the amateur gardener against this pest but if the canes are thoroughly sprayed with the organic insecticide rotenone, extensive damage may be avoided. The aim is to kill the young larvae while they are feeding on the outside of the fruits, so timing of the control measures is very important. On raspberries, spray when the first pink fruits are seen and again two weeks later. On hybrid berries spray at 80% petal fall and again two weeks later. On blackberries a single application should be made before the first flowers open.

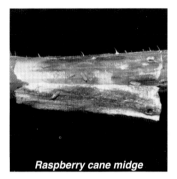

**Raspberry cane midge**

**RASPBERRY CANE MIDGE** — The raspberry cane midge is a widespread pest of summer fruiting raspberry varieties. The midges emerge from the soil at the end of May and beginning of June and lay eggs under the bark of the new canes where natural growth splits have occurred or the surface of the cane has been damaged. There may be several hundred larvae per cane. The failure of canes to break into leaf at the end of the winter and the wilting of the fruiting canes at any time between bud burst and picking, are the obvious signs that there had been an infestation by cane midge during the previous summer. The tissue in the feeding areas will become discoloured and turn brown or black. More importantly, the feeding of the larvae enables various fungal pathogens to infect the canes. These diseases may kill the fruiting canes and thereby considerably reduce fruiting potential for the following year. This pest does not affect autumn fruiting varieties (unless the canes are allowed to give a second crop the following summer) because the fruiting canes are cut out and burned once they have finished fruiting. This operation interrupts the life cycle of the midge before it has the opportunity to build up large populations. Cane vigour control, by which the first flush of new canes are removed, gives very good control against this pest (see page 100). The later and weaker growing canes do not split their bark and therefore do not provide egg laying sites for the adult midges. Cultivating the soil around the bushes during the winter will also help reduce overwintering populations and hence infestation levels the following spring. There are no label approved chemicals available to the amateur gardener against this pest. Several applications of the organic insecticide rotenone to the new canes when they are about 20-30cm high (usually in the first week of May) and again two weeks later may give some measure of protection. In southern areas an application may also be made in August or September when third generation midges are active.

**RASPBERRY LEAF AND BUD MITE** — The raspberry leaf and bud mite is a widespread and often common pest of raspberries and occasionally blackberries and hybrid berries. The mite is too small to be seen with the naked eye. It passes the winter under the bud scales and in April migrates to and feeds on the undersides of the newly opened leaves of the new and fruiting canes. Mites are most numerous in late summer and early autumn. Outbreaks are worst where raspberries are grown in very sheltered situations near tall trees and in hot dry summers. A severe infestation gives rise to crumbly fruit, a reduced crop and stunted canes. On raspberries, the feeding on the leaves gives rise to distortion and irregular yellow blotching on the upper surface of leaves which to the

**Raspberry leaf & bud mite damage**

inexperienced observer can be confused with virus infection. Leaf hair development beneath the yellow patches is abnormal, the appearance of these areas changing from greyish to pale greenish. Apical buds of young canes are sometimes killed, leading to the development of weak lateral shoots. Attacks on fruits cause irregular drupelet development, uneven ripening and malformation. Some varieties are more susceptible than others. 'Malling Jewel' for instance, is particularly liable to be attacked. On blackberries, heavy infestations may cause mildew blotches to develop on the upper surface of leaves and malformation of the hairs on the underside of the leaves. Unfortunately, no chemicals are available to the gardener for the control of this pest. It is therefore very important to buy Ministry certified stocks in the first place to obviate the risk of importing the pest into the garden. Where bushes are severely attacked, the drastic measure of cutting down all the canes to ground level and burning them but leaving their root systems 'in situ' should be taken. This means the complete loss of crop for one year but the only alternative would be to scrap the plot and replant with certified canes. Consideration should also be given to growing an autumn fruiting variety. The fruiting canes of such varieties are cut out and burned once they have finished fruiting (unless the canes are allowed to give a second crop the following summer). This operation interrupts the life cycle of the mite before it has the opportunity to build up large populations.

*Brown Scale*

*Woolly Currant Scale*

**SCALE INSECTS** — There are many different types of scale insects. The most common are the woolly currant scale which is a pest of currant and gooseberry bushes and Brown scale which attacks a wide variety of hosts including currant, gooseberry, blackberry, raspberry, plum and peach.The Woolly currant scale becomes active in early spring. The adult female is 4-6mm long, dark brown and roughly oval shaped. In May each adult female spins a sac of white waxen threads which over a period of two to three weeks, approximately one thousand eggs are deposited. The adult then dies and soon afterwards the egg mass forces the hind part of the scale away from the branch. The presence of the pest then becomes very obvious as the woolly secretion beneath the scale wafts around in the wind, covering many of the shoots and branches of infested bushes. The eggs hatch over a six week period. After a few days the young nymphs wander over the young shoots and leaves to begin feeding. Heavy infestations will weaken the bush and the strands of 'wool' are a nuisance during picking. The Brown scale adult female is 4-6mm long, oval shaped and reddish brown. She deposits several hundred eggs in May and June and then dies. She remains on the plant however, protecting her eggs (she may persist on the host plant for several years). The eggs hatch from about mid-June to mid-July. The young nymphs then wander over the young shoots and leaves and feed on the sap. Heavy infestations weaken the host plant and causes premature leaf fall. Attacks tend to be heaviest in sheltered, unsprayed sites. Spray the infested plants with Bio Organic Pest Control (the active ingredient is rape seed oil). This product can be used on edible plants right up to harvest.

**SLUGS & SNAILS** — Slugs and snails cause most damage to strawberry fruits, eating the flesh and making them susceptible to grey mould which can then spread by contact to sound fruits. Slugs also graze on newly planted strawberry runners, checking their growth or killing them. The smaller snail species climb up into blackcurrant bushes to feed on the leaves and berries. Occasionally slugs feed on the new canes of raspberries and hybrid berries, eating away large areas of the bark. This weakens the canes so that they break easily or become infected by various fungi. Slugs and snails can never be completely eliminated from the garden. On the strawberry bed they can be controlled by broadcasting slug pellets at the beginning of June before strawing down. If, later in the month, glistening slug trails are seen on the soil or on the plants, a second application should be made at least seven days before the fruit is expected to ripen. In gardens where slugs and snails are known to be numerous, slug pellets should be broadcasted under blackcurrant bushes at the 'grape stage' of flower development (i.e. when they are in tight green bud). Preventative measures for cane fruits should only be taken when damage to the canes is seen to be occurring. Slug pellets can kill cats and dogs, so care should be taken in their use. Slug and Snail Traps are a pesticide free alternative, harmless to wildlife and pests. An attractant is used to bait the traps which will attract slugs and snails from a distance of 1-2m. Slugs can also be controlled by the natural predator *Phasmarhabditis hermaphrpdita*. It needs to be applied to moist, well-drained soils during the spring and autumn. Under suitable conditions the nematode can significantly reduce the number of slugs for at least six weeks. It is however, less effective on snails.

**SPIDER MITES** — There are many different species of spider mite but the most important ones as far as gardeners growing fruit are concerned are the **fruit tree red spider mite** and the **two-spotted spider mite.** Both types live on the undersurfaces of leaves, feeding on the sap from the leaf cells. The **fruit tree red spider mite** is a widespread and important pest of apple and other fruit trees, including plum and damson and to a lesser extent cherry and pear. It also occurs on raspberry and loganberry canes as well as currant and gooseberry bushes. The mites are less than 1mm long, spider-like and blackish-red in colour. The **two-spotted spider mite** is an important pest of a wide range of glasshouse crops. It also attacks fruit crops grown outside,

*Two-spotted spider mite damage*

including raspberry, blackberry, strawberry, blackcurrant and gooseberry and fruit trees grown trained against walls, particularly peaches, nectarines and apricots. It can also occur on apples, pears, cherries and plums. The mites are less than 1mm long, spider-like, yellowish-green with two large dark markings towards the head end of the body. They only become orange-red in the autumn and winter. When plants are heavily infested, mites can be seen crawling over a fine silk webbing spun between the leaves and stem. The **fruit tree red spider mite** sucks out the sap, causing a fine mottling of the foliage at first, but as mite populations and damage increases, leaves become dull green, brownish and finally silvery bronze. Such foliage is brittle and may drop prematurely. On the lower leaf surfaces,

*Fruit tree red spider mite damage*

large numbers of tiny mites and spherical eggs will be visible. Leaf symptoms are usually most evident from July to September. Heavy infestations affect fruit yield and fruit bud formation, so the following year's crop may be reduced. The **two-spotted spider mite** causes fine pale mottling of the foliage which becomes firstly dull green and later increasingly yellowish white. The leaves dry up and fall prematurely. Fruit yields and plant vigour will be reduced with serious infestations. On strawberry plants, severe attacks before harvest will also reduce fruit size and quality. In the glasshouse, spider mites can often be successfully controlled biologically with the predatory mite *Phytoseiulus persimilis* if it is introduced before a heavy infestation has developed. The same predatory mite can also be used on outdoor plants during the summer. Alternatively, plants can be sprayed with bifenthrin or rotenone. Several applications will be necessary. Avoid unnecessary spraying against other pests as this often kills beneficial insects, allowing spider mites to breed unchecked.

**STRAWBERRY BLOSSOM WEEVIL** — The strawberry blossom weevil — or elephant bug as it is sometimes called because of its long snout that looks like a trunk — appears to be present on many strawberry plants in the south of England but has more localised distribution in the north. At flowering time, the presence of a number of capped flower buds which fail to open and shrivel, is the first sign of the presence of this pest. If these capped

*Strawberry blossom weevil damage*

blossoms are carefully examined, small white grubs may be found inside the flower, feeding on the stamens and ovaries. The flower is prevented from opening, by the adult weevil boring a hole in the stalk 10mm below the flower bud. Unfortunately there is not an insecticide available to the amateur gardener for controlling this pest.

*Strawberry seed beetle damage*

**STRAWBERRY SEED BEETLE** — The strawberry seed beetle is quite large, 12-18mm in length, with a black body. During the daytime it hides under stones and leaves and come out to feed at night. The beetles remove the seeds from the fruit, damage and eat the flesh. Linnets also eat strawberry seeds but the birds usually remove the seeds without damaging the flesh and normally from the upper surface of the fruit. Beetle damage is usually situated on the undersurface nearer the soil. There is no method of chemical control available to the amateur gardener. The strawberry bed should be kept free from weeds, to discourage a build up of this pest, since out of the strawberry season the beetle will feed on weed seeds.

**STRAWBERRY TARSONEMID MITE** — This is a microscopic pest that can just be seen with a 20x lens and in recent years has become quite a common pest of strawberries. Signs of an attack can be seen in the spring but they are more severe in August after picking, particularly after a hot summer. The plants are stunted, the leaves small and wrinkled and turn brown. There are no chemicals available to the amateur gardener for controlling this pest. The mite can be kept in check by burning the straw over the plants immediately after harvest. The straw should be picked up with a fork and spread over the plants and allowed to dry. On a day when there is a fair wind blowing down the rows, the straw should be set alight on the windward side, so that there is a quick fire that burns the leaves without damaging the crowns. If it is impossible to fire the bed, the only remedy would be to dig up and replant the bed with new stock.

*Strawberry tarsonemid mite damage*

**Tortrix moth larva**

**TORTRIX MOTH** — There are several different species affecting both top fruits and soft fruits. On strawberry plants the young caterpillars which have black heads and bodies that are white, green or grey, depending upon the species, cause most trouble during April and May. They spin the leaflets together with silken threads and feed on the leaf blades. A number of caterpillars bore through the sepals and petals of the unopened flower buds and feed on the ovaries, stigmas and stamens. The flowers open in the normal way but the berries are distorted and susceptible to grey mould infection. It is important to spray strawberries early with bifenthrin before the caterpillars spin the leaves together and bore into the flower buds. The buds of the flower trusses should be sprayed as they separate from each other and the application repeated after ten days. On blackcurrants they live similarly on leaves at the tips of the shoots, spinning the leaves together and killing the growing points as a result of which the shoots branch. This does not reduce the crop but it is a nuisance to have a lot of forked branches. On cane fruits the caterpillars spin the leaves together at the tips of new cane and fruiting laterals. This is seldom harmful and shoots and laterals usually grow away from the trouble. Fruit tree tortrix moths hibernate as young caterpillars in winter in cocoons attached to the branches. They emerge in late March, boring into fruit buds and then feeding on developing leaves, often spinning them together. They commence to pupate from late May from between the spun leaves after which the moth makes its appearance. Large numbers of moths are on the wing in late June or July, depending on the season and they lay their eggs in flat green batches on the leaves. The fruit tree tortrix moth is best controlled by the sprays recommended for the codling moth.

**VINE WEEVIL** — This is a very important pest of glasshouse plants. It also attacks soft fruit crops outdoors. Plants grown in containers are particularly at risk. The adult beetles are up to 9mm long with dull black, pear shaped bodies. The larvae are legless grubs, up to 10mm long, creamish to brownish white with a brown head. The adults can be seen at any time from spring to autumn. They emerge at night and feed on the leaf margins of strawberry plants but this is rarely serious. Larval damage is usually seen between early autumn and mid-spring. The larvae live in the soil and feed on the roots, which are severed or on woody plants that have the outer bark removed. Consequently the plants make slow growth and eventually collapse and die when insufficient roots remain

**Vine weevil larva**

to sustain the plant. The insecticides available to gardeners usually give disappointing results. The best method of controlling the larvae is biologically with pathogenic nematodes. Nematodes can be used outside between March and May or between August and mid-October. In greenhouses they can be used all year round. However, soil temperatures must be above 10°C (50°F) for the nematodes to be effective. Nematodes work best in open compost or light soils and it is important the soil is not very dry or waterlogged at the time of application. Avoid mixing with pesticides as many affect the nematodes. Adult weevils can be searched for by torchlight in the evening and removed from plants.

hibernating in buds which had become infected the previous season. The spores on the leaves of these primary infected shoots become dispersed by the wind and cause secondary infection of the leaves, shoots and fruit during the spring and summer. Badly infected shoots are often leafless and appear shrivelled and whitish-brown all over. Buds may be killed outright but usually they survive, only to develop into mildewed shoots the following year. Infection of the fruit is not usually very serious; infected twigs may be recognised in winter by their pale grey colour. They should all be pruned out and burned before the trees come into leaf. In spring when the foliage appears, all shoots with mildew should be removed and burnt and not left lying around. Dust with green sulphur or spray with myclobutanil.

*Apple mildew*

*Apple scab*

**APPLE SCAB** — Apple scab (black spot) is the most troublesome disease of apples and pears. It affects the foliage and on young twigs, causes lesions which may allow the canker fungus to gain entrance. The greatest destruction it causes is, however to the fruit. The fruit may become scabbed at all stages in its development. When the young fruits are attacked they may fall early and if they remain on the tree they become misshapen and often cracked. If fruits are affected later in the season, they too become disfigured. Scab is first seen as dark spots consisting of radiating branched lines. Later the spots become more corky and greenish. The spots produced early often serve as sources for later infection. Scab may also develop when the fruit is stored. All varieties of apple and pear may become infected but some are more prone to infection than others. 'Cox's Orange Pippin' and 'Worcester Pearmain' are particularly vulnerable to infection. The degree of infection will depend on the weather conditions at the time of fruit development. Wet cloudy weather during the blossoming period will encourage an outbreak of this disease. Diseased twigs should be cut away and burnt before the buds burst and fallen leaves should be raked up and destroyed in order to prevent the liberation of spores. Most reliance should however be placed on spraying with myclobutanil or mancozeb, which if carried out properly will reduce infection considerably. Spray at the first sign of symptoms and at fourteen day intervals. In some seasons it may be necessary to continue spraying until late July.

**APRICOT DIEBACK** — This is one of the most common diseases affecting apricots. Apricot dieback is usually caused by fungi but occasionally adverse weather conditions. If growth starts very early in the spring and frosts occur, the tree will suffer from injury and this can trigger dieback. First one branch and then the whole side of the tree dies. Cut back all dead wood to healthy tissue and paint the wounds with a protective paint. Give adequate feeding, watering and mulching to encourage plenty of replacement growth. As a preventative measure, apricot trees should always be protected from spring frosts.

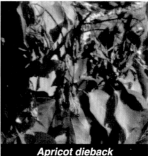

*Apricot dieback*

**BACTERIAL CANKER** — Bacterial canker is a serious but common disease affecting all stone fruits. Trees are particularly susceptible during their early years before cropping. Infection is most likely to occur during autumn and winter but the first signs are not noticeable until the spring. Elongated, flattened cankers which ooze gum appear on the bark and affected branches die back. Leaves on affected branches either do not develop or are small and yellow and soon die. During the summer, the organism infects the leaves and sometimes the shoots. Round, brown spots appear on the leaves and subsequently develop into holes. Bacterial canker can easily be confused with gummosis, a disorder of stone fruits that usually occurs after freezing weather. The patches of gum appear on the surface of branches and trunks. With gummosis, the gum arises from

*Bacterial canker*

healthy wood whereas with bacterial canker the gum oozes from diseased tissue. Bacterial canker must be tackled quickly in order to save the tree. Cankered branches should be removed and burned and the wounds painted with a protective paint such as Arbrex. It is very important that the pruning tools are then properly disinfected by immersing the blades in boiling water for five to ten minutes before using them on other trees. If canker occurs on the main stem, the entire tree will die. In such a case, it is necessary to uproot and burn the tree immediately to prevent the canker from spreading to other trees. Trees affected by canker should also be sprayed with Bordeaux mixture in mid-August, repeating in mid-September and again in mid-October. Always avoid pruning stone fruits during the winter since the wounds formed may allow the entry of the disease. Any necessary pruning or cutting back should be carried out either by the end of August or otherwise left until late April or early May of the following year.

*Bitter pit*

**BITTER PIT** — Bitter pit is a common disorder affecting the fruits of apples, particularly large fruited varieties such as 'Bramley's Seedling'. It is caused by a deficiency in calcium and/or a too high concentration of potassium or magnesium within the fruits but its incidence is influenced by various factors which affect the movement of calcium into or out of the fruits while on the tree. Bitter pit appears to be connected with water shortages at critical times and is generally worse in seasons when there are wide fluctuations in rainfall and temperature. Excessive tree vigour, excessive fruit thinning, and too much nitrogenous fertilizer are also factors which predispose fruits to bitter pit. It is also prevalent in fruits which are immature when picked. Bitter pit usually develops during storage, producing hard, slightly sunken pits on the surface of the skin and lines of brown tissue beneath the pits through the flesh, rendering the fruit bitter and inedible. Soil analysis may indicate a necessity for applications of lime or other minerals. Bitter pit can be prevented to a certain extent by careful cultivation. The object should be to maintain uniform and steady growth throughout the growing season. Special care should be taken to prevent water stress during fruit formation. Soil moisture should be conserved by mulching above the roots with some kind of humus but straw should not be used as this can aggravate the problem. The mulch should be forked in at the end of the season. Light pruning should normally be practiced but on a vigorous growing tree which only produces a few large fruits, late summer pruning would be beneficial. All shoots which have grown out during the current season should be cut right back to their point of origin, except where a replacement leader is required to fill the gap. If Bitter pit becomes a regular problem, it may be necessary to spray the tree several times with calcium nitrate from mid-June at the manufacturer's recommended rate. This will increase the concentration of calcium nitrate within developing apples. Calcium nitrate can be obtained from Ken Muir Ltd.

**BLUEBERRY DIEBACK & ROOT ROT** — This fungus thrives in waterlogged soils, both in containers and in the open ground. The variety 'Top Hat' is particularly susceptible to this disease. As the infection spreads, the roots of the plant collapse and decay. The plant will display a general lack of vigour, the leaves will turn yellow, then red, before excessive defoliation occurs. The plant will eventually collapse and die. Once established in the soil, this disease is difficult to eradicate. Lasting control is accomplished by improving drainage.

**BLUEBERRY STEM BLIGHT** — This disease is most common on one and two year old plants. The sudden wilting and death of an isolated stem is usually the first sign that this fungus is present. This is often followed by death of the entire plant as the fungus spreads down to the base of the plant. Infected stems will have a light brown discolouration down the infected side of the stem. Stems recently killed by the fungus do not drop their leaves, resulting in a brown-leafed 'flag' which stands out against the green healthy portions of the bush. After a few weeks the stems drop their leaves and turn almost black in colour. Infections are usually associated with a wound caused by pruning damage, insect damage or late season frost damage to young shoots. Spores are carried by wind and rain from infected stems to the wounds on healthy plants. Controlling the disease requires cutting out infected stems to well below the infected tissue. After a stem is cut off, the cut end of the stem should be examined. If any brown areas are visible in this cross section, the cut must be made again further down the stem until all infected tissue is removed. The prunings should be removed well away from the plant and burned.

**BROWN ROT** — The brown rot fungi affects almost all top fruits, particularly apples, pears, plums, peaches and nectarines. The fungi gains entry through injured skin. Bird pecks, frost crack, cracking due to irregular growth and scab infections can all cause the initial injury. The fungus can spread to adjacent healthy fruit by direct contact, or by insects, birds or rain splash that has come into contact with the source of infection. Fruit can also contract the disease in storage. Brown rot occurs as brown decaying patches (which later bear white concentric rings of spores) on ripening fruits. Infected fruits usually drop off, but sometimes remain attached to

*Brown Rot*

the tree and become mummified. There are no chemicals available to control this disease. However, preventative measures can be taken. All overwintering sources of infection should be removed and destroyed by the early spring. Fallen fruits, mummified fruits and the short section of the spur to which the fruit was attached should be removed and burned immediately. From May onwards the crop should be examined at regular intervals and any infected fruits should be destroyed. Avoid or minimise possible causes of injury to fruits by taking appropriate measures in pest control. Fruit thinning will also reduce the spread of brown rot from one fruit to the other by contact. Fruit that is put into storage should be unblemished and checked at regular intervals.

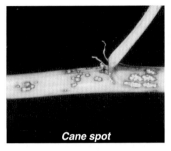
*Cane spot*

**CANE SPOT** — This disease can first be seen from May onwards on the leaves and canes of raspberries, blackberries and hybrid berries. The disease first occurs as small purple spots which enlarge into circular spots on the leaves and elliptical spots on the canes. Later the centres of the spots turn silvery-white in colour but retain their purple margins. Severe infections on the leaves can stunt growth and reduce yields. The disease can also severely disfigure the fruits. The new canes become infected from the fruiting ones on which the fungus has passed the winter. Badly spotted canes should be cut out and burned in the autumn. Raspberries should be sprayed with copper oxychloride at bud burst and every two weeks until the end of flowering. The fungicide must cover all parts of the bush. There are no approved chemicals available to the amateur gardener for use on other fruits.

**CROWN ROT** — This disease affects strawberry plants. The varieties 'Mae' and 'Rosie' are particularly susceptible and many other popular varieties may also become infected. The disease is worse on susceptible varieties in the warmer parts of the country and when strawberries are grown in peat based composts. The symptoms are similar to verticillium wilt and are seen in midsummer or earlier if the plants are grown under glass. First the younger leaves wilt, then the older leaves and the whole plant turns to a yellowish colour and then collapses and dies. A closer examination will reveal that the crown of the plant has rotted as well as the lower part of the stalks of the wilting leaves emanating from the infected crown. Infection comes from the soil but it can be introduced on

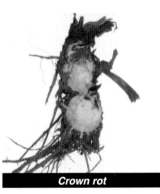
*Crown rot*

infected runners. Chemicals are ineffective against this disease. Infected plants should be removed and burnt and new plants should be planted on fresh soil, selecting a variety that is tolerant to the disease.

*Fireblight*

**FIREBLIGHT** — This can be a particular problem with pears but can also affect most other tree fruits. The disease is spread by rain splash and un-sterilized pruning tools. This disease infects the flowers which become blackened and shrivelled and then spreads down the shoots causing leaves to be brown and withered as if scorched. The bark sinks inwards on young branches and if pared back, a red discolouration will be noticed on the wood. Cankers formed at the base of the diseased tissue ooze in the spring. The tree may show extensive dieback and be killed within a few seasons. Trees with Fireblight cannot be cured but the disease can be controlled. Affected branches should be removed to 90cm (3ft) below the infection and if badly affected, the entire tree should be removed and burnt. All prunings should be burned and tools should be sterilized in boiling water for five or ten minutes after use on an infected stem.

**GRAPE POWDERY MILDEW** — This disease is common in the U.K. and is particularly troublesome on grapes grown under glass when the weather is wet and cold. It is also common on outdoor vines grown in very dry positions. A white powdery coating of fungal spores appears on the young shoots and leaves. The diseased areas then show a grey or purplish discolouration. The fungus can attack the flowers and fruits causing them to drop. At a later stage the fruits may become hard, distorted and split and can become infected with grey mould. The disease can be prevented to a certain extent by avoiding dryness at the roots. Plants should therefore be adequately mulched each season with well rotted

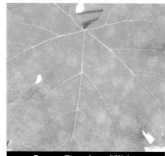

*Grape Powdery Mildew*

manure or garden compost to prevent the soil from drying out. Avoid overcrowding of the shoots and leaves to ensure good air circulation. In a cold greenhouse in dull weather, it may be necessary to provide some temporary heat to avoid excessive dampness and promote adequate circulation of air. Some of the more modern varieties have good resistance to powdery mildew. If symptoms appear, dust the plants with green sulphur. Up to four applications during the growing season may be necessary.

**GREY MOULD (BOTRYTIS)** — The berries of all kinds of soft fruit may become infected with this disease. Grey mould is very common and since it can live on most living and dead plant material, its spores are almost always present in the air. The disease is worse in wet summers, where excessive amounts of fertilizer have been applied and when excessive numbers of new shoots have been allowed to grow in the bushes. Grey mould may attack any part of the plant that is above the ground, usually gaining entry through wounds or points of damage. The infected plant tissue usually discolours and growth above points of infection may deteriorate with leaves turning yellow and wilting and flowers or fruits dying off. Both

*Grey Mould*

immature and ripe berries become covered with a dense grey fungal mycelium that causes premature drop of the former and makes the latter inedible. The spores are readily spread by rain or water splash and on air currents. The fungus may also overwinter in the soil or on infected plant debris. It is difficult to control this disease as there are no chemicals available to the amateur gardener. All dead and injured plant material should be removed before it becomes infected. Infected areas should be removed immediately, cutting back into healthy growth. Overcrowding of plants should be avoided and care should be taken that they have sufficient aeration. Harvested fruits should be promptly refrigerated and consumed within a few days.

**HONEY FUNGUS** — This can affect all fruit crops. Creamy-white patches of fungus appear beneath the bark on the roots and on the trunk just above ground level and tough, brown to black rhizomorphs (fungal strands that resemble old tree roots) are also produced. Clumps of honey coloured toadstools may appear at the base of the tree in late summer or the autumn. Death may be quite rapid, or an infected plant may take several years to die. Infected plants may set an unusually good crop of fruit before dying. Spread occurs either by root contact or by rhizomorphs which grow through the soil at the rate of about 1m a year and latch on to the remains of dead or living plants. Infected plants should be removed and burned straight away, digging out stumps and as much of the root system as possible.

**LEAF SPOT** — This disease infects blackcurrants, gooseberries and redcurrants and to a lesser extent, strawberries. It can cause premature defoliation of the bushes as early as late July, thereby reducing yields of fruit the following year. It is worse in wet summers. Infection commences in late April on leaves at the bases of the bushes. The first signs of the disease are small angular brown spots accompanied by a yellowing of the surrounding leaf areas. Under favourable conditions the number of spots rapidly increases and coalesce until all the leaf is infected and killed. Collect and burn all diseased leaves in order to prevent spring infection. Feed the bushes well to help encourage new growth. Early applications of mancozeb will control this disease. It is essential that good cover is obtained on the underside of the leaves.

*Leaf spot*

**PEACH LEAF CURL** — This is a serious fungal disease found on peaches, nectarines and sweet almonds. It is particularly troublesome in the U.K. climate but one that can be avoided. It is first noticed early in the spring. The leaf-blades become puckered and are often severely distorted. At first, leaves are pale green or yellowish but later, large reddish blisters develop. The upper surface of affected leaves become covered with a whitish bloom as the fungus begins to produce its spores. The affected leaves are finally killed and fall early, resulting in severe defoliation; often new leaves develop towards the end of the season. The vigour of the tree is consequently impaired and the crop suffers in quality and amount. The fungus over-winters in the bark and between the bud scales, not on fallen leaves. When the attack is slight, all infected shoots or leaves should be removed and burned as soon as the disease is identified so that the risk of infection the following season is kept to a minimum. Keep the tree well watered and fed to encourage the development of new replacement growth. As a preventative measure, trees should be sprayed with Bordeaux mixture or copper oxychloride just before the buds begin to swell, usually in late January and again fourteen days later.

*Peach leaf curl*

Spraying must be completed before the flower buds open. Spraying in the autumn just before leaf fall is also effective. For fan-trained trees, a clear polythene cover with the sides open and a gap of 30cm (1ft) at the bottom for ventilation, put on in December and removed in mid-May, should prevent peach leaf curl. The polythene will exclude the rain, thereby denying the moisture the peach leaf curl spores need to germinate. The extra warmth will also protect the blossom from being damaged by frost as well as improving fruit set. Ideally the polythene needs to be supported on a timber framework (see page 67). Containerised trees can be moved into a cold greenhouse or polythene tunnel during the winter months.

**POWDERY MILDEW** — This disease affects raspberries and strawberries. It appears on the plants from late April onwards, particularly during periods of dry weather. Purple spots appear on the upper surfaces of the strawberry leaves and on the undersides a white, mealy fungus

*Powdery mildew*

will be found. As the disease progresses, the leaves dry up and their edges curl upwards, giving the infected plants a characteristic appearance as if they are suffering from drought. In severe attacks the flowers themselves become mildewed; such flowers are deformed, often having dark pinkish petals and sometimes the petals do not open. The fungus later spreads to the fruits, causing distortion and giving them a dull appearance with protruding seeds. If the fruit is infected early, it may dry up before it ripens. On raspberries, the mycelium is present on the undersides of the leaves but causes a yellowing of the veins on their upper surfaces which is very difficult to distinguish from virus infection. The effect on growth of the new canes is rarely, if ever, serious. The white mycelium growing on the surface of the berries detracts from their appearance, reduces size and can cause distortion. With strawberry plants, very susceptible varieties should be sprayed with myclobutanil or dusted with green sulphur when the first flowers open in the spring, as a matter of precaution.

**PURPLE BLOTCH** — This disease affects blackberries and hybrid berries. It is usually seen first in midsummer when lengths of the new cane turn purple in colour. The blotches which are up to 8mm long, later turn whitish but remain bordered with purple. The disease is usually worse near to the stool but all parts of the bush can become infected. In the fruiting year, growth of the laterals on infected canes is poor and buds in the infected areas may be killed. In order to control the disease, seriously damaged canes should be cut out and the new canes should be trained above or away from the fruiting canes and sprayed with a copper-based fungicide when the buds on the canes have grown to 1cm.

*Purple blotch*

*Quince leaf blight*

**QUINCE LEAF BLIGHT** — This problem affects quinces and occasionally pears and medlars. It is caused by a fungus which may overwinter on infected shoots. Numerous dark spots appear on the leaves. These soon turn black and may join together. The foliage turns yellow and then brown and often falls prematurely. Occasionally similar spots develop on the fruit and brown rot often gains entry, causing the fruit to rot. Shoot tips may also be infected and develop dieback. Rake up and burn any fallen leaves and remove any infected stems, leaves and fruit. There are no label approved chemicals available to the amateur gardener for use against this disease. Bordeaux mixture can be used on pears and may give some measure of control if it is sprayed as soon as the disease is apparent. Repeat this again the following spring before bud burst and the disease makes its appearance.

*Raspberry cane blight*

**RASPBERRY CANE BLIGHT** — Cane blight is a serious fungal disease which affects raspberry canes. The fungus infects young canes through wounds which are initially caused by raspberry cane midge attack, late spring frosts or pruning. The disease may be serious enough to kill the young canes and consequently reduce fruiting potential for the following year. The fungus causing cane blight is carried by rain and infects canes when it splashes onto open wounds. A dark area can be seen on the canes just above ground level. Canes become brown and the bark starts to rupture. The shoots or the whole cane start to die back over the summer. Infected canes become very brittle and may snap off just above ground level. Tiny, black fungal fruiting bodies develop on dead areas and exude spores which are forcibly ejected into the air. Prune out infected canes and cut away any discoloured wood from the crowns. Spray the crowns and any new growth with copper oxychloride. As the fungus can gain entry through wounds caused by the raspberry cane midge, control measures should be used for this pest if found to be present (see page 175).

**RASPBERRY DIEBACK AND ROOT ROT** — This disease, new to the U.K, has made its appearance in recent years on raspberries. The first signs of its presence are that the fruit buds fail to grow out or the fruiting laterals wilt and die at any time between bud burst and berry ripening. Few, if any, new canes grow and any that do, wilt or show early autumn colouring and prematurely drop their leaves. As the disease can be carried on planting canes, only Ministry certified canes should be purchased and planted. The disease is also associated with poorly drained and heavy soils that are liable to waterlogging. Before planting raspberry canes, all soils should be double dug two spades deep. In addition, on the heavier soils, they

*Raspberry dieback*

should be planted on a raised bed or ridge. A bed may be formed by digging trenches 45cm (18in) wide, 60cm (2ft) from the intended raspberry row and spreading the soil over the bed. Alternatively, a planting ridge may be formed by digging the soil towards a centre line on which the canes are to be planted.

*Raspberry spur blight*

**RASPBERRY SPUR BLIGHT** — Spur blight is a fungal disease that affects raspberries and occasionally loganberries. It is usually most troublesome in wet weather. Plants that have been fed excessive quantities of nitrogen or which are overcrowded, are more prone to infection and encourage the disease to spread rapidly. Small dark purple blotches develop around the buds of new canes in the early autumn. These increase in size and spread up and down the canes causing extensive discolouration. In August, when they become very conspicuous, they are 5-8cm long and sometimes join together to form a discoloured length of cane measuring approximately 15cm in length, which may eventually girdle the cane. During the autumn and winter the blotches turn silver and become covered in numerous, minute, raised black spots which are the fruit bodies of the spur blight fungus. Buds wither and die or produce shoots which die back during the spring; infected shoots that persist crop very poorly. As a precautionary measure, young canes superfluous to requirements should be removed early in the season so as to avoid overcrowding. Diseased canes should be cut out and burned as soon as the patches start to appear. There are no label approved chemicals available to the amateur gardener for use against this disease. Copper oxychloride may give some measure of control. Spray at fourteen day intervals from bud burst until the blossom appears.

*Redberry disease*

**REDBERRY DISEASE** — Redberry disease in blackberries and hybrid berries is caused by the blackberry mite. The condition is most common on wild blackberries but is starting to become more widespread in cultivated bushes. Affected fruits do not ripen fully. Some drupelets, (usually those at the base of the fruit) remain red, or greenish red and hard. The damage increases as the picking season progresses, with late fruit being the most seriously affected. The mite which causes the damage is tiny (less than 0.2mm long) and overwinters beneath the bud scales and within old fruit that is left on the cane. It re-emerges in the spring to breed on the plant's new growth. The mites enter the flowers at blossom time and feed on the developing drupelets. An enzyme is injected during the feeding process and it is this that prevents the affected drupelets from ripening. Numbers of the mite increase rapidly as temperatures rise and there are a number of generations throughout the summer. However, few mites survive to overwinter. There is no satisfactory method of chemical control against this pest and where the damage to the fruit is severe, the only remedy is to cut out all of the canes, both old and new and burn them. Once the life-cycle of the pest has been interrupted in this way it should not be necessary to resort to burning again unless re-infestation occurs. As a preventative measure and if there is sufficient space, it is worth considering planting two bushes and cropping them in alternate years to interrupt the life cycle of the mite (see page 94).

**REDCORE** — Redcore is a disease of the roots of strawberries, so called because in late autumn or spring, when affected roots are split open longitudinally, the centres, instead of being white, are reddish-brown in colour. The disease is usually brought into a garden on infected uncertified runners and can remain in the soil for more than ten years. It is worse on heavy soils that are poorly drained but can also occur on lighter soils where a hard pan prevents water from draining away. First indications of the presence of redcore occur in dry weather during May or June when a number of plants will be seen to be growing less well than their neighbours. All the leaves will have a bluish-grey tinge and the outer leaves will turn yellow, orange and red in colour. The

*Redcore*

berries ripen prematurely, are small in size and negligible in weight if the infection is severe. There are no methods of chemical control available. Infected plants should be removed and burned immediately, together with the soil in the vicinity of their roots. Strawberries should not be grown on that site again. Only Ministry certified plants should be purchased in order to reduce the risk of introducing the disease into the garden. Before planting, make sure that the soil is well drained by double digging to a depth of 45cm (18in). Heavy soils should have a tile or plastic drain installed so that surplus water is rapidly removed from the strawberry plot. The worst effects of the disease can be avoided on heavy soils by planting on 10-15cm (4-6in) high ridges or adopting the 'table-top' method of growing strawberries (see pages 154-157).

**'Reversion' virus**

**'REVERSION' VIRUS** — 'Reversion' virus affects blackcurrants. It is spread largely by the gall or 'big bud' mite as it is more commonly called, an important and widespread pest of blackcurrants. Plants produce leaves with slight yellowing and unusually small veins. The leaves are shaped differently from healthy ones. The flowers are bright-red coloured instead of grey and cropping is reduced. There is no cure, and infected plants gradually degenerate. Sometimes the symptoms will appear on some shoots, whereas others look perfectly healthy. However, eventually the disease will spread all over the plant. As there is no cure for 'reversion' virus, infected bushes should be dug up and burned as soon as the symptoms of the disease are diagnosed, since they may act as a source of infection for other healthy bushes. Ensure that new bushes are Ministry certified. Consider growing 'Ben Hope', a new blackcurrant variety, resistant to the blackcurrant gall mite. As the disease is spread from infected bushes by the blackcurrant gall mite, control measures should be used for this pest (see page 169).

**RUST** — Rust disease affects currants, blackberries, raspberries and plum trees. It is readily recognised in its early stages by the bright orange coloured spots produced on the leaves from late spring onwards. Later the spots turn dark brown and appear to be woolly or coarsely hairy. It is only in recent years that the disease has become serious on raspberries, causing premature leaf drop and reduction in vigour. On blackberries the disease is similar to that on raspberries but the colour of the spots on the upper surfaces of the leaf is dark-red or purple. On raspberries and blackberries, the fungus overwinters on the leaves and in the spring, secondary spores are produced which infect the young leaves. In severe cases, the disease causes the defoliation of currants. When plum leaves are severely infected they turn yellow and fall prematurely. Such defoliation tends to weaken the tree but as infection is confined to the leaf, the tree will not be permanently damaged. Currants and gooseberries can be sprayed at regular intervals with Bordeaux mixture or copper oxychloride until there is no risk of further infection. There are no chemicals approved for use on other crops. If the symptoms are not too severe, rust can

**Rust**

be controlled by picking off and burning infected leaves. Fallen leaves should also be raked up and burned.

*Silver leaf*

**SILVER LEAF** — This is a very serious disease affecting all species of top fruit and particularly stone fruits. The spores enter the tree through a wound. Trees are subject to infection throughout the year except during June, July and August. Silver leaf causes dieback of a tree, branch by branch. Leaves appear silvery and a brown stain is produced in the inner tissue. The silvery leaves themselves are not infectious; their abnormal appearance is due to a condition brought about by fungal infection of the wood of stems and branches. Often the fungus is not visible on the exterior, even on trees showing pronounced silvering. However, as the infected branches die, the fungus bursts through the bark and appears at the surface. The bracket-like toadstools are often numerous and more or less overlapping, varying in size from 8mm to 5cm across. Silver leaf is often confused with 'false silver leaf', a common disorder which as the name suggests looks like silver leaf at first glance. Leaves are silvery, but the effect appears all over the tree rather than progressively along a branch. A cut branch reveals that the staining of silver leaf disease is absent. The cause of 'false silver leaf' is starvation or irregular watering. If silver leaf is diagnosed, affected branches should be cut out at least 15cm (6in) behind where the stain ceases and burned immediately. If they are left lying about, the fungus will continue to develop and scatter its spores. It is very important that the pruning tools are then properly disinfected by immersing the blades in boiling water for five to ten minutes before using them on other trees. All pruning wounds should be painted with a protective paint such as Arbrex. To lessen the risk of silver leaf infection, stone fruits should never be pruned during the dormant season.

**STAMEN BLIGHT** — This disease affects raspberries and blackberries. Infected flowers are slightly larger than healthy ones, and the stamens are covered with masses of white spores which give the flowers a mildewed appearance. Berries that develop from infected flowers ripen earlier than healthy ones, are deformed, the drupelets ripen unevenly and the berries are difficult to pick. Spores from the flowers infect the buds on the new canes. In order to control the disease, infected flowers should be picked off and burned as soon as they are seen.

**VERTICILLIUM WILT** — This disease affects strawberry plants. It is usually worse in the maiden year, during June and July. Verticillium wilt can be passed onto healthy strawberry plants from potatoes grown as the preceding crop. Some varieties are more susceptible than others if the disease is already present in the soil. The plants wilt, the older leaves turn reddish-brown and the undeveloped leaves are yellow. Black streaks may be seen on the leaf stalks and runner stolons and if the crown is cut across, a dark brown discolouration of the conducting tissues will be seen. Severely infected plants die, whilst mildly infected

*Verticillium wilt*

ones recover and crop fairly normally in the following year. There is no method of chemical control available. Only Ministry certified plants should be bought in order to reduce the risk of introducing the disease into the garden. Strawberries should not be planted in ground known previously to have been used to grow potatoes. If this is unavoidable, a far safer approach would be to grow strawberries on the 'table-top' system (see pages 154-157).

*Virus disease on raspberry*

**VIRUS DISEASES** — One of the main causes of fruit stocks failing to crop satisfactorily is infection by virus diseases. Viruses differ from other pathogens in three important ways; firstly, they are so small that they cannot be seen even with the aid of an optical microscope; secondly, once a plant becomes infected there is no practical method of ridding the plant of the virus; thirdly, every part of the plant is infected by the virus. The main effects of virus infections are that the plants become less vigorous, yields decline, growth may be distorted, the leaves may develop yellow blotches and streaks and some viruses kill outright. Viruses are spread from infected to healthy plants by greenfly but also by eelworms, leaf hoppers, mites and even bees carrying infected pollen. Good pest control, particularly of greenfly, will help to slow down the spread of viruses within a plot of fruit plants. Fortunately the majority of viruses are slow to cause serious reductions in vigour and fruit production. Provided healthy stocks were planted in the first place, cane and bush fruits normally go on cropping for ten to twelve years (strawberries for three to four years) before virus infections make their retention no longer worthwhile. Tree fruits are not drastically affected by viruses but they may cause slight reductions in yield or vigour. Viruses of tree fruits are mainly graft transmitted and so if healthy stock is obtained the tree should remain 'virus free' for the rest of its life.

**WALNUT BLIGHT** — This causes small black spots on the leaflets, leading to large withered areas. It can also cause dieback of the new shoots and damage to the fruits, notably blotches and holes. A large part of the crop is likely to be lost in a serious attack, especially when the male catkins are affected. The disease is most prevalent in periods of cold, wet weather around flowering time. Controlling the disease requires cutting out infected branches to well below the infected area. The prunings should be burned. Preventative measures include guarding against excessive nitrogen feeding and pruning the tree sufficiently to give an open structure for good aeration.

**WALNUT LEAF BLOTCH** — This causes the leaves to develop brown necrotic blotches and the leaves to fall prematurely. Similar lesions may appear on the fruits, causing them to turn from green to black. Symptoms usually appear in late May and early June. Infected trees should be sprayed with Bordeaux Mixture as soon as the first signs are seen and the application should be repeated again two weeks later. As the fungus overwinters on fallen leaves, they should be raked up and burned.

# GROW YOUR OWN FRUIT

## ACKNOWLEDGMENTS

I would like to express my thanks to Jim Arbury at the R.H.S. Garden, Wisley, for his immeasurable assistance in drafting large sections of the original handbook. Jim Arbury is the Superintendent of the Fruit Department at Wisley and is responsible for the technical running and supervision of the Fruit Collection and the Model Fruit Gardens. His sound practical experience of growing fruit in a garden environment, gained from many years experience at Wisley, has ensured that the reader has been presented with an up-to-date knowledge of the subject in a form which is both easy to follow and accurate in its content.

I am also grateful to Harry Baker, former Fruit Officer at Wisley, for casting an eye over the text before it was printed and making several useful comments to help improve the content even further.

I would like to say thank you to Mary Tomlin for providing most of the illustrations and to Claire Higgins for the many hours spent editing the text.

Finally, whilst most of the photographs were provided from our own library, from transparencies taken by Ed Gabriel (Photos Gt.Britain) and Claire Higgins, I would nevertheless like to record my thanks to David Alford, Peter Blackburne-Maze, Nick Dunn, the Central Science Laboratory, the Harry Smith Collection, the Scottish Crop Research Institute and the Royal Horticultural Society for the use of some of their pictures.

KEN MUIR
January 2007

First edition 1994
Second edition 1999
Third edition 2003
Fourth edition 2007